Dialectic

A scholarly journal of thought leadership, education and practice
in the discipline of visual communication design

Volume I, Issue I—Winter 2016-17

Dialectic is a fully open access, biannual journal devoted to the critical
examination of issues that affect design education, research, and inquiry into their effects on the practice of design. Michigan Publishing,
the hub of scholarly publishing at the University of Michigan, publishes
Dialectic on behalf of the AIGA (American Institute of Graphic Arts)
Design Educators Community (DEC).

ISBN: 978-1-60785-415-9

http://dialectic.aiga.org is the URL for *Dialectic's* home page on the web.

Contents

Dialectic Volume I, Issue I: An introductory letter from Dialectic's Managing Editor and its Producer

It's time to stir the pot...

KEITH M. OWENS[1] AND MICHAEL R. GIBSON[2]

1. The University of North Texas, Denton, Texas, USA

2. The University of North Texas, Denton, Texas, USA

SUGGESTED CITATION: Owens, K. M., & Gibson, M. R. "It's time to stir the pot..." *Dialectic,* 1.1 (2016): pgs. 5-8. DOI: http://dx.doi.org/10.3998/dialectic.14932326.0001.101

It's time to stir the pot...

KEITH M. OWENS

MICHAEL R. GIBSON

Yet another scholarly journal. Haven't we enough of them—habitats where academic minutiae quietly flourish? Volumes of vast but narrow knowledge of little practical use to most. Perhaps. Yet, the best of these types of publications have proven, in different ways and by fulfilling different roles, their usefulness to scholar and practitioner alike. Some serve as forums where all that is new relative to a specific area of thought or study is brought to light for critical examination and reflection—places where dynamic idea exchange sparks the kindling of future learning. Many function as repositories of collected wisdom—bodies of knowledge built up through slow-learned accretion. Still others endeavor to set and shape, or *re*-set and *re*-shape, the boundaries and focus of disciplinary theory and practice—forging the whats, whys and hows of scholarly investigation within and between areas of study. Moreover, with the popularization of content unfettered by the worldwide web, scholars, students, and, more recently, professionals can now access knowledge and insights through a proliferation of open access journals.

Dialectic, this journal, aspires to fulfill the dual role of provocateur and standard bearer. It seeks to occupy a place where the status quo is always in question, and to provide a forum where asking "why?" will be more fundamental and vital than asking "how?" or "what?" It will value the inquisitive and the analytical over the merely descriptive, and will foster a setting within which rigorous examination and interrogation are guided by high standards of analysis and reasoning. *Dialectic* will be an *open access* gathering place for those who wish to critically and thoughtfully propose, question, and argue about the ideas, systems and processes central to the nature of design education and practice.

Simply stated, there is much to hash out. By simultaneously being a part of *and* molding a discipline as comparatively new and fungible as

7

design(ing), design education has more blanks waiting to be filled in than do the educational domains of other academic and professional disciplines. One of the more prominent of these vacancies is framed by the following fundamental question: what is, or what should be, the unifying phenomenon of study for design education and research? Inherent in this query are challenges for designers that examine how we design, who we design for, and the 'things' we design. This begs a series of follow-on questions:

- if we so freely borrow theory and methods from other disciplines, what constitutes our unique domain of knowledge?;
- must our pedagogy merely ape design practice, so that educators are restricted to operating the classic—and still largely prevalent—atelier model, or should our approaches to teaching design evolve (and, if so, *how* and *how not*)?;
- on what basis does design education claim legitimacy within the academy (specifically, should our legitimacy be rooted in knowledge creation and dissemination, like the other scholarly disciplines, or should it arise out of service to our profession, as claimed by business or law schools)?;
- should our educational focus be on nurturing our students to effectively engage in the best practices of our industry as defined by those who practice within it, or on tipping the sacred cows now grazing in the increasingly co-opted fields of design practice.

The one trait common to all of these questions is that there exists no consensus about how to address any of them. We have yet to effectively describe, much less *attain*, any of the 'settled matters' that form the basis and boundaries of an established discipline and its practices.

And so...*Dialectic*. A place where those who wish to stir the pot, and perhaps add new ingredients to it, are welcomed. And, unlike academic journals in thrall to the written word as the sole standard bearer of knowledge creation and dissemination, *Dialectic's* editors and reviewers will embrace all manner of academic expression, be they written or visual or some combination of these. The standard of scholarly inquiry *Dialectic* will endeavor to maintain will not dictate that academic expression must exist in written form alone, but, rather, that academic expression, in all of its many forms, be critically rigorous in nature.

Journaling through the Back Door

STEVEN MCCARTHY[1]

1. Professor Graphic Design Program, University of Minnesota

SUGGESTED CITATION: McCarthy, S. "Journaling Through the Back Door." *Dialectic,* 1.1 (2016): pgs. 10-13. DOI: http://dx.doi.org/10.3998/dialectic.14932326.0001.102

Journaling through the Back Door

STEVEN MCCARTHY

For the first third of my academic career, roughly the 1990s, I taught undergraduate graphic design in a university art department; I maintained a fledging professional practice (with clients mostly in the arts and publishing); and I made speculative, self-authored works — primarily artist's books. The job emphasis was clearly on classroom teaching — the load was three courses per semester — but the occasional exhibit, publication, or competition that I got into built self- esteem and was appreciated by my students, colleagues and superiors.

When I joined the faculty at the University of Minnesota eighteen years ago, my job took a 'research turn' as I now teach two courses per term, advise graduate students, and am expected to produce significant scholarship. I was the first tenure-track hire with an MFA in the Department of Design, Housing, and Apparel (with programs in interior, apparel, product and graphic design, plus housing studies and retail merchandising). Most of my new colleagues, including those teaching graphic design, had PhDs. My colleagues tend to define themselves intellectually as social scientists,

engineers and humanists, with few design practitioners and artists among them.

I had departed a culture that valued individual artistic expression, studio production, professional practice and exhibitions and joined one that privileged qualitative and quantitative research methods, collaboration, interdisciplinarity and peer-reviewed publishing. I had to quickly adapt to this new culture *and* I had to educate my colleagues about other ways that design faculty could create scholarship. The Department's tenure and promotion guidelines acknowledged the parity of juried exhibits to journal publishing, but the culture maintained a pecking order, and journal publishing ruled.

Since then, here is what I have learned about journal publishing.

Publishing in academic journals, while daunting to consider initially, is not that difficult. Unlike most design competitions and art exhibits, which give a straight 'thumbs up' or 'thumbs down' judgment, the peer review process means that submitters receive the critical commentary of others to better shape their writing and research. Unless rejected outright, manuscripts can be revised and resubmitted. In my personal experience, the odds of journal acceptance are more likely than that of juried exhibition or design competition acceptance.

There are plenty of design journals, representing diverse design ideologies, interests, theories, critical discourses and so on. Finding a venue for publishing one's writing is made easier when the scholar directs their efforts towards a journal that — through the topics covered, its mission statement, the composition of its editorial board, or its theme-based call for submissions — seems to be a good fit for the paper. And because many international academic journals are published in English, there are ample calls for papers from journals published abroad.

Trade magazines are not academic journals. While design journalism is a legitimate pursuit (I've written a number of essays for *Eye*), unless the reviewers are peers (typically, advanced degree-holders) and unless the process is blind (anonymity between author and reviewer), the interests of most commercial magazines are not to create new knowledge for the discipline through research. Those magazines that host annual design competitions have found a profitable way to showcase professional practice that has more to do with entry fees and advertisements than critical discourse. That said, it would be a welcome convergence if the rigor of journal publishing were matched by the broad readership of design magazines and websites.

Not all journals are equal. Some have higher prestige; some have more selective acceptance rates; some have longer histories; some are published by notable university presses; and some have the institutional support of a major organization. The only effort I'm aware of to rank design journals has been by Ken Friedman, et al., in *Design Research Journal Ranking Study: Preliminary Results* (2008). Since then, Ico-D's new journal *Communication Design, Interdisciplinary and Graphic Design Research* and AIGA's *Dialectic* have been launched. How will these newcomers fit in to the reputations earned by *Design Issues, Visible Language, Design and Culture, Visual Communication, Design Studies, The Poster, The Design Journal, Book 2.0* and numerous others?

Journal publishing takes time. The typical cycle of research, writing, submitting, revising, resubmitting, editing and publishing can take the better part of a year. (I had one paper take five years from manuscript to print!) This means that tenure track design faculty need to have multiple 'irons in the fire' annually to be productive. One thing that ought to be revisited is the convention in academic publishing that manuscripts can only be under review at one journal at a time; this is in the best interest of the journal but to the detriment of the scholar. Clearly, publishing in two journals simultaneously should be forbidden, but why shouldn't a scholar have their paper published in the first journal that gives them the 'thumbs up'? This would add an element of competition to peer turn-around, and incentivize timely responses.

One doesn't need a PhD to publish in journals. Using effective research methods, the ability to think critically, good writing skills, and command of the subject matter are strengths of many design faculty with other advanced degrees. Mastering the style guides required for specific publications (APA, MLA, Harvard, etc.) can be a minor challenge, but getting the citations right lends credibility to one's argument.

Here is what I hope I have taught my departmental colleagues.

Scholarship in graphic design can take many forms, and can be disseminated in myriad venues. Juried and invitational exhibits, media festivals, performances, presentations, curatorial projects, entrepreneurial ventures, institutional collections, and more, are viable and appropriate for graphic design. Like journal articles, the design (image, product, experience, service, tool, environment, etc.) should undergo peer review to qualify as scholarship. Even the magazine competitions that I criticized earlier have an acceptance rate of around 5% (perhaps for economic reasons), which is highly competitive, and depending on the nature of the faculty member's creative practice, a potentially appropriate venue.

Graphic design has another quality that makes it well-suited for making scholarly inquiry manifest: it is self-exemplifying. The ability of graphic design to add meaning to content through visual form should not be overlooked. The typefaces, images, layouts, colors, patterns, paper choices, printing techniques, binding structures and so on that contribute to visual, spatial and tactile form serve to amplify, clarify, dramatize or add critical commentary to texts. The same applies to screen-based content, with design features like animation, navigation, sound and other interactive qualities.

Graphic design journals must be well-designed; anything less is hypocritical. *Zed,* a visually sophisticated journal published seven times by Virginia Commonwealth University in the 1990s, understood this. *Visible Language's* recent website overhaul presents an archive of its articles in an intelligent and handsome manner.

My department now considers what might be termed an 'inclusive scholarship life-cycle': faculty effort, scholarly product, the selection process, the dissemination venue, and the resulting impact. For example, using this sequence: research and writing/a paper/that is blind peer-reviewed/and published in a journal/that was cited by other scholars. This same model can apply to graphic design: creating/a design/ that is juried/into an exhibition/and acquisitioned into a museum's permanent collection. Considerations like rigor, scope, quality, originality and authorial role pertain equally to judging the merits of both outcomes.

I'll conclude with this statement by Meredith Davis, North Carolina State University professor emerita: "There are many paradigms for design research and it is the obligation of institutions to sort out where they stand on these issues. 'Smart' is not the opposite of 'beautiful.' Knowledge does not undermine creativity." (2016)

Graphic design scholarship is uniquely positioned to combine, and challenge, knowledge with creativity — hence the dialectic.

References

Friedman, K., Barron, D., Ferlazzo, S., Ivanka, T., Melles, G. and Yuille, J. (2008) Design Research Journal Ranking Study: Preliminary Results. http://researchbank.swinburne.edu.au/vital/access/manager/Repository/swin:10413 (online 28 May 2016)

Davis, M. (2016) Tenure and Design Research: A Disappointingly Familiar Discussion. Design and Culture, the Journal of the Design Studies Forum. Routledge. 8:1, 123-131.

A New North American Design Research Organization

JOHN ZIMMERMAN[1], CARLOS TEIXEIRA[2],

ERIK STOLTERMAN[3], JODI FORLIZZI[1]

1. Carnegie Mellon University
2. Illinois Institute of Design
3. Indiana University Bloomington

SUGGESTED CITATION: Forlizzi, J., Stolterman, E., Teizeira, C., & Zimmerman, J. "A New North American Design Research Organization." *Dialectic,* 1.1 (2016): pgs. 14-17. DOI: http://dx.doi.org/10.3998/dialectic.14932326.0001.103

A New North American Design Research Organization

JOHN ZIMMERMAN, CARLOS TEIXEIRA,
ERIK STOLTERMAN & JODI FORLIZZI

The last two decades have witnessed skyrocketing interest in design, designers, and *design thinking*. Businesses worked to promote and integrate design thinking into their innovation cultures (SAP, IBM, IDEO); tech companies purchased startups for their UX design teams; [1] banks and other service enterprises purchased design consultancies to help spark innovation; [2] and business consultancies acquired design agencies to extend their reach and offerings. [3] This demand for design talent has helped drive rapid growth in professional master's programs focused on information design, UX design, service design, and strategy. Within several North American universities, designers joined English departments, information schools, computer science departments, and medical schools. These actions demonstrate the increasing importance that industry and the academy place on design and design thinking as it relates to and affects innovation.

Paralleling this growing interest in design, over the last two decades a new type of scholarly design research emerged, distinct from design studies and from the clinical design research conducted by practitioners. Referred to as both *Research through Design* and *Constructive Design Research,* this approach promotes design inquiry (making new things to make sense of the world) as a form of scholarly research, distinct from engineering and scientific research. [4] When following this approach, researchers make things in order to reframe problematic situations, probe speculative futures, and reveal new preferred states; futures that could and should be. Technical advances, particularly around communication technology, have driven this growing interest in design.

1 Segall, L. (April 6, 2012) Silicon Valley is desperate for designers. CNNMoney Startup RADAR, Retrieved from http://money.cnn.com/2012/04/05/technology/ startups/designers/
2 Ha, A. (October 2, 2014) *Design Firm Adaptive Path Acquired By Capital One*. TechCrunch, Retrieved from https://techcrunch.com/2014/10/02adaptive-path-acquired-by-capital-one/
3 Hurst, N. (May 15, 2013) Big Corporations are Buying Design Firms in Droves. *Wired,* Retrieved from http://www.wired.com/2013/05/accenture-fjord/
4 Zimmerman, John, Jodi Forlizzi, and Shelley Evenson. (2007, April) Research through design as a method for interaction design research in HCI. In *Proceedings of the SIGCHI Conference on Human Factors in Computing Systems* (pp. 493-502). ACM Press, http://dx.doi.org/10.1145/1240624.1240704; Koskinen, Ilpo, John Zimmerman, Thomas Binder, and Johan Redström (2011) *Design research through practice: From the lab, field, and showroom. Elsevier.*

Industry and departments outside of design want help from designers to make sense of what technology might be, to give it meaningful forms, and to envision how it can enrich people's lives.

Interestingly, the growing interest in design and design thinking as a driver of innovation has not led to increased funding for design research or a substantial investment in design education. Neither U.S. government agencies—the National Institutes of Health, the National Science Foundation, the Department of Education—nor foundations have turned to design practitioners, educators, or researchers for their expertise. Large-scale, interdisciplinary projects focused on wicked societal issues such as sustainability or obesity rarely, if ever, seek out the input of designers. The increased interest in design and design thinking has also had little impact on the number and size of design PhD programs in North America. These programs, which should be a locus for advancing design education and research, remain nearly non-existent.

To help address this situation, we are founding a design research organization for North America. These organizations and societies exist in Asia and Europe, providing a community for design researchers and educators and promoting PhDs in design. We envision an organization headquartered here in the U.S. that focuses on design education both within and outside of design schools, one that promotes the establishment and growth of PhD programs within design schools, and one that focuses on advancing constructive design research both here and around the world.

This organization would extend the growing impact of design by:

- *Creating a viable, resilient community for design researchers and educators.* This includes designers teaching and doing research in design schools, in academic departments outside of design, and in other organizations including industry, government, foundations, and NGOs. The organization would provide a venue for design

researchers and educators to collectively generate priorities and share their latest advances.

- *Mentoring universities to create PhD programs.* The organization would help universities establish standards for a North American PhD in design, promote integration of design into interdisciplinary research, promote teaching of design skills and thinking to students in many other fields, and help to develop mechanisms for funding PhD work.

- *Facilitating research opportunities.* The organization would lobby government, industry, and foundations as funding sources for design research and education, promoting the benefits of design as a mode of inquiry by showing the impact it has made. In addition, the organization would facilitate linking design researchers with large-scale interdisciplinary projects that would benefit from input provided by design thinking experts.

- *Bridging design research, education, and practice.* The organization would provide a venue for practitioners to discuss changing needs that affect design education, and the persistent challenges faced in practice that re-search rarely addresses. Design educators could share best practices, especially around teaching new practices and advances in the learning sciences related to design. Design researchers could share their latest findings related to practice and education, and they could collectively generate research priorities with input from education and practice experts.

Readers of and contributors to *Dialectic,* this new journal being published by and for the AIGA Design Educators Community (DEC), are experts in communication and information design education, and therefore must play a critical role in creating this organization. This new Design Research organization needs your expertise to address emerging challenges around big data, information visualization, and the need to effectively facilitate collaboration between machine learning systems and people. Communication and information designers will shape the future through development of dashboards that help people make sense of data, through invention of new communication forms that harmonize dynamic data, text, images, audio, and video. These designers also have the capacity to further affect positive change by reframing how people read, communicate, coordinate, collaborate, and critique in small groups and at city, country, and global scales.

We will launch this new North American Design Research Organization at the IASDR 2017 Conference hosted by the University of Cincinnati from October 31 to November 3, 2017. <http://www.iasdr2017.com/>. Until then, there is much work to do to understand the needs of the North American design research, education and practice communities. We would love for you to contribute to a broadly informed dialogue to share your ideas, your hopes, your concerns, and your fears.

Join the conversation: #NA_DRO

References

Ha, Anthony. (October 2, 2014) Design Firm Adaptive Path Acquired By Capital One. TechCrunch, Retrieved from https://techcrunch.com/2014/10/02 adaptive-path-acquired-by-capital-one/

Hurst, Nathan. (May 15, 2013) Big Corporations are Buying Design Firms in Droves. Wired, Retrieved from http://www.wired.com/2013/05/accenture-fjord/

Koskinen, Ilpo, John Zimmerman, Thomas Binder, and Johan Redström (2011) *Design research through practice: From the lab, field, and showroom.* Elsevier.

SAP (2016) Design Thinking with SAP, Retrieved from https://designthinkingwithsap.com/

Segall, Laurie. (April 6, 2012) Silicon Valley is desperate for designers. CNNMoney Startup RADAR, Retrieved from http://money.cnn.com/2012/04/05/technology/startups/designers/

Zimmerman, John, Jodi Forlizzi, and Shelley Evenson. (2007, April) Research through design as a method for interaction design research in HCI. In *Proceedings of the SIGCHI Conference on Human Factors in Computing Systems* (pp. 493-502). ACM Press, http://dx.doi.org/10.1145/1240624.1240704

The Concept Of The Design Discipline

PAUL A. RODGERS[1] AND CRAIG BREMNER[2]

1. Imagination, Lancaster University, UK

2. Charles Sturt University, School of Creative Industries, Australia

SUGGESTED CITATION: Rodgers, P.A., & Bremner, C. "The Concept of the Design Discipline." *Dialectic,* 1.1 (2016): pgs. 19-38. DOI: http://dx.doi.org/10.3998/dialectic.14932326.0001.104

Abstract

In their previous work, the authors have demonstrated that the discipline of design has been superseded by a condition where conventionally set design disciplines have dissolved. [1,2,3] In this age where design is typified by fluid, evolving patterns of practice that regularly traverse, transcend and transfigure historical disciplinary and conceptual boundaries, the authors have argued that globalization and the proliferation of the digital has resulted in connections that are no longer 'amid,' cannot be measured 'across,' nor encompass a 'whole' system. In short, this 'disciplinary turn' has generated an 'other' dimension—an alternative disciplinarity. [4] Moreover, this reliance on the 'exhausted' historic disciplines has become obsolete as the boundaries of our understanding have been superseded by a boundless space/time that we call '*alterplinarity*.' [5] The fragmentation of distinct disciplines has shifted creative practice from being 'discipline-based' to 'issue- or project-based.' [6] Consequently, this paper presents a manifesto for the future design discipline that emphasizes disposing carefully of what you know, teaching what you do not know whilst always taking design seriously, protecting us from what we want, objecting to sustaining everything, designing without reproach, ensuring that objects are invisible but designed with care and within history whilst exploring design as an *idea* rather than an ideal.

1 Rodgers, P.A. & Bremner, C. "Alterplinarity—'Alternative Disciplinarity,' in Future Art and Design Research Pursuits." *Studies in Material Thinking,* 6 (2011).

2 Rodgers, P.A. & Bremner, C. "Exhausting Discipline: Undisciplined and Irresponsible Design." *Architecture and Culture,* 1.1 (2013): pgs. 138-158.

3 Ibid.

4 Rodgers, P.A. & Bremner, C. "Alterplinarity—'Alternative Disciplinarity,' in Future Art and Design Research Pursuits." *Studies in Material Thinking,* 6 (2011).

5 Rodgers, P.A. & Bremner, C. "Exhausting Discipline: Undisciplined and Irresponsible Design." *Architecture and Culture,* 1.1 (2013): pgs. 138-158.

6 Heppell, S. *"RSA Lectures: Stephen Heppell: Learning 2016,"RSA Lectures,* 30 June, 2006. Online. Available at: http://www.teachers.tv/video/4957 (Accessed December 22, 2010).

The Concept Of The Design Discipline

PAUL A. RODGERS

CRAIG BREMNER

Introduction

Since the 1950s, the adoption and application of the word *design* has been expanding continuously both in type and remit, and now extends from the design of objects and spaces that we use daily to cities, landscapes, nations, cultures, bodies, genes, political systems, and the way we produce food, to the way we travel, build cars and clone sheep. [7] The reach of design has expanded way beyond Ernesto Rogers' description from *"...from the Spoon to the City"* (*"...dalla cucchiaio alla citta"*) [8] to the way we formulate business and, more recently, think. [9] With accelerated design activity anticipated well into the 21st century, it is clear that an increasing number of researchers and practitioners across a diverse range of creative and other disciplines routinely regard their methods as rooted in design practice or are using methods, techniques and approaches that could be considered *"designerly."* [10] It is equally clear that design is expanding its disciplinary, conceptual, theoretical, and methodological frameworks to encompass ever-wider disciplines, activities and practice. As a result, design is either copious and being smeared as a viscous layer over the problems of the world, or what we call design is being stretched into an impermeable film expanding to keep in capital and consumption.

The boundaries of what were once recognized as discrete design disciplines such as product, graphic, textile, and fashion design have been and continue to dissolve. [11] Key amongst these changes is the realization that an indeterminacy of professional boundaries now exists, and fluid patterns of employment within and between traditional design disciplines is commonplace. Moreover, many modern day design pursuits have a core of designerly activity

[7]

Latour, B. "A Cautious Prometheus? A Few Steps Toward a Philosophy of Design (With Special Attention to Peter Sloterdijk)." In Proceedings of the 2008 Annual International Conference of the Design History Society, edited by F. Hackne, J. Glynne & V. Minto, pgs. 2-10, 2008.

[8]

Sudjic, D. The Language of Things: Understanding the World of Desirable Objects. New York, NY, USA: W.W. Norton, 2009.

[9]

Kimbell, L. "Rethinking Design Thinking: Part I." Design and Culture, 3.3 (2011): pgs. 285-306.

[10]

Cross, N. Designerly Ways of Knowing. London, UK: Springer, 2006.

[11]

Rodgers, P.A. "Design Now." In Perimeters, Boundaries and Borders, edited by J. Marshall, pgs. 8-11.

12
Schouwenberg, L. and Jongerius, H. Hella Jongerius. London, UK: Phaidon Press Ltd., 2003.

13
Bouroullec, R. & Bouroullec, E. Ronan and Erwan Bouroullec. London, UK: Phaidon Press Ltd., 2003.

14
van Hinte, E., ed. 1:1 Marti Guixe. Rotterdam, The Netherlands: 010 Publishers, 2002.

15
Myerson, J. IDEO: Masters of Innovation. London, UK: Laurence King Publishing, 2005.

16
West, D. "A New Generation." ICON, 43 (2007): pgs. 56-64.

17
Rodgers, P.A. & Bremner, C. "Alterplinarity—'Alternative Disciplinarity,' in Future Art and Design Research Pursuits." Studies in Material Thinking, 6 (2011).

backed by other subject specialist areas such as fine art, engineering, anthropology, computer science and business. The edges between product design and service design, for example, continue to be increasingly fuzzy. Mobile phone companies now offer more than a mere physical artefact (*i.e.* a phone), rather, they now regularly offer users the opportunities to subscribe to their services comprised of music and video downloads, among many others. Similarly, the work of design companies and designers such as Hella Jongerius, [12] Ronan and Erwan Bouroullec, [13] Marti Guixe [14] and IDEO [15] now all regularly transcend historical disciplinary frameworks such as interior design, fine art, product design, and graphic design.

Thus, design today is characterized by fluid, evolving patterns of practice that regularly traverse, transcend and transfigure disciplinary and conceptual boundaries. This mutability means that design research, education, and practice is continually evolving. Tony Dunne, Professor of Interaction Design at the Royal College of Art, London, states: *"New hybrids of design are emerging. People don't fit in neat categories; they're a mixture of artists, engineers, designers, thinkers."* [16]

This paper posits that the terrain of design practice, education, and research, and its subsequent points of inquiry, are continuing to shift and extend well beyond the boundaries of the (single) discipline. That is, the discipline that was once recognized and acknowledged as design, which was born of the split of idea from manufacture, now has little to do with manufacture and a single idea. Now the idea of design includes multiple disciplinary perspectives (*i.e.* multidisciplinarity) to cross-disciplinary pursuits, to the get-together of interdisciplinarity to the bricolage of transdisciplinarity and now beyond—to alter-disciplinarity, where globalization and the explosion of digital possibilities has resulted in connections that are no longer 'in the middle of...,' cannot be measured 'across,' nor encompass an 'entire system.' As such, the digital has generated an 'other' dimension, so we might now need to consider 'alter-disciplinarity' or 'undisciplinarity' as the most effective approach in the research required for a future of design.

An Alternative Disciplinary ('Alterplinary') Future Manifesto

As a way forward for the discipline of design, the authors propose an 'alterplinary' manifesto (a portmanteau of 'alternative' and 'disciplinary'). Alterplinarity is the condition contemporary design finds itself in. [17] The fluid, evolving muddle of practice that regularly cross, exceed and alter historical disciplinary and conceptual boundaries has resulted in research, education, and practice that is constantly shifting, creating, contesting and negotiating new terrains of opportunities and re-shaping the boundaries of design. This "other" dimension [18] or, as we propose, an "alternative disciplinarity"—an "alterplinarity" that does not rely on historic disciplines of design as the boundaries of our understanding has been superseded. The digital has modified the models of design thought and action, and, as a result, research and practice should transform from a convention domesticated by the academy to a reaction to globalization that is yet to be disciplined.

This Is The 'Alterplinary' Manifesto:

01   Dispose Carefully of What You Know

All design thought and action should emanate from a point of not knowing. Socrates, the Greek philosopher, is attributed to have said that: *"The only true wisdom is in knowing you know nothing."* This resonates well with Kenya Hara's notion of *"Exformation"*, where he makes clear that *Exformation* doesn't mean making known, but understanding how little we know. [19] If we can recognize that we know so little, a method for finding out how little we know will become clear to us as well. Kenya Hara believes that comprehension and recognition of the unknown is a necessary for the beginning of any design project. *Exformation* should be considered the direct opposite to the familiar, meaning exploration of the unknown. Hara emphasizes how our lives are full of wonders and the unknown, and how, as a race, we need to constantly wake up and consider new perspectives. He believes that *"known"* and *"understood"* are both horrible concepts, which usually means that your works (designs) have nothing new to offer the world. Alternatively, to succeed, Kenya Hara suggests, one has to look for the unknown consciously. The concept of *"not knowing"* is increasingly being acknowledged as a critical skill to tackle the complex problems we face in contemporary societies. That is, we should not fear heading uncomfortably toward the unknown. Rather, by developing a relationship with *"not knowing,"* we may discover new ways of designing, living, working and thriving in our modern world. Not knowing can be an exciting proposition where we are no longer

18

Bourriaud, N. Altermodern. London, UK: Tate Publishing, 2009.

19

Hara, K. Designing Design. Zurich, Switzerland: Lars Muller Verlag, 2007.

limited by what we already know, which allows for richer possibilities and more varied wisdom to prosper. [20]

02   Teach What You Don't Know

When confronted with the problem of teaching a language he did not speak, the eighteenth century educationalist Joseph Jacotot discovered it was possible to teach what you don't know. In Jacque Ranciere's reprise of Jacotot's relevance in his book, *The Ignorant Schoolmaster*, he reminds us that everyone is taught to forget that we all possess the ability to learn. [21] For almost a century design has been taught from the perspective of the Bauhaus, which relied on pedagogy that forgot the machine had already made the idea into an image of itself, setting design education on a path resulting in imitation and derivation (rather than invention or innovation), which remain the prevalent models today. Design has evolved to require a completely different logic from that which is informing its current learning models, where so many degree programs are guided by professionally licensed trajectories that are more germane to history than the possible future scenarios we now need to envisage to live in a rapidly changing world. Similar to Jacotot's experiences, Therese Huston's book, *"Teaching What You Don't Know,"* provides clear evidence that teaching outside of one's area of competence is typically the norm in the U.S. academy. [22] Rather than viewing this as a weakness, however, Huston suggests that teaching what you don't know may have certain advantages. Huston argues that novice tutors tend to show more empathy and have more realistic estimations of the time it takes new learners to complete tasks. Expert tutors, on the other hand, often expect more than new learners can handle. It is also suggested that novice tutors can better envision the steps that a beginner will take, what kinds of mistakes he or she will make, and which steps he or she may have to repeat. Furthermore, novice tutors are more likely than expert tutors to relate difficult concepts to everyday life, and to make use of common knowledge to facilitate this (*i.e.*, to relate these concepts to things that the learner likely already knows). Given the perilous state design currently finds itself in, teaching what we don't know may herald a refreshing alternative to design's historical preoccupation with the modern project.

20
D'Souza, S. & Renner, D. Not Knowing. London, UK: Lid Publishing, 2014.

21
Ranciere, J. The Ignorant Schoolmaster: Five Lessons in Intellectual Emancipation. California, CA, USA: Stanford University Press, 1991.

22
Huston, T. Teaching What You Don't Know. Harvard, MA, USA: Harvard University Press, 2012.

23

Warman, M. "Dieter Rams: Apple has Achieved Something I Never Did," The Telegraph, 7 June, 2011. Online. Available at: http://www.telegraph.co.uk/technology/apple/8555503/Dieter-Rams-Apple-has-achieved-something-I-never-did.html (Accessed 11 March 2014).

24

Rams, D. et al. "The Munich Design Charter." Design Issues, 8.1 (1991): pgs. 74-77.

One could be forgiven for forgetting this, however. We are told by Donald A. Norman (and others) in the Epilogue to his book *Emotional Design: Why We Love (or Hate) Everyday Things* that we are all designers, yet arguably one of the greatest designers of all time, Dieter Rams, has stated that he is "...*troubled by the devaluing of the word design*" and that he finds himself "...*now being somewhat embarrassed to be called a designer.*"[23] To combat the devalued meaning, Dieter Rams suggests treating the discipline of design seriously, understanding that design "...*is not simply an adjective to place in front of a product's name to somehow artificially enhance its value.*" As a signatory to the "The Munich Design Charter," published in Design Issues in 1991, Rams knows design's responsibilities in all parts of contemporary life all too well. Rams knows that design must concern itself with "...*economy as well as ecology, with traffic and communication, with products and services, with technology and innovation, with culture and civilization, with sociological, psychological, medical, physical, environmental, and political issues, and with all forms of social organization.*" It is unfortunate and depressing that, now, 25 years later, Rams needs to remind us again "...*that design is a serious profession, and for our future welfare we need to take the profession of design seriously....*"[24] Recently, however, there is some evidence to suggest that design is being taken more seriously by both those who practice and teach it and by at least some portions of the societies that it affects and, in turn, affect it. In the UK, for example, the British government now appears to understand that design can make a significant difference in major infrastructure projects. Sadie Morgan, co-founder of the London architecture firm dRMM, effectively became one of the most powerful figures in British architecture recently when she was named as the only creative on the British government's National Infrastructure Commission. (This group will advise the UK government on how to distribute £100 billion of investment over the next five years.) She holds this post in addition to her appointment as Chair of the design panel for HS2, a high-speed rail link that is currently the UK's biggest infrastructure project. Morgan believes these appointments signify a clear message that they—those that constitute the government of the UK—are starting to take design seriously, and that Britain's government is beginning

25

to recognize that design can actually make a crucial difference in the positive evolution of the UK. [25]

Protect Us From What We Want

A new strategy for design is required that reconnects design with its historic project—to imagine change. Design must re-engage with the eternal scenario conjured by the unavoidable question *what kind of world do we want?* A question also known historically as the basis of the modern project—a project whose result we have always known, but whose every thought and action still requires the application of infinite care and the assumption of great responsibility. The result is, of course, the creation of the totally artificial world, and it is from this prospect that design needs to protect itself in light of its contract with capital that is fueling the manufacture of a world no one wants (unless, of course, you want everything at the expense of everything). So what do we, as design researchers, educators, and practitioners want? Recent catastrophic events and unanticipated consequences of our current modes of living, such as the global financial meltdown of 2008-09, have left many around the world feeling very anxious about the future. This has led to a general lack of confidence in our collective ability to act for the collective good. This collective anxiety is rooted in the idea that we seem not to have developed a coherent vision of a desirable future and, worse still, doubt our ability to bring it about. Perhaps we need to look back to a time period over 40 years ago when Bruce Archer (eminent Professor of Design at the Royal College of Art, London) informed a UK government sponsored conference about design education that it was his *"...sincere conviction that a massive broadening and deepening of design education is overwhelmingly the most urgent need for the survival, as well as the happiness, of mankind."* [26] Archer made these claims in 1973 against a background of globally widespread economic difficulties, environmental crises, and social uncertainties not too dissimilar from today's situation. Archer spoke of the four great crises facing mankind, which are just as recognizable today as they were in 1973: (i) the crisis of overpopulation, (ii) the crisis of pollution, (iii) the crisis of depletion of natural resources, and (iv) the crisis of control. Today, the disappointment and alienation that many people experience in contemporary society

25

Winston, A. "UK Government is Starting to take Design Seriously." Dezeen (blog). 19 November, 2015. Available at: http://www.dezeen.com/2015/11/19/uk-government-starting-take-design-seriously-interview-sadie-morgan-drmm-national-infrastructure-comission-hs2-rail/ (Accessed 2 September 2016).

26

Archer, B., Baynes, K. & Roberts, P. A Framework for Design and Design Education: A Reader Containing Key Papers from the 1970s and 80s. Wellesbourne, UK: Design and Technology Association, 2005.

27
Meadows, D.H., Meadows, D.L., Randers, J. & Behrens III., W.W. Limits to Growth. New York, NY, USA: Universe Books, 1972.

28
Zalasiewicz, J. et al., "Are We Now Living in the Anthropocene?" GSA Today, 18.2 (2008): pgs. 4-8.

29
Corcoran, P.L., Moore, C.J. & Jazvac, K. "An anthropogenic marker horizon in the future rock record." GSA Today, 24.6 (2014): pgs. 4-8.

revolves around their insecurities about the future. Clearly, it is time for design to deliver coherent visions of desirable futures that address our dissatisfaction, our unhappiness, and our isolation, and bring those visions about.

05   ## Object to Sustaining Everything

Rather than trying to channel all design thought and action through the unsustainable framework of sustainability, it is clear that we have yet to design any viable response to the shift from rural to urban living occurring around the world. On a day in 2007, it is generally accepted that the population of our planet shifted from predominantly rural to predominantly urban living, and that by mid-century, 75% of the world's population will live in cities. 60% of humanity will live in urban slums by this time. Well before the UN produced this prediction, and around the time of the discovery of limits to growth articulated in the 1972 book *The Limits to Growth* by the Club of Rome,[27] the fields of design had begun to rally around the notion of the need for more effective stewardship of the planet. That is, there was concerted advocacy for the infinite possibilities of design to be balanced by the infinite responsibilities of designing. It is very clear that design latched on to the infinite possibilities portion of this principle, but shrugged off the responsibilities. That ill-considered course of action cleared the path for championing *sustainability,* so very quickly, rather than *stewardship* by those who were seeking to change the world. Sustainability was dumped on everyone, and, for much longer than the designers of this ruse imagined, the whole world was made responsible for sustaining unsustainable ways of procuring, living, making and distributing. Having finally seen through this subterfuge, those in the know—some of whom are designers and design educators—are now regrouping their collective efforts under the banner of the word *resilience.* As a reaction to a wide variety of planetary crises, resilience is more riddle than reprieve. It is a riddle because it is hard to imagine an elastic planet bouncing back from its current evolutionary path being forced onto a new one by the steady advance of the Anthropocene.[28] This is our planet's current geologic era that is marked in the geologic record by the recent discovery of plastiglomerate, or plastic rock.[29] Sadly, the staunchest adherents to the project

27

30
Fry, T. "Design: On the Question of
The Imperative." Design and Culture,
7.3 (2015): pgs. 417-422.

31
Moos, M.A. Marshall McLuhan Essays:
Media Research Technology, Art,
Communication. London, UK:
Routledge, 1997: p. 78.

of sustainability appear to reside in design schools, whose curricula have been appropriately recycled into socially and politically palatable constructs and have now all been rendered in shades of worthy grey. Design should reject sustainability and instead concentrate on what we might need to do to recover from being together on such a populous planet in such unprecedented proximity staring at a growing number of quickly evolving anthropocentric crises.

06 Design Without Reproach

Design's raison d'etre is to disrupt, contest, invent, direct, coordinate, respond, provoke and project. As such, contemporary design projects require undisciplined and irresponsible designers who are capable of purposely blurring social, economic and political distinctions, and who are able to shift methods from being 'discipline-based' to 'issue- or project-based.' These designers will be most effectively placed to make connections that generate new methods, and to identify 'other' dimensions of design research, activity and thought that are needed for the complex, interdependent societal issues we now face. Tony Fry, in his critical analysis of contemporary design education, proposes significant redirection in the education of designers. Fry claims that one of the key problems of conventional forms of design education is that it is bound up in its professional practices, processes, and political ideology. This has led to a rupture, Fry proposes, that is now evident in many forms of design education, research, and practice globally, between what designers have long been educated to design and what now needs to be designed instead to create the kind of world that will sustain our life on this planet into the future. [30]

07 Objects are Invisible

In answer to an interview question posed to him in 1968, 'Will there ever be silence?,' Marshall McLuhan replied *"Objects are unobservable. Only relationships between objects are observable."* [31] Mass consumer of information that he was, McLuhan was paraphrasing the discovery of uncertainty caused by the operation of observational practices in quantum mechanics (that would lead to the reluctant realization that matter has memory). Of the countless aphorisms from McLuhan, this one seems to have been largely overlooked, and should have been used to warn design that all the effort and energy it has put into the production of stuff failed to take into account that it was invisible as a process, as a causal factor or agent. Not long after McLuhan's puzzling interview, Gregory Bateson published *Towards an Ecology of the Mind*, in which he wrote that ecology was a way of looking at the relationships between the *"messages and pathways outside the body."* [32] The discovery by design much later of the user and their relational experience to that which has been designed probably should be heralded here, but it coincided with the substitution of objects by services, and the mistaken notion that with each design iteration, the world will be designed to be used in better and better ways. However, placing the user at the center of the design process tends to characterize him or her as one of the "problems" that design must "solve." Despite the lack of any evidence that the world is getting better, design still considers that it can formulate and operate its processes to manipulate the user into the ideal circumstances for using, which shares some of the lingering characteristics of marketing, wherein the primary goal is to manipulate a given consumer into consuming. In this sense, usability is essential to generate both profit and pleasure, and, in this vein, the service industry has been trying to maximize pleasure to increase its profits. As a willing proxy, design was conscripted to condition consumers to use services, but now it is time for design to service the deteriorating conditions on the one planet we share. However, as a framework for design thought and action, and as a notion lending legitimacy to design outcomes, usability runs into another major problem: it doesn't account for fashion. The world of fashion is certainly the most volatile battleground for the contest between the different projects of the user and designer. The phenomenon of fashion points to new possibilities for the notion of usability, wherein people might now have to craft their own personalized and customized world. [33]

Design with Care

With the failure of the structural mega-programs of the twentieth century, there is a need to transgress frigid technological perfection into genial ecological possibilities, and this has to be done with *care*. In this context, care refers to designing with the macro and micro social, technological, economic, environmental and political effects

32
Bateson, G. Steps to an Ecology of Mind. New York, NY, USA: Ballantine Books, 1972.

33
Bremner, C. "Usability." In Design Dictionary: Perspectives on Design Terminology, edited by T. Marshall & M. Erlhoff, pgs. 425–428. Basel, Switzerland: Birkhauser, 2008.

08

34
National Institute on Aging. Global Health and Aging, Washington D.C., USA: National Institute on Aging and National Institutes of Health, U.S. Department of Health and Human Services, 2011.

of design decision-making well in mind. Because we now operate in a globalized state of culture, design needs to seek new territories to off-set the relentless uniformity derived from our current cycle of mass culture/consumption. As defined here, care cannot follow trends that become out-dated after a short time, and therefore reflects a profound evolution in our vision and perception of the world and our way of inhabiting it. Because our universe has become a territory, all dimensions of which may be traveled both in time and space, it is only with care that design can make contributions towards the maintenance of a stable environment and sensible material situation worldwide. Further, design needs to take as much care as possible as it evolves its educational and professional practices because it can now only try to make sense from journeying through a chaotic and undisciplined ecology layered with non-essentials. It must be stressed that care is not a service product designed primarily to be served. Like design, the purpose of care is to affect the way we live. In our increasingly population-aging world, within which we are about to cross a demographic landmark of huge social and economic importance—the proportion of the global population aged 65 years and over is set to outnumber the population of children under five years of age for the first time—how we design and care for unprecedented numbers of pensioners and retirees will bring with it huge challenges for policymakers, designers, healthcare providers, and families. [34] There will be more than 1 billion people living in the world who will have effectively aged out of its workforce by 2040. With care, however, design can play a major role in transforming how health and social care looks and feels for many of these people. Working collaboratively, designers, together with clinical directors, health and social care experts, families, and others will co-develop high quality care that is focused around meeting the needs and desires of individuals and that puts them in control of their own care. As both the proportion of older people and the length of life increase throughout the world, arguably design's greatest purpose will be to ensure we are cared for in ways that maintain longer periods of good health, along with a sustained sense of well-being, and extended periods of meaningful social engagement and productivity. Design's major incentive in the decades ahead, then, is to develop and establish physical and social infrastructures that will foster better health and well-being in older age.

09 **Design Within History**

Perhaps design needs an alternative history. Not a counter-cultural version of a history of design, but another way to present what most designers avoid contemplating—the past. That is, for most designers, design has no history; it is enacted in the permanent present, and if in some way they are reminded of its history, most designers cannot see any future in this past. Design has never been connected to its broader, more deeply defined temporal dimensions. Time, from the point of view of design, is now. Design has even failed to come to grips with its one means to control time: posing the question "what next?," or, more precisely, "what-might-become?" Viewed in this way, the history of design is captured in several time loops, all of which are concurrent. To locate the history of design in the *simple present*, it is necessary to look at the origins of design in the way it is understood/ misunderstood as a product of the split of idea from manufacture. It is from this split that design willingly assumed the responsibility of communicating the *idea* to manufacture, but also failed to critically observe or attempt to deeply understand the workings of the machinery of manufacture, and in so doing turned the idea into an image of itself that had no need for design. In the commonplace history of design, the most familiar time period is the *simple past*, where design was given the project of producing competitive advantages in the market which, constrained by the machine, led to imitation (rather than ideas), fuelling the now globalized cycle of production and consumption. Underlying this cycle of produce/consume was an almost unshakable faith in material progress that resulted in Foucault's maxim *"We know what we do but do not know what we do does."* [35] This is further supported by the *past perfect* that describes the history of design framed by one investment. This investment is rooted in our faith in technological progress, the technological progress that made all our imaginings *and* the technological progress we imagine will fix all that fails to meet our needs or desires in the future. There is also the *present perfect*, where digital flows make it possible to reconnect ideas to manufacture and manufacturing processes, but that in fact

35
Foucault, M. Madness and Civilization: A History of Insanity in the Age of Reason. New York, NY, USA: Pantheon Books, 1971: p. 187.

31

turns everyone into a producer of nothing and a consumer of many things, services and experiences. Additionally, there is the *simple future,* where the digital production of nothing crafts new producers, and ideas are reduced to derivatives of what we already know and are comfortable with. The main issue in all of this is that imitation is built into the digital system of production on a number of levels. On one level, software imitates conceptual thought. On another level, and probably because of the former level, software enables the endless digital reproduction of the same 'thing.' On yet another level, and because of our use of software to imitate conceptual thought and enable endless digital reproduction, the endless digital circulation of derivations is encouraged. In the *future perfect,* a future is still framed by one investment—faith in technological progress, but, in this case, it is a digitally networked progress. In order to imagine a viable future, it has now become necessary to navigate the competing time frames of the digital cataloguing of the past and the digital reproduction of the future. Finally, there is the problem of the *future in the past,* or the history/theory of design (i.e. something we will look at sometime in the future), or the core problem of design's carelessness with its history in leaving us with but one problem to solve—the contest between being and becoming.

10 Design: Idea versus Ideal

Because of its media definition, the very idea of design invites pursuit of the ideal—once an action in pursuit of representation, now a representation in pursuit of better (or just more) representation. Additionally, educational enhancement has laid the path to the realization of the ideal designer—a course of exercises to build job-winning capability. Enhancement was developed around the regime of organization and has become classically scientific. The regime is now so successful that it is imitated ubiquitously—now visible everywhere making hamburgers, athletes, and lots of other stuff. Therefore, the idea that design produced the imitation of both the regime (once designed it is imitated by almost every school) and the designer (almost every graduate emerges from his or her course of study with the same capabilities). The imitation is now the ideal, and the media transmit this creation—the ideal is vaunted by a daily regime of web

36
Rodgers, P.A. & Bremner, C. "Exhausting Discipline: Undisciplined and Irresponsible Design." Architecture and Culture, 1.1 (2013): pgs. 138-158.

37
Ibid.

magazines enhancing their own design capabilities. Therefore, design no longer needs an idea, giving rise to a question vexing all dimensions of design—if the ideal (a representation) no longer needs an idea (what needs to be done), can design (serial digital reproductivity) produce an idea of design? An answer requires knowing what to look for, and perhaps we shouldn't look at the means of enhancement (talent identification and education), or enhancing the means (augmented digital representation), which both pursue the ideal. If we look from outside the regime, then the ideal designer is playing to a skeptical public ("Nothing seems to be getting better...") with little trust in the idea of design (especially since everyone knows what needs to be done). So without an idea of design, the ideal (an imitation of design) is now a fragile media invention with no moral reference. Further, now that the idea of the discipline of design doesn't seem to exist, and its ideal exists on an *other* playing field defined by the media—an alternative playing field playing an alterplinary discipline. [36] The net result is the ideal has no feel for the idea, and the idea has no effect on the ideal. If we accept this scenario, we have to ask whether we still participate in the idea of design?

Conclusions

We have argued that the discipline of design has been superseded by a condition where the conventionally defined design disciplines have been dispersed. Moreover, this reliance on the 'exhausted' historic disciplines as the boundary of our understanding has been superseded by an unlimited expanse that we call *'alterplinarity.'* [37] As a consequence, this paper presents a manifesto for a future design discipline where the emphasis is on understanding how little we know and recognizing that the unknown is a necessary condition for the beginning of any project. That is, as design researchers and educators, we should focus on what we do not know and move away from current models of design education that largely result in imitation and derivation as the norm, whilst also reminding ourselves that design must be taken seriously at all times. This seriousness is inherent in the new strategy we require for design. A strategy that reconnects design with its historic project—to imagine change and to answer the unavoidable question—what kind of world do we really want to live in? Contentiously, perhaps, we also propose that we need to object to sustaining everything. Design would be better off rejecting sustainability and concentrating on finding ways of us being together on such a populous planet in such unprecedented proximity staring at many other major crises. As such, design now needs to disrupt, contest, invent, direct, coordinate, respond, provoke and project. The complex and interdependent issues we face today need undisciplined and irresponsible designers who act in productively irresponsible ways. With that stated, we must also endeavor to design with care and remember that, like design, the purpose of care is to affect positively the way we live. Finally, designers need to confront what most of them avoid—the past—and also accept that if design no longer needs an idea, should design still participate in the idea of design?

References

Archer, B., Baynes, K. & Roberts, P. *A Framework for Design and Design Education: A Reader Containing Key Papers from the 1970s and 80s.* Wellesbourne, UK: Design and Technology Association, 2005.

Barrett, E. & Bolt, B., eds. *Practice as Research: Approaches to Creative Arts Enquiry.* London, UK: I.B. Taurus, 2007.

Bateson, G. *Steps to an Ecology of Mind.* New York, NY, USA: Ballantine Books, 1972.

Bauman, Z. "Utopia Without the Topos." *History of the Human Sciences,* 16 (2003): pgs. 11.

Borer, A. *The Essential Joseph Beuys.* Cambridge, MA, USA: The MIT Press, 1997.

Bouroullec, R. & Bouroullec, E. *Ronan and Erwan Bouroullec.* London, UK: Phaidon Press Ltd., 2003.

Bourriaud, N. *Altermodern.* London, UK: Tate Publishing, 2009.

Bremner, C. "Usability." In *Design Dictionary: Perspectives on Design Terminology,* edited by T. Marshall & M. Erlhoff, pgs. 425-428. Basel, Switzerland: Birkhauser, 2008.

Bremner, C. & Rodgers, P.A. "Design without Discipline." *Design Issues,* 29.3 (2013): pgs. 4-13.

Buckley, B. & Conomos, J., eds. *Rethinking the Contemporary Art School: The Artist, the PhD and the Academy.* Nova Scotia, Canada: Nova Scotia College of Art & Design University Press, 2009.

Corcoran, P.L., Moore, C.J. & Jazvac, K. "An anthropogenic marker horizon in the future rock record." *GSA Today,* 24.6 (2014): pgs. 4-8.

Cross, N. *Designerly Ways of Knowing*. London, UK: Springer, 2006.

de Duve, T. "When Form Has Become Attitude–And Beyond." In *The Artist and the Academy: Issues in Fine Art Education and the Wider Cultural Context*, edited by S. Foster & N. deVille, pgs. 19-31. Southampton, UK: John Hansard Gallery, 1994.

D'Souza, S. & Renner, D. *Not Knowing*. London, UK: Lid Publishing, 2014.

Elkins, J., ed. *Artists With PhDs: On the New Doctoral Degree in Studio Art*, Washington D.C., USA: New Academia Publishing, 2009.

Emmott, S. *10 Billion*. London, UK: Penguin, 2013.

Feyerabend, P. *Against Method*. London, UK: Verso, 2010 (4th edition).

Fry, T. "Design: On the Question of The Imperative." *Design and Culture*, 7.3 (2015): pgs. 417-422.

Hara, K. *Designing Design*. Zurich, Switzerland: Lars Muller Verlag, 2007.

Heppell, S. (2006). "*RSA Lectures: Stephen Heppell–Learning 2016*." Available at: http://www.teachers.tv/video/4957 (Accessed December 22, 2010).

Huston, T. *Teaching What You Don't Know*. Harvard, MA, USA: Harvard University Press, 2012.

Kimbell, L. "Rethinking Design Thinking: Part I." *Design and Culture*, 3.3 (2011): pgs. 285-306.

Latour, B. "A Cautious Prometheus? A Few Steps Toward a Philosophy of Design (With Special Attention to Peter Sloterdijk)." In *Proceedings of the 2008 Annual International Conference of the Design History Society*, edited by F. Hackne, J. Glynne & V. Minto, p. 2-10, 2008.

MacRae, F. "Quarter-life crisis hits three in four of those aged 26 to 30," *Mail Online*, 5th May, 2011. Online. Available at: http://www.dailymail.co.uk/news/article-1289659/Quarter-life-crisis-hits-26-30-year-olds.html (Accessed 12th February, 2014).

Madoff, S.H., eds. *Art School (Propositions for the 21st Century)*. Cambridge, MA, USA: The MIT Press, 2009.

Marshall, J. & Bleecker, J. "Undisciplinarity." In *Digital Blur: Creative Practice at the Boundaries of Architecture, Design and Art*, edited by P.A. Rodgers and M. Smyth, pgs. 216-223. Oxon, UK: Libri Publishers, 2010.

Meadows, D.H., Meadows, D.L., Randers, J. & Behrens III., W.W. *Limits to Growth*. New York, NY, USA: Universe Books, 1972.

Moos, M.A. *Marshall McLuhan Essays: Media Research Technology, Art, Communication*. London, UK: Routledge, 1997: p. 78.

Myerson, J. *IDEO: Masters of Innovation*. London, UK: Laurence King Publishing, 2005.

National Institute on Aging. *Global Health and Aging*, Washington D.C., USA: National Institute on Aging and National Institutes of Health, U.S. Department of Health and Human Services, 2011.

Norman, D. *Emotional Design: Why we Love (or Hate) Everyday Things*. New York, NY, USA: Basic Civitas Books, 2004.

Norman, D. "Why Design Education Must Change." *Core77* (blog). 26th November 2010, Available at: http://www.core77.com/blog/columns/why_design_education_must_change_17993.asp (Accessed 11th September, 2012).

Rams, D. et al. "The Munich Design Charter." *Design Issues*, 8.1 (1991): pgs. 74-77.

Ranciere, J. *The Ignorant Schoolmaster: Five Lessons in Intellectual Emancipation*. California, CA, USA: Stanford University Press, 1991.

Rodgers, P.A. "Design Now." In *Perimeters, Boundaries and Borders*, edited by J. Marshall, pgs. 8-11. Manchester, UK: Fast-UK Publishers, 2008.

Rodgers, P.A. & Bremner, C. "Alterplinarity – 'Alternative Disciplinarity' in Future Art and Design Research Pursuits." *Studies in Material Thinking*, 6 (2011).

Rodgers, P.A. & Bremner, C. "Exhausting Discipline: Undisciplined and Irresponsible Design." *Architecture and Culture*, 1.1 (2013): pgs. 138-158.

Royal College of Psychiatrists. *Mental Health of Students in Higher Education*. London, UK: Royal College of Psychiatrists, 2011.

Scharmer, C.O. "Leading from the Emerging Future." *Minds for Change–Future of Global Development Ceremony to mark the 50th Anniversary of the BMZ Federal Ministry for Economic Cooperation and Development*, Berlin, Germany, 13th November, 2011.

Schouwenberg, L. and Jongerius, H. *Hella Jongerius*. London, UK: Phaidon Press Ltd., 2003.

Smith, H. & Dean, R.T., eds. *Practice-led Research, Research-led Practice in the Creative Arts*. Edinburgh, Scotland: Edinburgh University Press, 2009.

Sottsass, E. "Conferenza al Metropolitan Museum 1987." In *Ettore Sottsass: Scritti 1946-2001*, edited by M. Carboni & B. Radice, pgs. 327-345. Milano, Italy: Neri Pozzi Editore, 2002.

Stearn, G. E., ed. *McLuhan Hot and Cool*. London, UK: Penguin, 1968.

Sudjic, D. *The Language of Things: Understanding the World of Desirable Objects*. New York, NY, USA: W.W. Norton, 2009.

Therborn, G. "Class in the 21st Century." *New Left Review*, 78 (2012): pgs. 29.

UNICEF. *The State of the World's Children.* New York, NY, USA: UNICEF, 1999.

United Nations Human Development Report (UNHDR). *United Nations Development Program.* 27th November, 2007.

van Hinte, E., ed. 1:1 *Marti Guixe.* Rotterdam, The Netherlands: 010 Publishers, 2002.

Warman, M. "Dieter Rams: Apple has Achieved Something I Never Did," *The Telegraph,* 7 June, 2011. Online. Available at: http://www.telegraph. co.uk/technology/apple/8555503/Dieter-Rams-Apple-has-achieved-something-I-never-did.html (Accessed 11 March 2014).

West, D. "A New Generation." *ICON,* 43 (2007): pgs. 56-64.

Winston, A. "UK Government is Starting to take Design Seriously." *Dezeen* (blog). 19 November, 2015. Available at: http://www.dezeen. com/2015/11/19/uk-government-starting-take-design-seriously-interview-sadie-morgan-drmm-national-infrastructure-comission-hs2-rail/ (Accessed 2 September 2016).

World Health Organization. *World Report on Violence and Health: Summary.* Geneva, Switzerland: WHO, 2002.

Zalasiewicz, J. et al., "Are We Now Living in the Anthropocene?" *GSA Today,* 18.2 (2008): pgs. 4-8.

Biographies

Paul A. Rodgers is Professor of Design at Imagination, Lancaster University, UK. He holds undergraduate and postgraduate degrees in Design from Middlesex University, London, and a PhD in Product Design Assessment from the University of Westminster, London. Prior to joining Imagination Lancaster he was Professor of Design Issues at Northumbria University School of Design (2009-2016), Reader in Design at Edinburgh Napier University (1999–2009) and a postdoctoral Research Fellow at the University of Cambridge's Engineering Design Centre (1996–1999). He has over 20 years of experience in product design research and has led several research projects for Research Councils in the UK and design projects funded by the Scottish government and The Lighthouse (Scotland's National Centre for Architecture, Design and the City). He is the author of more than 150 papers and 7 books including The Routledge Companion to Design Research published in 2015. His research explores the

37

discipline of design and how disruptive design interventions can enact positive change in health and social care and elsewhere.

Craig Bremner holds joint positions as Professor of Design at Charles Sturt University, Australia and Professor of Design at the University of Southern Denmark. Prior to this he held the positions of Professor in Design Pedagogy at Northumbria University School of Design and Professor of Design at the University of Canberra. With an Arts degree in English literature, he then studied design in Milan and completed a Ph.D. in architecture at Royal Melbourne Institute of Technology. His research deals with developing methods to discover how and why we don't know much about the experience of design, as well as finding ways to clarify the reason why not knowing is an essential and valuable starting point. His research has traced the experience of living in Glasgow, using banks and driving motorcars. In his private practice, he has curated design exhibitions that have toured Australia, the USA and Japan.

First Issues, First Words: Vision in the Making

JESSICA BARNESS[1]

1. Kent State University, Kent, Ohio, USA

SUGGESTED CITATION: Barness, J. "First Issues, First Words: Vision in the Making." *Dialectic*, 1.1 (2016): pgs. 39–60. DOI: http://dx.doi.org/10.3998/dialectic.14932326.0001.105

Abstract

This study connects design history with design practice, and focuses on editorial introductions found within the first issues of a broad cross section of design periodicals launched around the world between 1902–2015. This body of literature includes a diverse range of scholarly/peer-reviewed journals, professional magazines, and designer-authored publications. All of these are somehow connected with visual communication design and related disciplines. Many design periodicals began publication to provide or facilitate thought leadership, criticism, research or scholarly inquiry within particular social, economic, and industrial contexts. Their introductory issues, and often the editorial mission statements contained within them, may be read as calls to action, or manifestos, among the various constituencies of the professional or academic design communities, or their clienteles, or among the broad array of vendors and manufacturers that the work of designers affects. As a means to critically examine these writings on what design is, does, and might be, this author prototyped a 'new' text, with lines extracted from these introductions. The resulting new text, *Vision in the Making*, makes visible a collection of design writings that contain informational as well as expressive content, and may not otherwise receive close attention. In this paper, this study's context and method are followed by *Vision in the Making* in the form of a visual essay.

Keywords

design history, design practice, design periodicals, manifesto, prototype

First Issues, First Words:

Vision in the Making

JESSICA BARNESS

Introduction

Some theoretical approaches to thinking about design and methods for designing begin quietly, while others roar into existence. In design writing, the definitive boundary that separates a 'manifesto' from an 'editorial' is often a matter of context, and intent. Published visionary statements are familiar territory for designers, and any one particular 'design manifesto' can mark the emergence or affirmation of a seminal (or trivial) design movement. Many of these focus attention on issues of design practice, and are written with a distinct social function toward bringing a community of like-minded individuals together. The word *manifesto* is akin to manifestation, which is to embody a theory or idea. Design manifestos of note include William Morris' *The Arts and Crafts of To-Day* (1889); Adolf Loos' *Ornament and Crime* (1910); Walter Gropius' *Bauhaus Manifesto* (1919); Naum Gabo and Antoine Pevsner's *Constructivist Manifesto* (1920); El Lissitzky's *Topography of Typography* (1923); Ken Garland's *First Things First* (1964, 2014); Dieter Rams' *Ten Rules of Good Design* (1987); Icograda's *Design Education Manifesto* (2000, 2011); Ellen Lupton's *Free Font Manifesto* (2006); and Allan Chochinov's *1000 Words: A Manifesto for Sustainability in Design* (2007). Through these statements, practitioners, educators, and scholars identify and often assert a shift in the scope and focus of the work that transpires within and around their communities. Practice—an act of manifesting—is one of the crucial defining points of design, and the poetics of these activities serve to inform the construction of who we are. Without them, we'd be "just a continuous stream of little designers". [1]

Within the context of 'affirmative manifestations,' I began studying a lineage of design periodicals launched from 1902–2015. This body of literature

[1] Vignelli, M. "Keynote Address." In Coming of Age: The First Symposium on the History of Graphic Design, April 20-21, 1983, Rochester Institute of Technology, edited by B. Hodik & R. Remington, p. 11. Rochester, NY, USA: Rochester Institute of Technology, 1985.

41

includes a diverse range of scholarly/peer-reviewed journals, professional magazines, and designer-authored publications, and these are all connected to communication design and related fields. [a] Specifically, I began reading through editors' introductions within the first issues of these publications. Here could be found the presence of cautiously assertive yet authoritative voices. Very often when there is a shift or debut of authority, something new ignites; these first words, written by editors and sometimes referred to as 'letters,' often read as calls to action.

Occupying a space between scholarly advocacy, professional correspondence, and manifesto, these texts hold a curious position within the greater scheme of periodical publication and within design history. They also serve to introduce a long-term project of mine that has been taking shape over countless hours (days, months, years...) of critiquing, curating, organizing, selecting, and authoring. These essays may be omitted from tables of contents and not referenced in other literature. Their authorship may be credited to named persons, initials, or simply "The Editors." In asserting a conceptual framework for the future and setting the public tone for a new periodical, they provide written evidence of new voices, new directions, and new goals for design. Pushing for change, an editor's first words are not quite research or practice, but they are certainly evidence of lived experience, and they reflect a critical observation of a discipline or field.

This study focuses on my investigation of a history of design through a critical review and re-contextualization of inaugural, publication-based reflections on design practice. This experiential framing offers a new way to understand what design is, does, and might be. It begins with an overview of English-language design periodicals situated within a historiographic framework. This is followed by observations about the meta-subjectivity, visual characteristics and linguistic variations found in these types of publications. I then document and reflect on a 'prototyping' process for cut-and-paste design practice in which I use extracted lines of text from first-issue editorial introductions to compose a new text. The result, *Vision in the Making,* is presented as an intertextual composition—a 'manifesto' made manifest in the form of a visual essay.

Design Periodicals

In the early twentieth century, writing in graphic design, advertising or commercial art periodicals in North America and western Europe lived largely

a *On a methodological note, the main challenge encountered throughout this study was accessibility: academic journals can generally be searched through a library database, but older issues of professional magazines and designer-authored publications are more difficult to obtain.*

under the guise of commercial art or graphic arts, and circulated through trade magazines. Monotype, a supplier of typesetting machinery and typefaces for the industry, began publishing *The Monotype Recorder and Monthly Circular* in 1902 (relaunched in 2014 as *The Recorder*). Popular WWII era trade periodicals *Print* (1940) and *Graphis* (1944), and, eventually, the *Journal of Commercial Art* (1959, later published as *Communication Arts*), served to elevate the importance of professional practice and provide information and news for the industry. More periodicals that reported on or critically analyzed issues in and around graphic design practice and criticism appeared over the next few decades. Among these, just two years after *First Things First* was published in 1964, *Dot Zero* (1966) was launched to integrate visual communication design practice with theory and criticism, and, the next year, the *Journal of Typographic Research* (1967) began publication and focused on the scholarly investigation of typography (later published as *Visible Language,* now the oldest peer-reviewed design journal in the world). Neither was a traditional graphic arts magazine and both introduced new ways to write critically and analytically about design (and to explore the visual design of writing). Shortly thereafter in 1971, *Icographic* was launched by the international design organization Icograda, followed by professional typography magazines *U&lc* (1973) and *Baseline* (1979). In 1982, *the Journal of Art and Design Education* began publication, and in 1984—the same year the Apple computer made its grand debut—the academic journal *Design Issues* and the designer-authored magazine *Emigre* published their first issues. Though aimed at different audiences, all three of these were interested in changing the landscape of design through the introduction and analysis of form and the essential ideas that guided formal configurations, as well as through criticism and a variety of types of editorial, scholarly, and research writing. The following years gave way to a flurry of periodicals, from *Fuse* (1991) to *Design Philosophy Papers* (2003) to *Shè Jì* (2015), and it became clear that different aspects of the growing knowledge base of and about design were being introduced within each title. These all began within a certain span of time and place, and in response to new practices, the need to examine graphic design through new theoretical lenses, and, sometimes, through new types of media.

Emerging from diverse social, economic, and industry contexts, design periodicals represent attitudes toward practices related to or embedded within a typology that includes but is not limited to visual communications, graphic design, industrial design, architecture, interior design, interaction design, typography, design history, material culture, design management, and now, with this inaugural publication of *Dialectic,* design education. Few definitive frameworks exist to categorize design periodicals according to the wide variety of discourses that now affect and are affected by design and the work of designers and their collaborators. They might be further sorted into types related to audiences (practicing designers or designers working in academia or design researchers), evaluative practices (editor reviewed or peer-reviewed), or content sources (designer-authored, commissioned, or submissions-based). The editor introductions I have chosen to examine address different facets of design and its discourses. For example, in the mid-1980s, three vastly different periodicals began publication: *HOW* was launched to provide industry professionals with "start-to-finish information and/or instructions that trace a project from concept, to production, to final costing;" [2] *Octavo* was conceptualized, published, and edited by the design practice 8vo to "investigate the way in which letterforms are used in the visual arts, poetry, architecture and the environment…[and] design education;" [3] and the academic journal *Design Issues* was founded at the University of Illinois at Chicago by design faculty members who believed that "before the design profession becomes too concerned with conclusions, a place for ongoing deliberation must be established." [4] A common thread running through these introductions is the desire to serve and facilitate inquiry toward the professional practice of design.

Design periodicals are artifacts and activities. At the same time, they are also meta-artifacts in that they manifest writing *about* artifacts and activities in design. The variances among the periodicals in attitudes, contexts, and practice reflect historiographic challenges in that "defining and explaining design and what a designer does are dependent not only on immersion in design practice, but also on the ability to see this practice in both historical and social perspectives." [5] The issues of periodicals—those addressed, and those of the paginated variety—are in continuous development. Design is difficult to define because it is constantly changing, which presents a problem: "How, then, can we establish a body of knowledge about something that has no fixed identity?;" [6] indeed, discussing these publications solely within a comprehensive, chronological arrangement may, "…assert a continuity among objects and actions that are in reality discontinuous." [7] Similarly, discussing singular meanings of design artifacts is "…ignoring the fact that design is a process of representation. It represents political, economic, and cultural power and values within the different spaces occupied, through engagement with different

2

Editors. "Welcome." How, 1.1 (1985): p. 19.

3

Johnston, S., Holt, M., Burke, M., & Muir, H. "86.1." Octavo, 1 (1986): n.p.

4

Margolin, V. "Editorial." Design Issues, 1.1 (1984): p. 3. Online. Available at: http://www.jstor.org/stable/1511538 (Accessed 20 September 2016).

5

Dilnot, C. "The State of Design History, Part I: Mapping the Field." Design Issues, 1.1 (1984): p. 6. Online. Available at: http://www.jstor.org/stable/1511539 (Accessed 20 September 2016).

6

Margolin, V. The Politics of the Artificial: Essays on Design and Design Studies. Chicago, IL, USA: University of Chicago Press, 2002, p. 225.

7

Margolin, The Politics of the Artificial, p. 191.

8

Buckley, C. "Made in Patriarchy: Toward a Feminist Analysis of Women and Design." Design Issues, 3.2 (1986): p. 10. Online. Available at: http://www.jstor.org/stable/1511480 (Accessed 20 September 2016).

9

Fallan, K. & Lees-Maffei, G. "It's Personal: Subjectivity in Design History." Design and Culture, 7.1 (2015): p. 15. Online. Available at: http://www.tandfonline.com/doi/abs/ 10.2752/175470715X14153615623565 (Accessed 20 September 2016).

10

Gemser, G., de Bont, C., Hekkert, P., & Friedman, K. "Quality percep- tions of design journals: The design scholars' perspective." Design Stud- ies, 33.1 (2012): pgs. 4–23. Online. Available at: http://dx.doi.org/10. 1016/j.destud.2011.09.001 (Accessed 20 September 2016).

11

Barness, J. "Letters are Media, Words are Collage: Writing Imag- es through A (Dis)Connected Twen- ty-Six." Message, 2 (2015): pgs. 47-48. Online. Available at: http:// www.jessicabarness.com/papers/Bar- ness_Disconnected26_Message2015.pdf (Accessed 20 September 2016).

[b] *Cut-up, in this context, describes writing that is composed by cutting, pasting, and arranging material from preexisting sources.*

subjects." [8] In this study, language used in editorial introductions represents the vision or self-awareness of its writer(s), and is thus concretely tied to the new periodical's imagined or proposed future; this vision is integrated with the subject matter of the publication, as well as with the facilitation of its specific discourse. As a result, a problem is encountered in this study: given the rather subjective nature of editorial introductions, how might these texts be effec- tively studied to expose their humanistic qualities, as well as their critical ob- servations on design? Discussion on subjectivity in design history suggests that artifacts speak and must be translated, but "...how far can we go in our trans- lations of 'thing talk?' Where is the border between imaginative interpretation and sheer flight of fancy?" [9]

Inquiry through Critical Making

A common element across design periodicals in their first issues is the existence of editorial 'calls to action.' An exhaustive list of titles is prac- tically non-existent, but a critical examination of a recent study, [10] combined with a cursory analysis of library databases and helpful colleagues provided a starting point. In total, 72 periodicals were surveyed, and 62 contained editori- al introductions in their inaugural issues. Of these, 50 editorial introductions contained visionary or self-aware language. Visionary discourse contains pow- erful or imaginative ideas on what a future will or might be like, and self-aware statements by particular editors and producers display the editorial knowledge and awareness of the individual character and purpose of their particular de- sign periodical, as well as its relative position within the "landscape" of other design periodicals.

To better understand and communicate my findings, I offer a first-is- sue text of a different kind: a new text prototyped with phrases extracted from these inaugural editorial introductions. The term 'prototyping' is used to describe the process of manifesting an idea through the construction of a pre- liminary model. In this case, a new cut-and-paste text was made to expose the types of visionary or self-aware language found within the inaugural writings. My approach combines social and historiographic inquiry with design practice. The decision to work this way follows my previous research on Dada language games, cut-up, [b] and DJ remix approaches to inform a framework for creating new messages. [11] However, rather than relying on elements of chance, this study involved close readings of the texts, followed by the deliberate extraction and arrangement of lines. This process of reading through cut-and-paste

12

Baker, S. "A Poetics of Graphic Design?" Visible Language, 28.3 (1994): p. 255. Online. Available at: http://search.proquest.com/docview/1297966689?accountid=11835 (Accessed 20 September 2016).

13

Drucker, J. Figuring the Word: Essays on Books, Writing, and Visual Poetics. New York, NY, USA: Granary Press, 1998, p. 74.

14

Ruecker, S. "A Brief Taxonomy of Prototypes for the Digital Humanities." Scholarly and Research Communication, 6.2 (2015): para. 7. Online. Available at: http://src-online.ca/index.php/src/article/view/222/415 (Accessed 20 September 2016). See also Boer, L. & Donovan, J. 2012. "Provotypes for Participatory Innovation" in DIS 2012: Proceedings of the Designing Interactive Systems Conference, 11–15 June 2012, Newcastle, UK: ACM press, 2012: pgs. 388–397. Online. Available at: http://dx.doi.org/10.1145/2317956.2318014 (Accessed 20 September 2016).

writing connects with a broader call for "...a non-linear and more visual form of history-writing, which we should perhaps not balk at calling a poetics of graphic design." [12] The construction of entire narratives using appropriated sources may be seen in books such as *Woman's World* made by Graham Rawle (2005) and Société Réaliste's *The Best American Book of the 20th Century* designed by Project Projects (2014). As described by Johanna Drucker, literature written through appropriation displays "...a recognition of the fact that language lives in the world and thus has a life beyond the original intention of its first author." [13]

In designing this new text, titled *Vision in the Making,* I deliberately draw attention to the existence of multiple editorial voices as founders, stewards, curators, and activists. These writings quietly expose the advances and shortcomings that have guided and are guiding scholarship and professional practices in and around design. This was approached as a provocative prototype, or 'provotype,' which is intended to "...challenge presuppositions, break down stereotypical understandings, and generally produce changes in the way people think about a particular topic or situation." [14] Through its narrative and bibliography, Vision in the Making makes visible a collection of design writings that may not otherwise receive close attention. Photocopies, scans, and photographs of originals (figure 1) were used as raw material that guided cut-and-paste processes that made use of both paper and digital components. These originals varied greatly in quality, depending on the original printing method used to publish them, as well as the nature of their distribution. These materials eventually yielded a diverse array of high-resolution digital files, scans of faxed material, visually disintegrated reproductions, and digital snapshots. Some letterform touch-up was necessary to ensure legibility, but the typographic character of each text has been retained. The individual lines, representing the earnestness and humor found throughout the literature, are no longer situated within their respective periodicals and discourses. Instead, they are contextualized alongside—and connected linguistically, conceptually, and physically with—the first words from editorial writings that were published in other first issues.

Vision in the Making is historiographic because of the nature of its contents and ahistorical in terms of its design. My process, which was subjective in that my voice is present as the designer-composer, was guided by visionary and self-aware language and not by historical markers (figure 2). As the composer making this new text, it was impossible to distance myself from the content.

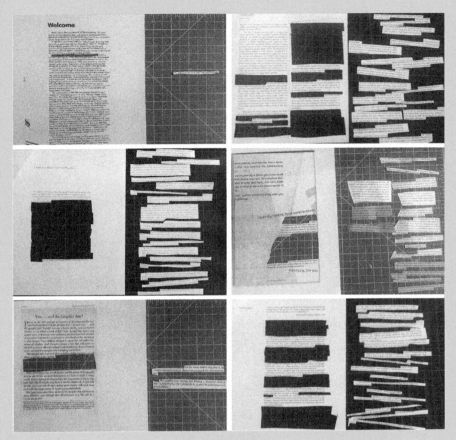

That this first number sees publication is, literally, a result of their interest and support.

The first issue of a new journal is a moment for celebration and a time for reflection.

Design has entered a golden age.

One thing is obvious from the past year's organizational work: there is no scarcity of fresh thinking and new ideas being generated in this field.

Our inaugural issue has no theme other than courage—that of Mitchell Wolfson, Jr. who dared to initiate it and contributors who dared to write for it sight unseen.

This scholarly journal on sustainable design is both important and timely.

I believe it to be a long overdue addition to the ranks of highly acclaimed and respected journals.

I welcome you on behalf of the Editorial Board to the readership of this new international journal.

It is always a special time when a new product is launched, a time like the dawn of a new day when the darkness of struggles past gives way to the bright hope of the future. The struggles that lie behind the start-up of this journal must still cast at least a faint shadow across the minds of those individuals whose vision, sweat, and perseverance have brought the journal, this new product, to its first light.

The launch of this new journal emerges from an extraordinary range of innovative research on material culture that has taken place across the humanities and social sciences during the last two decades.

Some of the material will be complex but that is the challenge of reflection. If the contemporary situation is so hard to grasp, how can its analysis be simple?

This journal was born in the context of our research mission.

Is this a utopian endeavour? Perhaps.

FIGURE 03

As a hybrid journal, **design practice**[29]

total design[30]

design activity will be addressed from an

educational, historical, technological or practical perspective.[31]

This requires research, discourse, and debate.[32]

Design has acquired not just a history but also a historiography.[33]

not only an increasing amount of critical analysis, but also of critical practice.[34]

There are no sharp breaks—no boundaries—where the realm of science
ends and those of the humanities and art begin [35]

The formation of a new set of directions for thinking about design is a long-term project.[36]

it will be critical that any new approaches and new solutions are inherently sustainable.[37]

Our project is, of necessity, a political one,[38]

The aim of this journal is to be provocative and to raise controversial issues.[39]

tacit knowledge, conditions for creative performance, serendipity, creativity

of teams, organizational culture and entrepreneurship make up

a sixpack brimfull of potential controversy.[40]

FIGURE 04

Those who can communicate succeed; those who can't, fail.[45] *the medium through which a message is communicated is as important as the message itself.*[46] (so) There will also be space in the journal for visual material — experimental typography, drawings, sketches for objects.[47] (and) **narrow questions of semantics to larger issues of identity**[48] (and) what has been called 'the meaning of things'.[49] Our fingers are also known as "digits" (...) to be digital is to be radical and new.[50] **instead of exposing practice as research, you could also stage, perform, curate, translate, unfold or reflect practice as research.**[51] (Design,) ebbing and flowing a thousand times a day, is long overdue for a chronicle to present its possessions and potentialities.[52] It connects goal to strategy, image to word, style to substance [53] (and it) infiltrates almost every aspect of our visual culture.[54] This dialogue on the historical, contextual, theoretical, institutional and interpretive modalities (...) will take on specific and interrelated forms.[55] (These) **are goals for humanity as a whole in the context of inclusive wellbeing.**[56] (We are) blurring the boundaries of public and privately consumed media (...) the collapsing of the creator and user into a single individual.[57] What will be the shape of our new world of design?[58]

The growth of any discipline relies on the accumulation of knowledge.[59] (But) **We have wrapped our conversations tightly around ourselves, blankets of white noise offered with expectations of sameness.**[60] Disciplines, with their boundary- maintaining devices, institutional structures, accepted texts, methodologies, internal debates and circumscribed areas of study tend, by virtue of their very constitution, to be rather conservative in nature.[61] *We have swallowed ideas and images that our grandparents would have choked on.*[62] (We) **remember it with mixed emotions—mainly a nostalgic association with green eye shades, garters on the sleeves, naked light bulbs and low pay.**[63] No longer do we need to restrict ourselves to particular viewpoints or methodologies in order to analyse, interpret and understand the visual world around us.[64]

In order to craft a manifesto that could potentially speak to anyone (or everyone) connected with design, I sought to bridge issues and attitudes; by doing this, various lineages converge, and it becomes a tapestry of discourses. Power shifts between scholarly and professional concerns are purposefully merged. Though liberties were taken in juxtaposing and combining phrases, all sources are referenced, and the bibliography itself is an homage to authors, generations, and audiences (figure 3). Transition words were added and some pronouns replaced to build a more fluid reading experience. Specific periodical names are substituted with "our project" or similar. These paper iterations took final shape through digital composition (figure 4).

Observations

Through this study, a number of observations emerged regarding visual character and use of language. These form a starting point for future in-depth analysis of and about these periodicals.

Visually, the texts may be described across a spectrum of graphic character. At one end of this spectrum is the editor introduction for the *Journal of Interior Design Education and Research* (1975), which "...has no budget whatever" and was begun as a response to "...a noticeable lack of serious and scholarly work addressed specifically to problems of the profession." [15] Its appearance suggests it was produced manually with a typewriter for a small community, was low-budget, and was without graphic embellishment of any kind. At the opposite end of the spectrum is *Zed* (1994), with its playful and rhythmic layout, a publication that sought to "identify and embrace the margins; to question, debate, and question again; to weigh the alternatives and consider the possibilities." [16] Its use of slightly distorted typefaces throughout the various layouts that constituted its seven issues, combined with formal imperfections (representative of 1990s typographic layout trends that themselves referenced American typographic layout trends from the 1930s fostered by the likes of Brodovitch and Fehmy Agha), trapezoid-shaped text columns, line art, angular shapes, and slanted lines of larger-size type visually indicate this was a periodical paving a new path. Though not to the same extent as Zed, the layouts of editor introductions within *Dot Zero* (1966), *Octavo* (1986), *Fuse* (1991) and *Iridescent* (2009) were also given consideration regarding white space and typographic variations.

The remaining texts fall in the middle of this spectrum, and are similar to one another in terms of their visual design. In this way, they maintain

15

Friedmann, A. "Introduction." Journal of Interior Design Education and Research 1.1 (1975): p. 2.

16

Salen, K. "Editor's Note," Zed, 1 (1994): p. 6.

the look and feel of what periodicals and editor introductions characteristically look like: single, two- or three-column layouts with consistent margins, serif typefaces, and a tendency to make use of only a few graphic elements per page spread. To a viewer-reader, these texts may appear 'standard,' as there is little to differentiate them from the pages of any other periodical. Some subtly set themselves apart by using sans serif typefaces (see examples within *Vision in the Making*), italics (*Graphis* 1944; *Dot Zero* 1966), or by including graphic imagery (*U&lc* 1973; *Fuse* 1991; *Visual Communication* 2002; *Journal of Visual Culture* 2002; *The Poster* 2010; *Communication Design* 2015), or, in one case, an editor's headshot portrait (*Design Management Journal* 2002). The introductions of *Design Studies* (1979) and *Journal of Decorative and Propaganda Arts* (1986) bear the signatures of their editors. Overall, these decisions may have been a result of a periodical's visual identity, a publisher's house style, or available production technology. Indeed, the assertion of particular visual characteristics and styles may have been a purposeful attempt to establish credibility and to meet expectations within the greater academic and professional communities. On the other hand, these 'standard' graphic layouts may contradict the editorial language they contain concerning innovation and new goals for design artifacts and activities.

Language also varies among the introductions. For the most part, the founding editors write to inform and make one or more emotional appeals. This approach was also used to guide the editorial and visual structure of *Vision in the Making*. The editors of the periodicals I have examined during my study acquaint audiences with their periodical's focus, perspective, and context. In so doing, one periodical is differentiated from the others that occupy its disciplinary landscape, and its practical function is established. Nonetheless, these texts also contain expressive language that encourages readers and entices potential contributors. The editors challenge ideas of the past while anticipating the future, and phrases such as 'we will,' 'we want,' 'the world needs,' 'our dream,' and similar permeate the introductions. Curiously, texts with more colorful language reside within 'standard' visual layouts. This includes editors' personal stories (*Ergonomics in Design*, 1993; *The Poster*, 2010; *Codex: The Journal of Typography*, 2011) and quirky, unexpected content (*Dot Zero*, 1966; *Journal of Art and Design Education*, 1982; *Journal of Product Innovation Management*, 1984). Some of these ideas were incorporated into *Vision in the Making*. Beyond these, two texts stand out. William Edward Rudge, the founding editor of *Print* (1940) alludes to an audience that is primarily male and middle-class.

This reflects pertinent aspects of design's history, but is not included in *Vision in the Making*. The inaugural issue of *Design Studies* (1979) contains persuasive language by its first managing editor Nigel Cross befitting a speech to motivate the masses, and pieces of this are included in the new text for emphasis.

Through its narrative and bibliography, *Vision in the Making* reveals that certain overarching visions and issues have remained constant in periodicals devoted to chronicling, analyzing and criticizing design for over one hundred years. These include the integration of theory, history, and criticism with practice, the challenges and opportunities that attach to utilizing new technologies, and a propensity among many editors for addressing educational concerns. At the same time, editors' perspectives reflect those of the audiences to whom they speak, and these introductions are akin to snapshots of a changing history. Early twentieth century printing trade concerns have given way to today's academic, global, multicultural, economic, industrial, and social issues in design (for example, see *Vision in the Making* lines 26, 38, 40, 43, 57, 69, 71, 74, 83, 97, 105, and 123). The editorial introductions reveal the evolution of what was a customer-centered industry into a more inclusive design community that includes and fosters critical, self-aware discourse.

Editor introductions anticipated and looked toward a future...which happens to be now: are we changing the paradigm (line 27)? Practicing in provocative ways and raising controversial issues (line 39)? Thinking deeply about design as a world-shaping force (line 77)? Questioning tradition and taking risks (line 116)? The launch of this first issue of *Dialectic* demonstrates that there is still new territory to investigate and document. The contents of design periodicals have certainly changed over time, yet the form of these meta-artifacts has changed little. Moreover, the design periodicals examined in this study are printed and bound or exist online in a print-friendly format, which presents yet another question: What shape or form might the future chronicles of our design knowledge take?

Conclusion

Vision in the Making is an intertextual composition of editors' introductions to first issues of design periodicals and, in effect, it manifests as an interplay of the voices that shepherd ongoing dialogue concerning what design is, does, and might become. This study forms a foundation for further inquiry about the nature of scholarship in design. It is intended to be read in a few of different ways: as an amusing narrative in its own right; as a starting point for learning titles, names, and dates associated with design periodicals through the bibliographic footnotes; and as a manifesto calling for awareness of the editorial voices and publication venues that have helped shape design practice and scholarship. Additionally, readers are asked to consider how close readings of other design texts might be facilitated through a similar cut-and-paste prototyping process. Ultimately, *Vision in the Making* strives to inspire. It demonstrates that nearly every editor's words allude to the same desire as the readers and authors—to engage in a practice through writing, theory, criticism, education, designed things, or something else entirely:

(a "provotype")

vision in *the* making

Jessica Barness

The first issue of a new journal is a moment for celebration and a time for reflection[1] (and) Our inaugural issue has no theme other than courage.[2] Is this a utopian endeavour? Perhaps.[3] (Our project) **is not a sudden venture**[4] (and) it belongs to no single person or entity.[5] It is always a special time when a new product is launched, a time like the dawn of a new day when the darkness of struggles past gives way to the bright hope of the future.[6] (We are) on the verge of tremendous growth.[7] Design has entered a golden age[8] (and) there is no scarcity of fresh thinking and new ideas being generated in this field.[9] **The launch of this new journal emerges from an extraordinary range of**[10] vision, sweat, and perseverance.[11] **There are already enough constraints imposed on our ability to think and to write fresh and creative work without inventing any new ones.**[12] speaking against power is always dangerous and repression breeds invention in the repressed.[13] *Before the paint is dry on the protest poster, the issue has shifted—so much has our rate of communication changed.*[14] (Our project) **is a springboard** (...) **an incitement** (...) **a laboratory**. It is an experiment in how we think.[15] As a designer (in a previous life) I was never really aware of the moral obligation imposed on me to act in a way that brought no harm to the world, let alone to promote good.[16] **It is time for a fresh approach.**[17] *Good design is no longer a matter of good taste and intelligence alone,*[18] for all too often design is seen as a prettifying profession.[19]

---

1 Ken Friedman, Yongqi Lou, and Jin Ma, "Editorial," *Shè Jì: The Journal of Design, Economics, and Innovation*, 1.1 (2015): p. 1.

2 Pamela Johnson, "From the Editor," *Journal of Decorative and Propaganda Arts*, 1.1 (1986): p. 5.

3 Editor(s), "Editorial," *Journal of Visual Culture*, 1 (2002): p. 5.

4 Stuart Macdonald, "Editorial," *Journal of Art and Design Education*, 1 (1982): p. 2.

5 Charlie Breindahl, Ida Engholm, Judith Gregory, Erik Stolterman, "The Computer and Design," *Artifact*, 1 (2007): p. 3.

6 Blair Little, "The Dawn of a New Journal," *Journal of Product Innovation Management*, 1.1 (1984): p. 1.

7 Marty Neumeier, "Welcome," *Critique*, 1 (1996): n.p.

8 Elizabeth Guffey, "Editorial Introduction," *Design and Culture*, 1.1 (2009): p. 5.

9 Merald Wrolstad, "A Prefactory Note to the First Number," *Journal of Typographic Research*, 1.1 (1967): n.p. Later published as *Visible Language*.

10 Editor(s), untitled, *Material Culture*, 1.1 (1996): p. 5.

11 Little, "The Dawn of a New Journal," 1.

12 Editor(s), untitled, *Material Culture*, 6.

13 Simon Downs, "Editorial," *The Poster*, 1.1 (2010): p. 6.

14 Robert Malone, "Editorial," *Dot Zero*, 1.1 (1966): n.p.

15 Editor(s), "Editorial," *Journal of Visual Culture*, pgs. 5–6.

16 Downs, "Editorial," 6.

17 John Wozencroft, "Fuse," *Fuse*, 1.1 (1991): n.p.

18 Malone, "Editorial," n.p.

19 Max Bruinsma, "Iridescent: A Prism on Design Research," *Iridescent*, 1 (2009): p. 10. Later published as *Communication Design*.

During the past three decades, there has emerged a wealth of thoughtful, mischievous, exacting and imaginative research and writing.[20] Few serious, critical or erudite articles appear in the professional magazines[21] (and our project) has evolved from a desire to see an independent publication which acts as a serious forum for the discussion of matters, both contemporary and historical.[22] But, then, we never thought that doing, activating, sounding out visual culture should be anything other than awkward, thought-provoking, captivating.[23] Since the early 20th century a great deal of theoretical thinking has taken place in the context of design *practice*, and today this is increasingly taken up and developed in the context of academic research.[24] As (our project) evolves, it will look even further afield to curate the work of men and women who spend every day of their lives creating.[25] No one, least of all the designer, can operate meaningfully in today's fast-changing economic and cultural situation without a well-defined sense of purpose.[26] We are changing the paradigm[27] (and the) changes are shaking us to our roots.[28]

As a hybrid journal,[29] **design practice** (...) **total design** (...) **design activity**[30] will be addressed an educational, historical, technological or practical perspective.[31] This requires research, discourse, and debate.[32] Design has acquired not just a history but also a historiography.[33] not only an increasing amount of critical analysis, but also of critical practice.[34] There are no sharp breaks— no boundaries— where the realm of science ends and those of the humanities and art begin.[35] The formation of a new set of directions for thinking about design is a long-term project[36] (and) it will be critical that any new approaches and new solutions are inherently sustainable.[37] **Our project is, of necessity, a political one**[38] (and furthermore) The aim of this journal is to be provocative and to raise controversial issues.[39] tacit knowledge, conditions for creative performance, serendipity, creativity of teams, organizational culture and entrepreneurship make up a sixpack brimfull of potential controversy.[40] **Design was once an art focused on the shape of things.**[41] **Nobody today is a commercial artist!**[42] This shift is a transformation from thinking of design as a

20 Editor(s), "Editorial," *Journal of Visual Culture*, 5.
21 Arnold Friedmann, "Introduction", *Journal of Interior Design Education and Research*, 1.1 (1975): p. 2.
22 Simon Johnston, Mark Holt, Michael Burke, Hamish Muir, "86.1," *Octavo*, 1 (1986): n.p.
23 Editor(s), "Editorial," *Journal of Visual Culture*, 5.
24 Carey Jewitt, Theo Van Leeuwen, Ron Scollon, Teal Triggs, "Editorial," *Visual Communication*, 1.1 (2002): p. 6.
25 John Boardley, "This Wonderful Affliction," *Codex: The Journal of Typography*, 1 (2011): p. 5.
26 Victor Margolin, "Editorial," *Design Issues*, 1.1 (1984): p. 3.
27 Sydney Gregory, "Design Studies: The New Capability," *Design Studies*, 1.1 (1979): p. 2.
28 Neumeier, "Welcome," n.p.
29 Peter Storkerson, "From the Editor," *Design Research Quarterly*, 1.1 (2006): p. 3.
30 D.F. Sheldon, "Editorial Comment," *Journal of Engineering Design*, 1.1 (1990): p. 3.

31 Rachel Cooper, "Design Research Comes of Age," *The Design Journal*, 0.1 (1997): p. 1.
32 Aleksandar Subic, "Editorial," *International Journal of Sustainable Design*, 1 (2008): p. 2.
33 Christopher Bailey, "Editorial," *Journal of Design History*, 1.1 (1998): n.p
34 Jewitt, Van Leeuwen, Scollon, and Triggs, "Editorial," 6.
35 Wrolstad, "A Prefatory Note to the First Number," n.p.
36 Margolin, "Editorial," 3.
37 Subic, "Editorial," 2.
38 Editor(s), untitled, *Material Culture*, 8.
39 Margolin, "Editorial," 3.
40 Susan Moger and Tudor Rickards, "Editorial," *Creativity and Innovation Management*, 1.1 (1992): p. 3.
41 Friedman, Lou, and Ma, "Editorial," 2.
42 Editor(s), untitled, *CA: Journal of Commercial Art*, 1.1 (1959): p. 2. Later published as *Communication Arts*.

craft-based artisan skill of designing things to thinking of design across a spectrum of target fields.[43] The remit of the designer has necessarily broadened from the design of the visual to also include the design of sound, haptics, experiences and services.[44]

Those who can communicate succeed; those who can't, fail.[45] the medium through which a message is communicated is as important as the message itself.[46] (so) There will also be space in the journal for visual material — experimental typography, drawings, sketches for objects,[47] (and) **narrow questions of semantics to larger issues of identity,**[48] (and) what has been called 'the meaning of things'.[49] Our fingers are also known as "digits" (...) to be to be digital is to be radical and new.[50] **instead of exposing practice as research, you could also stage, perform, curate, translate, unfold or reflect practice as research.**[51] (Design,) ebbing and flowing a thousand times a day, is long overdue for a chronicle to present possessions and potentialities.[52] It connects goal to strategy, image to word, style to substance.[53] (and it) infiltrates almost every aspect of our visual culture.[54] This dialogue on the historical, contextual, theoretical, institutional and interpretive modalities (...) will take on specific and interrelated forms.[55] (These) **are goals for humanity as a whole in the context of inclusive wellbeing.**[56] (We are) blurring the boundaries of public and privately consumed media (...) the collapsing of the creator and user into a single individual.[57] **What will be the shape of our new world of design?**[58]

The growth of any discipline relies on the accumulation of knowledge.[59] (But) **We have wrapped our conversations tightly around ourselves, blankets of white noise offered with expectations of sameness.**[60] Disciplines, with their boundary- maintaining devices, institutional structures, accepted texts, methodologies, internal debates and circumscribed areas and circumscribed areas of study tend, by virtue of their very constitution, to be rather conservative in nature.[61] *We have swallowed ideas and images that our grandparents would have choked on.*[62] (We) remember it with mixed emotions—mainly a nostalgic association with green eye shades, garters on the sleeves, naked light bulbs and low

43 Friedman, Lou, and Ma, "Editorial," 2.

44 Teal Triggs, "Research Notes: Communication Design," *Communication Design*, 3.1 (2015): p. 1. Continuation of *Iridescent*, beginning as vol. 3.

45 Daryle Jean Gardner-Bonneau, "Comment from the Editor," *Ergonomics in Design*, 1.1 (1993): p. 3.

46 Masoud Yazdani, "Editorial," *Intelligent Tutoring Media*, 1.1 (1990); p. 2. Later published as *Digital Creativity*.

47 Margolin, "Editorial," 3.

48 Editor(s), untitled, Material Culture, 8.

49 Bailey, "Editorial," n.p.

50 Editors(s), "Editorial," *Digital Creativity*, 8.1 (1997): p. 1. Continuation of *Intelligent Tutoring Media*, beginning as vol. 8.

51 Michael Schwab, "Editorial," *Journal of Artistic Research*, 0.1 (2011): para. 3.

52 William Rudge, "You... and the Graphic Arts," *Print: A Quarterly Journal Of The Graphic Arts*, 1.1 (1940): n.p. Later published as *Print*.

53 Neumeier, "Welcome," n.p.

54 Emma Tucker, "Editor's Letter," *Monotype Recorder*, 1 (2014): n.p.

55 Editor(s), "Editorial," *Journal of Visual Culture*, 5.

56 Friedman, Lou, and Ma, "Editorial," 4.

57 Julia Knight and Alexis Weedon, "Editorial," *Convergence*, 1.1 (1995): p. 8.

58 Gregory, "Design Studies: The New Capability," 2.

59 Lin-Lin Chen, "International Journal of Design: A Step Forward," *International Journal of Design*, 1.1 (2007): p. 1.

60 Katie Salen, "Editor's Note," *Zed*, 1.1 (1994): p. 6.

61 Editor(s), untitled, *Material Culture*, 5.

62 Malone, "Editorial," n.p.

nostalgic association with green eye shades, garters on the sleeves, naked light bulbs and low pay.[63] No longer do we need to restrict ourselves to particular viewpoints or methodologies in order to analyse, interpret and understand the visual world around us.[64]

As such we have no obvious genealogy of ancestors to whom we should pay homage, and are not concerned to invent any.[65] Part of our task is to trace them.[66] It's what a research journal should do: filter the luster and see what it is composed of [67] (so that) valuable time will not be unduly encroached upon.[68] All of us can contribute to building a common theoretical foundation, one which can then be passed on to future generations of designers.[69]

Design is a global topic,[70] as both a social activity and as a subject for critical enquiry.[71] as 'doers' and 'thinkers' [72] call it what you wish.[73] This journal has, as its over riding purpose, the creation of provision for the interchange of ideas on an international basis,[74] a panoramic window, a showcase (...) a clearing house for the international exchange of ideas and information.[75] It will attempt to serve as an organ expressing the designer's point of view in the new scene.[76] Broadly, (our project) is about getting more people to think deeply about design as a world-shaping force, be stopped in their tracks by this recognition and then to participate in developing more informed design thinking and action.[77] let's go back to the drawing board and do it,[78] whether it has come within the range of " practical politics " from their point of view or not.[79] (We may be) anglophone but not anglocentric, as we hope to show in this first issue.[80] The world is constituted through a continuous dynamism,[81] (and) It is this spirit we hope to make visible in our journal: shared interests and concerns, distinctly different voices and approaches.[82] In contrast (...) a multiplicity of voices shapes our view design and its discourse today[83] (and) there are important relationships that have not been expressed and categories that overlap or defy easy classification.[84] We are confident that the articles, debates, interviews and reviews published in these pages will take account of the complex and inter-animating series

63 Editor(s), untitled, *CA: Journal of Commercial Art*, 2.

64 Jewitt, Van Leeuwen, Scollon, and Triggs, "Editorial," 5.

65 Editor(s), untitled, *Material Culture*, 5.

66 Editor(s), "Editorial," *Journal of Visual Culture*, 5.

67 Bruinsma, "Iridescent: A Prism on Design Research," 10.

68 Editor(s), "The Monotype Recorder," *The Monotype Recorder and Monthly Circular*, 1.1 (1902): n.p.

69 Chen, "International Journal of Design: A Step Forward," 2.

70 Cooper, "Design Research Comes of Age," 1.

71 Paul Stiff, "Typography papers," *Typography papers*, 1 (1996): n.p.

72 Schwab, "Editorial," para. 10.

73 Editor(s), untitled, *CA: Journal of Commercial Art*, 2.

74 John Heywood, "Editorial," *International Journal of Technology and Design Education*, 1.1 (1990): p. 2.

75 Herb Lubalin, Aaron Burns, Ed Rondthaler, Jack Anson Finke, "Why U&lc?" *U&lc*, 1.1 (1973): p. 2.

76 John Hallas, "Introduction," *Icographic*, 1.1 (1971): p. 1.

77 Anne-Marie Willis, "Opening Lines on Unsustainability," *Design Philosophy Papers*, 1.1 (2003): p. 1.

78 Editor(s), untitled, *CA: Journal of Commercial Art*, 2.

79 Editor(s), "The Monotype Recorder," 1-2.

80 Stiff, "Typography papers," n.p.

81 Editor(s), untitled, *Material Culture*, 6.

82 Jewitt, Van Leeuwen, Scollon, and Triggs, "Editorial," 5.

83 Guffey, "Editorial Introduction," 6.

84 Merald Wrolstad, "Visible Language: The Journal for Research on the Visual Media of Language Expression," *Visible Language*, 5.1 (1971): p. 5. Continuation of *Journal of Typographic Research*.

of relations that exist between history, theory and practice.[85] **After all, any journal article is *not* the research, but a deliberately created (re)presentation of research within a restricted format.**[86] (There are) New materials, new tools, new ways to plan work[87] (and) Design is no exception.[88] We have a world to win.[89]

The best design is done with intensity and commitment and[90] The success of any journal is dependent on the success of the community it aims to serve.[91] (This project) is, then, for academics, scholars, students, and practitioners struggling with the questions, the challenges, and the possibilities.[92] because design research is dispersed in journals across many different fields, it is difficult for design researchers to locate and read each other's works,[93] challenging conventional theories of representation.[94] The very breadth of the discipline, however, is problematic;[95] But the whole field is dissociated, its energies uncoordinated, its efforts unencouraged, its voice inarticulate.[96] At the same time, as design programs proliferate throughout the United States, many educators have realized that design education lacks the dimension of history, theory, and criticism that can foster more sophisticated and critical responses to new situations.[97] **Consequently, designers speak to other designers, academics to other academics, and students to no one in particular, or any who might listen.**[98] It would be presumptuous to say that (this project) has been created to solve this problem[99] (but) We intend to live up to your high expectations.[100] (This project) is a kind of experiment in which we hope to accommodate many possibly discordant voices[101] (and) *Plans made for an uncertain future can now begin to take on solid form.*[102]

(We) must keep continually alert to new research in every related area, and the best internal communication channel for new ideas is an active, vocal readership[103] in the context of protectable intellectual property[104] *that is historical/futuristic/comparative/ qualitative/quantitative/ethnographic/ethics-based/practice-led.*[105] (This) has often had a neurotic edge, which presents in obsessive formalisms, and in the self-satisfaction

85 Editor(s), "Editorial," *Journal of Visual Culture*, 6.
86 Schwab, "Editorial," para. 8.
87 Lubalin, Burns, Rondthaler, and Finke, "Why U&lc?" 2.
88 Chen, "International Journal of Design: A Step Forward," 1.
89 Gregory, "Design Studies: The New Capability," 2.
90 Margolin, "Editorial," 3.
91 Yazdani, "Editorial," 2.
92 Editor(s), "Editorial," *Journal of Visual Culture*, 6.
93 Chen, "International Journal of Design: A Step Forward," 1.
94 Michael Bull, Paul Gilroy, David Howes and Douglas Kahn, "Introducing Sensory Studies," *The Senses and Society*, 1.1 (2006): p. 5.
95 Thomas Walton, "Design Management as a Business and Academic Discipline," *Design Management Journal*, 1.1 (2000): p. 5.

96 Rudge, "You... and the Graphic Arts," n.p.
97 Margolin, "Editorial," 3.
98 Salen, "Editor's Note," 6.
99 Margolin, "Editorial," 3.
100 The Editors, "Welcome," *How*, 1.1 (1985): p. 19.
101 Stephen Scrivener, "Editorial," *CoDesign*, 1.1 (2005): p. 2.
102 The Publishers, "Introducing Graphis," *Graphis*, 1.1 (1944): p. 3.
103 Wrolstad, "A Prefatory Note to the First Number," n.p.
104 Moger and Rickards, "Editorial," 2.
105 Omar Vulpinari, "The Essentials," *Iridescent*, 1 (2009): p. 9. Later published as *Communication Design*.

of the comfortable just as much as in the self-inflation of the *nouvelle*.[106] we particularly encourage debate,[107] provocation and contestation,[108] to create a centre for discussion which which at present occurs, if it occurs at all, on the margins.[109] **And so the margins grow**[110] **in the form of editorial notes on 'burning issues' that are worth printing and that meet the aims of the journal.**[111] At the same time, if you take issue with anything, let us hear about it![112]

the concept for this journal was borne out of a perceived gap, or margin, in the current design dialogue.[113] Not quite as exciting as the arrival of one's first child, I guess[114] (but) The offspring is in your hands, and its growth and nurturance are largely up to you.[115] The best way to encourage a new generation of (...) designers is to break open (the) closed circle, to question its traditions and to support risk taking.[116] not enough progress has yet been made to shift from a teacher-led environment to one enabling a student-focused approach.[117] **its future depends upon their continued interest and writings, or as a harassed editor should say, upon their typings, triplicate, one-sided, marginate, and double-spaced.**[118] Although (we) worked long and hard, (we) saw the stars and (we) had the pleasure of an inherently satisfying task—building something new while aspiring to serve others.[119] Following this short celebration, we will turn the pages of (this project) over to thinkers whose work has helped to define the design field today, building bridges to innovation, value creation, the productive economy, and the world we build together.[120] This journal is one of the first of its kind[121] (yet) **It is simply a beginning—a concept that will ideally grow and transform as needs are identified and new energies explored.**[122] (It is) is a lens through which emerging discourses in contemporary communication design research and professional practices are made manifest, critically examined and developed.[123] (It) **does not need to be an 'ultimate statement',**[124] *There is nothing here intended to be final or definitive;*[125] a new level of thinking is not expected to emerge full-blown like Athena from the head of Zeus.[126] We hope you enjoy our first issue.[127] It is a start.[128]

106 Stiff, "Typography papers," n.p.
107 Storkerson, "From the Editor," 3.
108 Editor(s), "Editorial," *Journal of Visual Culture*, 5.
109 Bailey, "Editorial," n.p.
110 Salen, "Editor's Note," 6.
111 Sheldon, "Editorial Comment," 3.
112 Wrolstad, "A Prefatory Note to the First Number," n.p.
113 Salen, "Editor's Note," 6.
114 Scrivener, "Editorial," 1.
115 Gardner-Bonneau, "Comment from the Editor," 3.
116 Wozencroft, "Fuse," n.p.
117 Editor(s), "Editorial," *Art, Design, and Communication in Higher Education*, 1.1 (2002): p. 5.

118 Macdonald, "Editorial," 2.
119 Little, "The Dawn of a New Journal," 1.
120 Friedman, Lou, and Ma, "Editorial," 1.
121 Sheldon, "Editorial Comment," 3.
122 Salen, "Editor's Note," 12.
123 Triggs, "Research Notes: Communication Design," 1.
124 Wozencroft, "Fuse," n.p.
125 Malone, "Editorial," n.p.
126 Margolin, "Editorial," 3.
127 Walton, "Design Management as a Business and Academic Discipline," 7.
128 Scrivener, "Editorial," 4.

References

Baker, S. "A Poetics of Graphic Design?" *Visible Language,* 28.3 (1994): pgs. 245–259. Available at: http://search.proquest.com/docview/1297966689?accountid=11835. Online. (Accessed 20 September 2016).

Barness, J. "Letters are Media, Words are Collage: Writing Images through A (Dis)Connected Twenty-Six." *Message,* 2 (2015): pgs. 46–53. Online. Available at: http://www.jessicabarness.com/papers/Barness_Disconnected26_Message2015.pdf (Accessed 20 September 2016).

Boer, L. & Donovan, J. 2012. "Provotypes for Participatory Innovation" in DIS 2012: Proceedings of the Designing Interactive Systems Conference, 11–15 June 2012, Newcastle, UK: ACM press, 2012: pgs. 388-397. Online. Available at: http://dx.doi.org/10.1145/2317956.2318014 (Accessed 20 September 2016).

Buckley, C. "Made in Patriarchy: Toward a Feminist Analysis of Women and Design." *Design Issues,* 3.2 (1986): pgs. 3–14. Online. Available at: http://www.jstor.org/stable/1511480 (Accessed 20 September 2016).

Dilnot, C. "The State of Design History, Part I: Mapping the Field." *Design Issues,* 1.1 (1984): pgs. 4–23. Online. Available at: http://www.jstor.org/stable/1511539 (Accessed 20 September 2016).

Drucker, J. *Figuring the Word: Essays on Books, Writing, and Visual Poetics.* New York, NY, USA: Granary Press, 1998.

Editors. "Welcome." *How,* 1.1 (1985): pg. 19.

Fallan, K. & Lees-Maffei, G. "It's Personal: Subjectivity in Design History." *Design and Culture,* 7.1 (2015): pgs. 5-27. Online. Available at: http://www.tandfonline.com/doi/abs/10.2752/175470715X14153615623565 (Accessed 20 September 2016).

Friedmann, A. "Introduction." *Journal of Interior Design Education and Research,* 1.1 (1975): p. 2.

Gemser, G., de Bont, C., Hekkert, P., & Friedman, K. "Quality perceptions of design journals: The design scholars' perspective." *Design Studies,* 33.1 (2012): pgs. 4-23. Online. Available at: http://dx.doi.org/10.1016/j.destud.2011.09.001 (Accessed 20 September 2016).

Johnston, S., Holt, M., Burke, M., & Muir, H. "86.1." *Octavo* 1 (1986): n.p.

Margolin, V. "Editorial." *Design Issues,* 1.1 (1984): p. 3. Online. Available at: http://www.jstor.org/stable/1511538 (Accessed 20 September 2016).

Margolin, V. *The Politics of the Artificial: Essays on Design and Design Studies.* Chicago, IL, USA: University of Chicago Press, 2002.

Salen, K. "Editor's Note," *Zed,* 1 (1994): pgs. 6–13.

Ruecker, S. "A Brief Taxonomy of Prototypes for the Digital Humanities." *Scholarly and Research Communication,* 6.2 (2015). Online. Available at: http://src-online.ca/index.php/src/article/view/222/415 (Accessed 20 September 2016).

Vignelli, M. "Keynote Address." In *Coming of Age: The First Symposium on the History of Graphic Design, April 20-21, 1983, Rochester Institute of Technology,* edited by B. Hodik & R. Remington, pgs. 8–11. Rochester, NY, USA: Rochester Institute of Technology, 1985.

Biography

Jessica Barness is an Assistant Professor in the School of Visual Communication Design at Kent State University. Her research resides at the intersection of design, humanistic inquiry, and interactive systems, investigated through a critical, practice-based approach. She has presented and exhibited her work internationally, and has published research in *Design and Culture, Visual Communication, SEGD Research Journal: Communication and Place,* and *Message,* among others. Recently, she co-edited (with Amy Papaelias) a special issue of *Visible Language* journal, "Critical Making: Design and the Digital Humanities". She has an MFA in Design from the University of Minnesota, Twin Cities. jbarness@kent.edu, jessicabarness.com

Tip of the Icon:
Examining Socially Symbolic Indexical Signage

TERRY DOBSON[1] AND SAERI CHO DOBSON[2]

1. Azusa Pacific University, Azusa, California, USA

2. Loyola Marymount University, Los Angeles, California, USA

SUGGESTED CITATION:

Dobson, T. & Dobson, S.C. "Tip of the icon: Socially Symbolic Indexical Signage." *Dialectic,* 1.1 (2016): pgs. 61-90. DOI: http://dx.doi.org/10.3998/dialectic.14932326.0001.106

Abstract

A probative look beneath the surface of modernist claims of facilitating universal communication through the use of human iconography reveals how the supposedly neutral and objective qualities of signage have become socially symbolic in their gender references. Graphic design has the power to make what is and has become socially and culturally acceptable in particular societies appear to be so ingrained that it should not be questioned, much less altered. The study described in this piece describes a means to correct at least some portion of the social and cultural transgressions attributable to graphic design in many developed countries over much of the last century. This effort was guided by the following research question designed to address one of the most titanic design issues confronting contemporary society: how can universal public restroom signage be redesigned to help positively transform the signification of gender identity in and around them, especially in ways that effectively address the needs of the transgendered?

To examine this question, this essay examines the shortcomings of culturally specific signage; the ways in which social issues can be negatively affected by the aesthetics of graphic form; and the ramifications of perpetuating stereotypes through continuing the history of employing universal graphic forms.

The result of this visual inquiry contributes to ongoing study in the field of visual semiotics by classifying a new hybrid type of "sign:" the 'symbolic-index.' By translating a graphic and historical analysis of signage systems into critical readings and writings about and, eventually, into the making of signage systems through a series of classroom experiments, the integrated learnings that result enable a design outcome that is both pragmatically clear and culturally acceptable.

This study builds upon the theories originating from two distinct schools of thought derived from semiotics' "founding fathers" (specifically, Ferdinand de Saussere and Charles Sanders Peirce). As such, it serves as an introductory primer that describes the context in which semiotics was first introduced as a discipline of study that helps theoretically frame how meaning-making is facilitated through graphic design.

The application of this theoretical speculation reimagines a new role for socially-symbolic restroom figures by proposing an all-inclusive, gender-neutral solution that harnesses the indexical "bathroom" connotation of the original sign. In achieving this, it demonstrates how designers can become stewards of intercultural communication by modifying the universal with the culturally specific.

Tip of the Icon:

Examining Socially Symbolic Indexical Signage

TERRY DOBSON

SAERI CHO DOBSON

Introduction

The graphic language of nonverbal signs plays a complicitous role in expediting our ever-accelerating, visually oriented culture. Through synthesis and reapplication, visual language becomes the constantly evolving shorthand for graphic designers who rely heavily on semiotic conventions to guarantee their messages can be decoded correctly. Since the meaning of visual language is open to wide interpretation, it is important to understand the valence of potential factors that influence connotation. The reduction of information into a single unmistakable sign needs to be both pragmatically clear and culturally acceptable. However, when graphic conventions are appropriated unquestioningly, unintentional connotation passes from one generation to the next, which causes signs to become outdated, obscured, and even offensive. As a corollary, social issues can be negatively affected simply by the uncritical aesthetics of graphic form. As culture becomes progressively more symbol-oriented, designers have a greater responsibility to evaluate the impact of their artifacts on society, and the study of semiotics [a] can help separate and analyze their "signs" of communication at a very basic level.

Meaning-making through "signs" is not solely the province of design, and scholarship outside design recognizes the role of culture in making and negotiating meaning. [b] The use of the word "sign" throughout this essay is thus differentiated to reflect its duality of meaning. When used with quotation

[a] *According to Philip Meggs and Alston W. Purvis, "The general philosophical theory of signs and symbols known as semiotics has three branches: semantics, the study of the meaning of signs and symbols; syntactics, the study of how signs and symbols are connected and ordered into a structural whole; and pragmatics, the study of the relation of signs and symbols to their users."* From Meggs, P. B., & Purvis, A.W. Meggs' History of Graphic Design, Fourth Ed. Hoboken, NJ, USA: John Wiley & Sons, 2006, pgs.357-358.

[b] *Semiology has provided a continuing critical base for social theory, deconstruction and "the interpretive turn" in the humanities. Semiotics is used in technical communication and semiotic concepts are used in human factors to decompose and analyze interpretation.* From Storkerson, P. "Antinomies of Semiotics in Graphic Design." Visible Language, 44.1 (2010): p. 7.

Swiss linguist Ferdinand de Saussure's primary contribution to the study of language was his definition of two components of a sign: the Signified (the person, thing, event, place or concept called forth by the stimulation of the signifier), and the Signifier (the sound, word, or image that recalls in our mind the signified, even in the absence of the real thing).
From Davis, M. Graphic Design Theory: Graphic Design in Context. New York, NY: Thames & Hudson Publishing (2012), p. 106.

French literary critic and semiologist Roland Barthes proposed his semiotic theory of connotation by describing the "Sign" as the sum of their relationship: not one or the other, but both at the same time working together in an inseparable bond "...the associative total of the first two terms."
From Barthes, R. Mythologies. New York, NY, USA: Hill & Wang (1995), p. 113.

1
Skaggs, S. "Visual Design Semiotic Primer," 27 July, 2011. Online. Available at: http://stevenskaggs.net/VDSP%20Chapt%201.pdf (Accessed 30 October, 2016).

2
Skaggs, S. Zed 4: Semiotics: Pedagogy and Practice. Richmond, VA, USA: Virginia Commonwealth University Press (1997), p. 5.

marks, it refers to its semiotic definition—something which stands for something else, such as "flowers are a sign of affection," or "The doctor sees signs of illness," whereas when it appears without quotation marks, it denotes the signage designers create as part of our visual information environment.

The first part of this essay examines some of the more prevalent ways ill-considered design choices can contribute to a failure to produce adequate or appropriate meaning in nonverbal signs. It presents the principle elements of semiotic theory that will be discussed and makes a case for their foundational role as a basis for design theory. It also provides an overview of *what we know* about how people extract meaning from "signs," and thus why designers need to be more thoughtful as they engage in the processes of designing and implementing them. Part two explores the contexts that have produced meaning from abstraction when "signs" are appropriated from one semiotic system to another. By providing an historical analysis of how we got to where we are, it speculates on where we might be headed next. The final part of this essay unpacks the meaning of the title. A closer look at what is going on beneath the surface of signage reveals how the supposedly neutral and objective qualities of Modernist icons depicting human figures have become socially symbolic in their gender references. By acknowledging the designer's complicity in subverting signage to mark members of society with all kinds of 'otherness,' it offers a prescriptive alternative for rethinking one of the titanic design issues confronting society today. All three parts of this article build upon what has previously been accepted by semiotic scholars as influential in the meaning-making process: namely time, context, and history. Together, they constitute a call for action to current design educators and practitioners to look more critically at contemporary practices of nonverbal encoding so they might recognize when signs are out of step with the culture of a particular population group that interprets them.

Part 1: Beneath The Surface of Signage

Contemporary American graphic design educator Steven Skaggs calls graphic design "naked semiotics." He sees graphic design as pure semiotics in action, and believes semiotics is critically foundational and more important than any other approach as a basis for design theory: "Semiotics is the explicit heart of graphic design theory, just as it is the implicit (subconscious) engine in graphic design practice. The central role of semiotics is therefore clear, as, from this perspective, every graphic designer is a semiotician." Yet, in order to inform what has historically been an intuitive-based discipline with theory to help contextualize the conceptual underpinnings of their profession, designers must reconcile the often contradictory[3] theories originating from two distinct schools of thought derived from semiotics' "founding fathers:" specifically, Peirce's *semiotics* and Saussure's *semiology*.[d] The brief historical interlude that follows is not meant to be an exhaustive account of names and events, but rather serves as an introductory primer to establish a context for how semiotics was first introduced as a discipline of study to help theoretically frame how meaning-making occurs in graphic design.

Semiotic theory in graphic design education dates back to when it began to be incorporated into the curriculum at *The Ulm School of Design* (*Der Hochshule für Gestaltung*) in Germany in the 1950s. (The design curriculum at Ulm revived and then examined anew some of the Bauhaus teaching principles in the context of more globally interdependent post-war world). One of the primary differences between the teaching practices operated at the Ulm School of Design, or HFG,[e] and those that had been operated at the Bauhaus was that several of the scholarly programs at Ulm incorporated the study of semiotics in their curricula. This pedagogic innovation is now widely acknowledged as being crucial to the introduction of semiotic analysis as a key educational component of graphic design education. In his book *Graphic Design: A New History*, design historian Stephen Eskilson writes, "What truly separated the professors[f] and students at the Ulm School from their contemporaries was their concern for the theoretical dimension of graphic design."[4] At that time, American graphic designers—who were mostly self-taught[g]—were far less engaged in trying to formulate or understand the intellectual structures and philosophical issues that epistemologically and ontologically framed and supported their work. By contrast, from 1953 to 1955, former Bauhaus professors Josef Albers and Johannes Itten (with Walter Peterhans) helped design a theoretically well-formed and framed set of curricula to guide the new design programs of the HFG. At about this same time—beginning in 1950—Albers *also* began to introduce more theoretically based approaches to guide design students' learning experiences as he took over the leadership of the Department of Design at Yale University in the U.S.[5] Although it was introduced at Yale during the 1950s, semiotics would not be accepted in the U.S. as a credible academic theory to help guide design practice until it was introduced in the curriculum of the Rhode Island School of Design in the early 1970s. Thomas Ockerse (MFA Graphic Design, Yale 1965), became one of America's foremost semiotic design education

[3] "The history of semiotics in design indicates that there is no one underlying problem, but a series of antinomies or contradictions." Storkerson, P. "Antinomies of Semiotics in Graphic Design." Visible Language, 44.1 (2010): p. 7.

[d] *Semiotics originated as a discipline of study at the turn of the twentieth century. The thinking that guided its instantiation originated from two scholars who were working on opposite sides of the Atlantic at about the same time. Each of them independently arrived at similar theories to explain how meaning-making occurs in the mind of a viewer, or an "observer," as she engages in the mental processes necessary to interpret words or visual forms according to her ability to associate these with her extant knowledge of the world. The study of what came to be known as 'the life of signs' was first explored in a linguistic context by Ferdinand de Saussure (1857–1913) in France and Switzerland in the first decade of the 20th Century, and almost simultaneously in a more visual context by Charles Sanders Peirce (1839–1914) in the United States. The work of both scholars was used to formulate a general theory of meaning construction based on cognition.*

[e] *One of Germany's preeminent semioticians, Martin Krampen (1928–2015) began studying graphic design and visual communication at the then newly-opened Hochschule für Gestaltung in 1953. The Bauhaus had been the first German design school to incorporate the moniker 'Hochschule für Gestaltung' into its title in 1919. After the Bauhaus was closed by the Nazis in 1932-3, this language stayed out of use among German art and design schools until it was used again to describe the new programs at Ulm beginning in 1953-4.*

[f] *In search of a theory to epistemologically contextualize a field of human practice characterized by a lack of conceptual discipline, designers, especially those educated in the Ulm School tradition, were willing to adopt semiotics as one of their primary foundational theories, provided that semioticians paid attention to the critical problems of design and avoided extending a more logocratic model of argumentation into situations where a more established explanatory framework seemed necessary or more easily applicable.*
Extracted from Maldonado, T. Uppercase 5: HfG Ulm. Tonbridge, Kent, UK: Whitefriars Publishing, 1961.

[g] *Paul Rand, Bradbury Thompson, Alvin Lustig, Alexey Brodovitch, Herbert Matter—some of the most admired and influential American graphic designers of the 20th century—did not have formal educations in design and were essentially self-taught.*
Kelly, R. R. "The Early Years of Graphic Design at Yale University." Design Issues 17. 3 (2001): p.13.

4
Eskilson, S. Graphic Design: A New History. New Haven, CT, USA: Yale University Press, 2007, p. 321.

5
Ibid., p. 1.

6
Friedman, K. "Theory construction in design research: criteria: approaches, and methods." Design Studies, 24.6 (2003), p. 507.

7
Ibid., p.507.

8
Davis, M. Graphic Design Theory: Graphic Design in Context. New York, NY: Thames & Hudson Publishing (2012), 104.

pioneers, who, along with Hans C. van Dijk, collaborated to design and implement a graphic design curriculum at RISD based on Peirce's typology of signs beginning in 1973. [h] Despite the fact that semiotics has played a seminal role in shaping some of the more prominent aspects of graphic design education for roughly half of the past 60-plus years of graphic design history in the U.S., it still has relatively low visibility and application here. This is due in part to a broad tendency among American graphic design educators and practitioners to divorce the practice of design from the theoretical knowledge and understandings that inform and guide it. One of the goals of this research is to at least address and perhaps undo this bifurcation by explicitly integrating research informed by semiotic concepts and principles into the making of graphic objects through a pedagogical approach that links tacit knowledge with discursive knowledge. By doing this, it is hoped that both emerging (i.e. student) and established graphic designers can become more adept at, as Ken Friedman opines, "solving problems, creating something new, or transforming less than desirable situations into preferred [ones]..." [6] Friedman goes on to bolster this point by offering, "To do this, designers must know how things work and why. Understanding how things work and why requires us to analyze and explain. This is the purpose of theory." [7]

As a way of calling attention to the issues that accompany the design of nonverbal signs as carriers of unintentional meaning, the overview that follows offers three observations that identify some of the shortcomings inherent in culturally problematic signage. The first two provide perspective on what happens when time moves on and signs do not: by anchoring meaning in outdated visual language, signs suffer from the obsolescence of styling. Additionally, by uncritically replicating signage conventions with historically outdated values, designers can unintentionally perpetuate negative stereotypes. The third observation demonstrates how the physical context of a sign influences its decoding by underscoring how dramatically the context of a sign's use can change its connotation.

Anchoring Meaning in Outdated Visual Language

Leading American design educator Meredith Davis has opined that the "...concern for meaning and how it is made and interpreted is as fundamental to graphic design practice as are the aesthetics of form." [8] A common misconception among non-designers about signs is that their visual meaning remains the same over time. Similar to verbal language, meaning transmitted through signs is

9

Lupton, E. Design Issues, MIT Press, 3.2 (Autumn, 1986), pgs. 50–51.

10

Abdullah, R. & Huber, R. Pictograms, Icons & Signs. London, UK: Thames & Hudson Publishing, 2006.

11

"Tie a Yellow Ribbon Round The Ole Oak Tree" by Dawn, featuring Tony Orlando, written by Irwin Levine and L. Russell Brown, recorded 1973. New York City, New York, USA: Bell Records, 45 rpm.

12

Fry, D. & Fry, V. "Continuing the conversation regarding Myth and Culture: An alternative reading of Barthes." American Journal of Semiotics, 6.2/3 (1989), pgs.183–197.

Obsolete Technology   Old-Fashioned Styling   Outdated Social Norms

FIGURE 1: Obsolescence of Styling: Iconographic visual signage is made obsolescent as technology and styles change, and social norms become outdated. *Source: Dobson, T. 2016.*

h *Charles Sanders Peirce developed a taxonomy of sign types, of which his second 'triad' comprised of icon, index and symbol has been the most relevant to design. "Peirce's classification of sign types is not mutually exclusive—we can have iconic symbols or indexical icons."* Davis, M. Graphic Design Theory: Graphic Design in Context. New York, NY, USA: Thames & Hudson Publishing, 2012, p. 127.

i *Style: A distinctive form or prevailing mode of expression, often associated with an era or a culture and having less to do with the subject matter of the communication than how it is represented.* Extracted from Davis, M. Graphic Design Theory: Graphic Design in Context. New York, NY, USA: Thames & Hudson Publishing, 2012, p. 145.

continuously redefined by contemporary society's usage of them. Design curator and author Ellen Lupton acknowledges the temporal nature of visual language: "To interpret is to recognize that signs are not absolute, neutral, and fixed, but are, rather, in historical flux." [9]. Since graphic style [i] also conveys meaning, the more neutral a sign appears, the more directly viewers can connect with its literal content. Pictorial signs are rarely devoid of style, and iconographic representations need updating over time in order to avoid falling into the trap of obsolescence facilitated by failing to update the styling of their essential forms (see fig. 1). Signs also need updating to avoid being misinterpreted as societal norms change. Rayan Abdullah and Roger Huber explain how, in the context of the third example depicted in Figure 1, "The old motif for the 'footpath' sign had to be changed—not for the sake of modernization—but because the man in the hat holding hands with the little girl suggests a possible abduction rather than a father taking his daughter for a walk." [10]

In the *American Journal of Semiotics*, Donald and Virginia Fry have documented the extent to which the connotative meaning of the same "sign" can be shifted over time. They traced the drift in meaning of "Tie a yellow ribbon..." from a poetic symbol of an American Pop song from the 1970s that emphasized a theme of forgiveness, [11] into a persuasive ideological "sign" of American solidarity regarding social and political attitudes about the Gulf war. [12] As subsequent generations of American designers repeatedly expropriated the symbolism of the yellow ribbon for their own uses over time, its original meaning became hollowed-out, leaving behind a timeless form without

67

Lupton & Miller point out how the only place the female icon appears in the Department of Transportation (D.O.T.) system aside from lavatory doors is in the sign for ticket sales, where the designers deemed it appropriate to show a woman assisting a man (fig. 2, center). Extracted from Lupton, E. & Miller, A. Design Writing Research: Writing About Graphic Design. New York, NY, USA: Kiosk Publishing, 1996, p. 42.

Figure 2. right, depicts how this sexist convention has been copied in Japan with a slight modification to the rendering of the woman's waistline, but ironically, with no attempt made to 'politically correct' the overt sexism inherent in this image.

Verbal language, literature, and legalese all emphasize his, rather than hers. Our everyday experience is saturated with androcentric language because, largely until the latter portion of the 20th Century, most developed societies in the world expected men to have a better formal education than women. Before universal literacy, far fewer women than men around the world were able to read and write, and thus written material tended to reflect a male point of view.

Part of the Special Olympics' mission is to lead the way around the world to change the term 'mental retardation' to 'intellectual disabilities.'

13
Griffin, E. A First Look at Communication Theory. New York, NY, USA: McGraw-Hill, 9th Edition, 2015, p. 333.

14
Ibid., p. 329.

substance. Not only does this example illustrate how a seemingly neutral or inanimate "sign" can accomplish so much, but it also demonstrates the communicative power of non-pictorial signs as purely abstract symbols.

Perpetuating Unintentional Stereotypes

The widespread depiction of stereotypes continually perpetuated through media, movies, music and advertising has a powerful influence over society. The role of design is also complicit, and though often inadvertent, public signage should be particularly accountable because of its seemingly neutral and objective qualities. Pejorative connotations can be unwittingly reinforced if designers adopt outdated graphic signifiers without considering how the meaning they convey has been developed in a given society, or how those meanings and their attendant social norms may have shifted over time. Despite wide visibility of initiatives encouraging intentional diversity and inclusion, figure 2 illustrates a sexist signage convention that designers continue to perpetuate. In many instances around the world, when the international sign for 'Assistance' is displayed showing one person offering a service to another, the convention is to show *women* assisting *men.*

Gender inequality is ingrained into iconographic visual language as much as it is in everyday verbal language, and all too often the verbal language used to describe marginalized groups in society results in their becoming stereotyped. Whereas verbal language can more easily be 'politically corrected,' in North America and other G20 nations our visual sign systems have not kept pace with changing social views. Communication Theory educator Em Griffin points out how this is precisely the problem with the connotative nature of signs: "They *go without saying.* They don't explain, they don't defend and they certainly don't raise questions." [13] Instead, the ideological baggage that signs "carry" wherever they go has the power to perpetuate the dominant values of society. French literary critic and semiologist Roland Barthes believed "...the significant semiotic systems of a culture lock in the status quo. The mythology that surrounds a society's crucial 'signs' displays the world as it is today—however chaotic and unjust—as natural, inevitable and eternal." [14]

Barthes' theory that addresses semiotics is rooted in connotation. It supports the idea that the outdated values and inherent social inequalities personified in a given society's everyday signage is indicative of a high level of social inequality within it. His model explains the process by which seemingly neutral "signs" function in society as ideological tools: they make what

Germany
1968

United States
1974

Japan
2013

FIGURE 2: Ambiguity of Meaning: The grammar of visual language becomes imprecise when the logic of a sign system is not consistently applied.
Source: Dobson, T. 2016.

is cultural seem natural. [15] For example, signs function to legitimize the stigmatizing of women as subordinate and the physically challenged as passive. In 2014, the implementation of a new law in New York State requiring the term *'Handicapped'* be removed from state signs or any other communication and be replaced by the word *'Accessible,'* has helped instigate and perpetuate a positive rather than pejorative connotation towards the physically challenged. The original 'International Symbol of Access'—unchanged since its design in 1968—now signifies *'static'* and *'incapable'* compared to a new sign, which designers have subsequently updated to reflect the more self-reliant mobility connotation of the term *'Handicapable'* (see fig. 3). If designers consider the broader cultural, social, historical and political connotations concerning the things they design, then just as verbal language can adapt to counteract its past transgressions, Barthes' *'connotative sidestepping'* model can be leveraged to proactively innovate more graphic opportunities to do the same.

Context Changes Connotation Completely
More broadly informed and deeply probed historical perspective and more thoughtful critical reflection can help designers avoid the unintentional pitfalls inherent in designing and implementing culturally problematic signage. One of the most important factors influencing how a sign will be decoded is its physical context. Figure 4 illustrates how the same sign can mean *Don't Touch* when juxtaposed against cacti, or *Don't Go* where there's visible danger of being

15
Barthes, R. Mythologies. New York, NY, USA: Hill & Wang, 1995, p. 115.

69

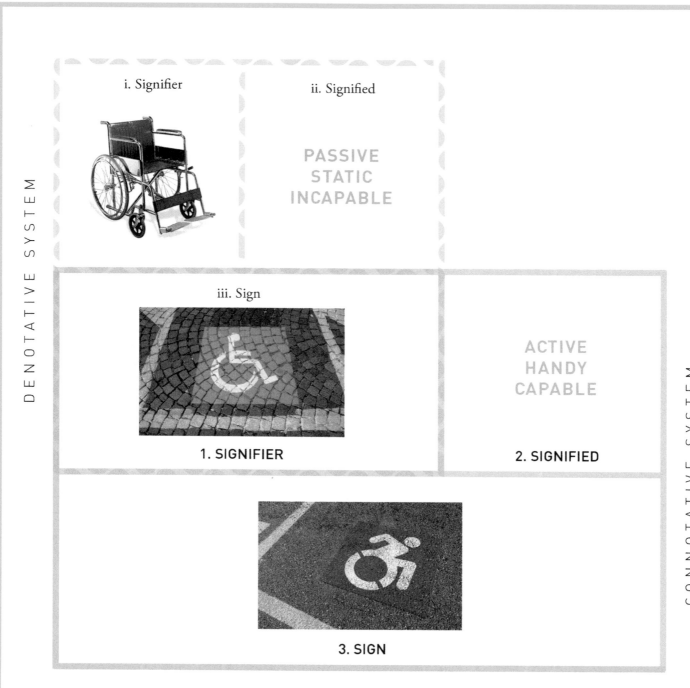

FIGURE 3: Perpetuation of Stereotypes: The evolution of sexist, iconographic visual signage is a result of prevailing graphic design conventions being passed on from one generation of designers to the next. *Source: Dobson, T. 2016.*

[m] *As a rule, the red circle-slash universally means NO and always negates that which it cancels: for example, "No Smoking" if it is juxtaposed over a cigarette, "No Parking" if it is juxtaposed over the letter 'P'. However, when the meaning of the circle-slash (Don't), is combined with the iconographic palm of an outstretched hand (which we've learned to connote symbolically as "STOP"), the resulting meaning becomes ambiguous. Without the context of any signifier to reaffirm meaning, the literal denotation could be misread as Don't Stop! rather than Don't Go!*

[n] *The hand gesture made by joining the thumb and forefinger into a circle signifies 'OK' in the UK and the USA but in France it signifies 'worthless' or 'zero,' and in Brazil, it is interpreted as an obscene gesture.*

struck by falling ice. But when the same sign is removed completely from the context of any signifier (fig. 4), the resulting meaning changes completely. [m] American design educator Garland Kirkpatrick points to the instability of a "sign's" meaning as centermost to the formulation and operation of semiotic theory: "One may be more dominant than another, but this instability or reactivity creates a valence of potential meanings." [16] A connotative response is less fixed than a denotative response, and the associations signified may well depend upon the social, cultural, economic and political values and realities operating within the contexts of an individual's perceptions, and his or her society's.

Italian semiologist and novelist Umberto Eco coined the term *'Aberrant Decoding'* to describe how context changes the interpretation of "signs." [17] His concept is useful to designers because it explains what happens when a message that has been encoded according to one socio-cultural code is decoded by means of another. When "signs" are appropriated from one culture into another or one system into another, often there exists the potential to propagate misunderstanding. [n] Whereas the rules of verbal language adequately serve as parallels for the first two observations in this essay, this third example differs because unlike words, the language of the visual world does not always become more emphatic when more "signs" combine to strengthen the communicative power of a message.

[16]
Kirkpatrick, G. 1+1=3: The Sum of the Parts is Greater Than the Whole. Forthcoming research (2005?).

[17]
Eco, U. "Towards a Semiotic Inquiry Into the Television Message." Working Papers in Cultural Studies, University of Birmingham, 3 (1972): pgs. 103–21.

[18]
Griffin, E. A First Look at Communication Theory. New York, NY, USA: McGraw-Hill, 9th Edition, 2015, p. 329.

[19]
Crow, D. Visible Signs: An Introduction to Semiotics in the Visual Arts. Switzerland: AVA Publishing, 2nd Edition, 2010, p. 7.

Part 2: No One Sign Fits All

The second part of this visual inquiry seeks to understand the contexts that have produced meaning from abstraction by tracing the origin of the circle-slash sign. Very little has been written about its etymology, but its development within the European road sign system since the mid to late 1920s seems to have codified the first ever rules for its usage. Since road signs in Europe have developed abstract iconographies from a milieu of cultural precedents, they offer a rich opportunity for researching meaning-making within an emergent semiotic system. Em Griffin points out, "A 'sign' does not stand on its own: it's part of a system," [18] and semiotician David Crow discourses on the ways in which "signs" are organized into systems reveals how underlying structures and patterns help to form meaning. [19] By unpacking the logic of the European road sign system, the origin of the circle-slash and the transformation of its visual meaning can thus be mapped.

The need for a universal picture language became necessary in the early 20th century as people living in industrialized societies began to

Don't Touch!   Don't Go!   Don't Stop!

FIGURE 4: Context Changes Connotation Dramatically: The same sign can mean Don't Touch when juxtaposed against cacti, or Don't Go where there's visible danger of being struck by falling ice. But when the same sign is removed completely from the context of any signifier, the resulting meaning changes completely.
Source: Dobson, T. 2016.

[o] *An international convention in Paris first addressed the problem of language-based signs in 1926, and a year later the convention of using pictographs on road signs was officially ratified in Vienna.*
Krampen, M. "Icons of the Road." Semiotica: Journal of the International Association for Semiotic Studies, 43.1–2 (January 1983), p. 74.

[p] *Krampen traces the origin of road-warning signs back to 1909, well before the broad introduction of Saussure's semiology. Detailed documentation of this process provides an empirical timeline of its evolution. Unlike the normal case in the diachronic study of other sign systems, in the study of the implementation of various iterations of the road sign system, changes can be pinpointed to exact dates in this century.*
Krampen, M. "Signs and Symbols in Graphic Communication." Design Quarterly, 62 (1965), pgs. 1–31.

[q] *Triangular-shaped signs were introduced to symbolize a warning of approaching danger because they were deemed more recognizable that signs rendered in other shapes. Round-shaped signs symbolized driver restrictions (maximum speed/height/weight limits etc.), as well as prohibitions, and the Paris convention stipulated that the color red should predominate on these signs* (Schipper 2009, p. 87).

encounter problems stemming from increasing globalization and the development and implementation of new transportation and communication technologies. In 1915, the early implementation of automobiles prompted the need to place the world's first stop signs on American streets, where traffic signs have continued to rely on words because English is the primary spoken language in the U.S. However, as automobile travel became widespread across Europe, a new method was needed to communicate to motorists that transcended language barriers. Initially, purely typographic or type-dominant road signs were created in each country, but only those who spoke the national language could understand them. [o] In the mid 1960s, a leading German semiotician, Dr. Martin Krampen—an alumnus of The Ulm School of Design—coined the term "semiotization" to describe the iterative process by which this system of road signs evolved from words to pictograms to symbols. [p] Along with the advent of symbolically shaped signs [q] came the introduction of the first abstract symbol: the circle-slash "NO" sign.

Krampen points to the *'red crossing-out mark'* as a unique example of how "...behavioral agreement among members of different language groups can also be attained with non-pictorial visual forms." The landmark significance of the design and implementation of the circle-slash as an abstract symbol illustrates how "...meanings can be directly expressed and transmitted by imitations of reality, or completely *'abstract'* visual forms." [20] In speculating about the pro-

20

Krampen, M. "Icons of the Road." Semiotica: Journal of the International Association for Semiotic Studies, 43.1–2 (January 1983), p. 164.

21

Krampen, M. "Icons of the Road." Semiotica: Journal of the International Association for Semiotic Studies, 43.1–2 (January 1983), p. 164.

venance of the red crossing-out mark, Krampen's conclusions fell short of providing any great significance to explicate the reason for adopting a *single* red slash-mark as the graphic convention for the cancellation device. He concludes that it "…probably originated with the need to cancel black written signs."[21] Another plausible explanation could be that the *single* slash-mark was already being used as a cancellation signifier in an extant European signage system.

Communicating A 'False Alarm'

One clue to the origin of the cancellation sign can be found within the history of long-distance visual signaling, which did not change for over 2,000 years. When the paranoid Emperor Tiberius ruled Rome from the island of Capri during the last decade of his life (26 AD to 37 AD), he built hilltop beacons as an early warning system to alert him of impending danger (see fig. 6). Similarly, in Elizabethan times, when the Spanish Armada was sighted off the South coast of England in 1588, a relay of beacons was lit across an approximately 60-mile succession of hilltops to transmit the warning all the way to London. These types of warning systems were plagued by a persistent problem: once the beacon was lit and the signal was sent, its operators had difficulty cancelling it in the case the impetus for triggering it was a false alarm? In the late 18th century, the French engineer Claude Chappe invented the precursor of what came to be known as semaphoric communication: a system of using manually facilitated signal flag-waving to communicate more complex messages across distances of

FIGURE 5: Along with the advent of symbolically shaped signs came the introduction of the first abstract symbol: the circle-slash "NO" sign, which solved the specific visual problem of prohibiting parking. The origin of the circle-slash sign within the European road sign system seems to have codified the first ever rules for its usage.
Source: Dobson, T. 2016.

Prohibit   Restrict   Annul   No   No More

73

Symbols are not as immediately efficient as icons from a designer's perspective because their relationship is governed by codes or cultural conventions that first need to be understood by the receiver. Since the relationship between symbols and what they stand for is arbitrary, their abstract meaning has to be learned, often by habitual exposure over time.

Gert and Derk Dumbar's 2007 "Safe Place" exhibition of new international pictograms for disaster areas featured this classic example of a prohibition sign that is supposed to prevent attempts at extinguishing electrical or chemical fires by dousing them with water. Extracted from Dumbar, G. & Dumbar, D., "A Safe Place: International System of Disaster Diagrams." Originally presented at The Utrecht Manifest: Second Biennale for Social Design, November 3, 2007, in Utrecht, NL. SIGNS4DISASTER, 30 October, 2013. Online. Available at: https://signs4disaster.wordpress.com/2013/10/30/a-safe-place-international-system-of-disaster-pictograms/ (Accessed November 9, 2016)

22
Barnard, M. Graphic Design As Communication. London, UK & New York, USA: Routledge, 2013, p. 45.

23
Atkin, A. "Peirce's three categories of Signs: icon, index, symbol," Stanford Encyclopedia of Philosophy, 15 November, 2010. Online. Available at: http://plato.stanford.edu/entries/peirce-semiotics (Accessed April 14, 2016).

a few hundred yards to about two miles. Chappe solved the problem of how to effectively communicate a cancel signal (see fig. 6). This meant implementing a pre-existing convention—of using a diagonal gesture to indicate the cancellation or annulment of a message—had already been established, that the road sign system could simply appropriate. The annul signal is both visually identical and symbolically synonymous with the meaning and direction of the *circle-slash* sign (see fig. 7).

Taken Out of Context

The evolution of the annul *signal* into the circle-slash sign helped galvanize the function of its non-arbitrary meaning as a universal *symbol*. However, "...to the extent that it is symbolic, it cannot be universal,"[22] and through inconsistent applications and implementations, the rules for how its cancelling authority should work in conjunction with a variety of pictograms to convey meaning within specific signs lacks clarity, convention and sometimes even logic. The interpretation of the meaning of signs ultimately depends upon the context of use in which they appear, and perhaps more so than any other sign, viewing the circle-slash out of context produces a myriad of illogical connotations (see Fig. 8).

The overly complex iconography warning against the danger of placing child car seats in the front of an automobile where airbags could inflate is graphically illegible, but arguably made more so if seen out of the context of that automobile (see fig. 8: left). The absurdly ambiguous 'In case of fire, don't attempt to extinguish with water!' sign (fig. 8: middle), is completely irrational without the context of electrical equipment or chemical substances to which it typically refers. Perhaps the most vexing example from a designer's perspective arises when multiple signs with duplicative meanings are amalgamated in a redundant way that seemingly contradict the connotation of the combined whole (fig. 8: right). This ubiquitous Italian 'No access to unauthorized persons' sign incorporates hybrid categories that combine all three classifications of Peirce's most notable semiotic taxonomy.[23] The *iconic symbol* of the outstretched palm (*Stop!*), is combined with the *indexical icon* of a man shouting (his mouth wide open, as if warning of some nearby unseen danger), and overlaid with a *symbolic index* that directly '*points to*' that which it prohibits (see fig. 9). When all three signs with similar signification are sequentially combined, the resulting denotative meaning should cancel itself out. Yet instead, logic is overruled, and although seemingly counter-intuitive, the three meanings merge to strengthen

Roman Hilltop Beacons

Chappe's Mechanical Semaphore

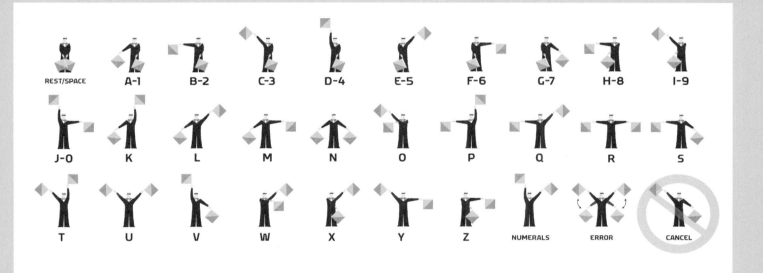

REST/SPACE   A-1   B-2   C-3   D-4   E-5   F-6   G-7   H-8   I-9

J-0   K   L   M   N   O   P   Q   R   S

T   U   V   W   X   Y   Z   NUMERALS   ERROR   CANCEL

FIGURE 6: Claude Chappe's mechanical communication stations solved the timeless conundrum of long-distance visual signaling: How to cancel a signal in case of a false alarm. Source: Liebig's trade cards (collection of the author). *2016.*

FIGURE 7: Semaphore's existing convention of signaling a way to cancel a message preceded the system of European road signs with an already established convention that is both visually identical and symbolically synonymous with the meaning and direction of the circle-slash sign. *Source: Dobson, T. 2016.*

Overcomplexity

Ambiguity

Redundancy

Indexical Icon

Iconic Symbol

Symbolic Index

FIGURE 8: Taken Out of Context: Circle-slash confusion results from their being used in ways that are overcomplex, ambiguous and graphically redundant. The circle-slash has become a symbolic index to signify 'NO' in the specific location in which it appears, which is why taking it out of context often renders it nonsensical.
Source: Dobson, T. 2016.

FIGURE 9: Hybrid Signs: Introduction of the 'Symbolic Index.' The classification of this new type of "sign" is particularly useful in both describing and creating signs that simultaneously harness symbolic and indexical qualities as predominant connotations.
Source: Dobson, T. 2016.

the overall graphic communication. The rules can be broken and even over-ruled—but almost never ignored. [u]

Despite the circle-slash confusion, the provenance and subsequent proliferation of this type of sign demonstrates how meaning can become symbolically reinforced over time, and even stabilized as a bi-product of reapplication from one sign system to another. The circle-slash has become a symbolic index to signify 'NO' in the specific location in which it appears. That is why taking it out of its context of use often renders it nonsensical.

The Mark of 'Otherness'

There's one final vestige of the circle-slash's circuitous past that warrants commentary on its residual meaning. An even older signage system that utilized a slash-mark running diagonally from upper-right to lower-left across a visual field exists within the symbolism of European heraldry (see fig. 10). A *barre-sinister* (from Latin verbiage meaning "left") was used as a visual mark to indicate the *end* of a lineage on the coat-of-arms [v] of an illegitimate child who could not inherent his father's ancestral titles or holdings. The power that symbols carry to mark members of society with 'otherness' has been exploited throughout history with dire consequences. The scarlet letter symbolizing sexual immorality in 17th and 18th century colonial New England foreshadowed the yellow badge as a mark of shame that Jews were forced to wear in Nazi Germany. Iconographic signage suggesting women are subordinate and the handicapped are passive are the modern-day manifestations of this same socially symbolic labeling. If we wish to become preventative stewards of culturally and socially responsible signage in the future global melting pot of signs, then we should seek inclusiveness as one of its universal hallmarks.

Part 3: Rethinking Restroom Signage

The final part of this essay is an historical analysis of another almost globally ubiquitous, if not universally agreed upon and understood system of signs: the iconic male and female restroom figures. Recognizing the power of their indexical connotation provides a strong rationale for reimagining their new roles as visual signifiers as restroom signage changes its functions in at least some parts of the world in the near future.

Perhaps the most egregious examples of socially and culturally problematic signs are those that continue to perpetuate exclusionary, discriminatory and stereotypical biases in ways that are not entirely coincidental.

[t] *Index is a term coined by Charles Sanders Peirce to describe signs that are non-arbitrarily associated with what they represent. Indexical signs are signs that acquire their function through a causal connection with what they signify, containing an indirect connection with what it represents, and what it signifies. Examples of Indexical signs are: a road sign of a knife and fork that tells a driver there is a restaurant ahead; a road sign depicting a bed, indicating there is a hotel ahead; a sign showing a toothbrush outside of a building, indicating that there is a dentist there; a sign at the beach showing a shark fin surfacing out of a ripple of water, meaning that the beach is dangerous because the waters that it abuts may contain sharks.* Extracted from Torres, E. "The three kinds of Signs in Linguistics," Linked-In SlideShare, 24 November, 2014. Online. Available at: http://www.slideshare.net/durakusnation/the-three-kinds-of-signs-in-linguistics (Accessed 17 September 2016).

[u] *Inspired by typographer David Jury's most noteworthy rule about design: "Rules can be broken—but never ignored."*

[v] *Traditionally, a coat of arms was a distinctive pattern of symbols and markings that allowed an individual knight to be recognized as distinct from similarly attired knights who appeared near him, especially in battlefield situations. These systems of symbols, or arms, were displayed on his banner, shield and horsecloth, as well as on his coat. Because no two men could display the same coat of arms simultaneously, even the eldest son (who would eventually inherit his father's arms) had to deploy a special mark to distinguish him from his father during his father's lifetime. These marks were called labels, and various other labeling devices were used throughout heraldry to denote wives, daughters and younger sons, as well as offspring from what came to be known as "the wrong side of the bed sheets." A band (or barre in French) running diagonally from top-right to bottom-left was the heraldic label used to signify an illegitimate child.*

FIGURE 10: Medieval, European heraldry exemplifies the power symbols carry to mark members of a given society with 'otherness.' Unless we sensitize ourselves with increased iconographic empathy, our sign systems will continue to perpetuate exclusionary social and cultural ideas, and remain as stereotypical in our future information landscape as they were during European design's often ignoble, heraldic past. *Source: Dobson, T. 2016.*

Figure 11 depicts examples of non-gender germane public signage in which the discriminatory use of the female icon becomes socially symbolic in their gender references. Subtle variations of this sexist design convention often go unnoticed. The warning sign on the Spanish subway system uses a stylized icon of a little girl to illustrate careless behavior that could lead to self-injury. The careless parent allowing this to happen is also depicted as a woman. This begs questions as to why girls and women—rather than boys or men—are depicted throughout a nationally sanctioned signage system as being prone to engaging in careless behavior. Informational signage in Chinese airports follow a design convention used widely around the world: icons depicting men are used for the majority of pictogram-based visual communications illustrating authoritative social roles, whereas icons depicting women are exclusively reserved to illustrate social and cultural roles that reinforce traditional childrearing and homebound stereotypes. Hospital signage in the UK prescribes the usage of male icons to depict the highly regarded social and cultural role of doctor, and female icons for the less socially and culturally esteemed roles of nurse and clinical technician. In each of these examples, the seemingly neutral and objective qualities of male and female iconography belie a normalization of gender roles, social hierarchies and stereotypical labeling. As David Crow reminds us: "Where there is choice, there is meaning." [24]

The visually persuasive power of everyday signage—though seemingly innocuous—can have a formative influence on the social and cultural

24
Crow, D. Visible Signs: An Introduction to Semiotics in the Visual Arts. Switzerland: AVA Publishing, 2nd Edition, 2010, p. 43.

Spanish
Subway Warning

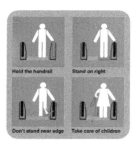

Chinese
Airport Graphics

British
Hospital Signage

FIGURE 11: Ethics of Everyday Icons: The visually persuasive power of everyday signage can have a formative influence on society. The seemingly neutral and objective qualities of male and female iconography are actually socially symbolic in their gender references, and belie a normalization of gender roles, social hierarchies and stereotypical labeling. *Source: Dobson, T. 2016.*

conventions that operate within a given society. By intentionally adopting stereotypical graphic tropes, designers reinforce impressions that are potentially detrimental to the normalization of social experiences, especially in children. In a research study testing perceptions of occupations typed by sex,[25] six to seven-year-old children were presented with counter-stereotypical imagery of a female doctor and a male nurse. When later asked what they had seen, they recalled the exact opposite: a male doctor and a female nurse. The children had relabeled the roles to make them more consistent with the gender stereotypes they had been exposed to through their social and environmental conditioning. If media, marketing and movies, as well as gender-specific toys,[26] can negatively affect a child's development through strong social reinforcement of stereotypes, then so too can the subtle influence of gendered typography, sexist signage, and the one-sided nature of verbal language. Even the replacement of gender-specific job titles like *Chairman, Air Hostess* and *Fireman,* with *Chairperson, Flight Attendant* and *Firefighter* has helped change preconceptions in children about the gender-appropriateness of potential future careers. Whereas gender neutrality has become an effective equalizer in the war on words, the same insurgence has yet to occur in the world of graphic signs. And this is just "the tip of the icon." With constant repetition and frequent exposure, signs with outdated social values continue to mark members of society with all kinds of 'otherness.'

25

Cordua, G. et al. "Doctor or Nurse: Children's Perception of Sex Typed Occupations." Child Development, 50.2 (June, 1979), pgs. 590–593.

26

Robb, A. "How gender-specific toys can negatively impact a child's development," Women In The World, 12 August, 2015. Online. Available at: http://nytlive.nytimes.com/women intheworld/2015/08/12/how-gender-specific-toys-can-negatively-impact-a-childs-development/ (Accessed 1 November 2016).

[W] *Ellen Lupton and Abbott Miller described the visually cognitive efficiency of Otl Aicher's visual vocabulary for the 1972 Munich Olympics as "...the semiotic climax of international pictures: a geometric body alphabet... deployed on a consistent grid."* Extracted from Lupton, E. and Miller, A., Design Writing Research: Writing About Graphic Design. New York City, New York, USA: Kiosk Publishing, 1996, p. 43.

[X] *Otl Aicher (1922–1991) and Inge Scholl (1917–1998) pioneered the semiotic analysis of graphic design at a time when few graphic designers working outside the HFG were using these types of theoretical approaches to inform their design processes.* Eskilson, S. Graphic Design: A New History. New Haven, CT, USA: Yale University Press, 2007, p. 321.

[Y] *In particular, it was Aicher's convention of using a detached floating head that has since become the most distinctive characteristic of neutral, modern, public signage. Before this point, road signs depicting a human form followed Neurath's style of utilizing simplified silhouettes (see fig. 13). The abstracted floating head made pictogram figures look anonymous, and thus became the quintessential hallmark of universality.*

Course-Correcting the Future

Affecting change in verbal and written language is understandably easier than reforming the existing landscape of visual signage. One of the most pressing design challenges of our time is the need to reimagine transgendered restroom signage here in the U.S. As voices emerge from various LGBTQ subcultural groups across America, the opportunity presents a challenge to designers to mitigate these issues through innovative and informed—rather than prejudicial and pigeonholed—use of visual language. To do this effectively, we first need to understand how the subtle design difference between the male and female graphic icons were conventionalized to begin with.

Graphic designers continuously seek new ways for how, when and why to use pictures in preference to words. Modernist attempts to design a purely universal picture language began with Austrian-born economist and philosopher Otto Neurath in the 1920s, and culminated with the geometric body alphabet [W] designed for the 1972 Munich Olympics by German graphic designer Otl Aicher [X] (see fig. 12). By eliminating all references to gender, his intent was to create a universal form of visual language to represent all of *humankind*. [Y] However, close observation of these figures that depicted Olympians reveals that even though the sports represented are played by both genders, the viewer sees ONLY male, rather than female, athletes.

We contend that one of the primary reasons for this can be traced to the introduction and subsequent ubiquity of male and female icons for international restroom signage that had been in use for over a decade in many industrialized nations before Aicher and his team began their work on these figures in the late 1960s. In an attempt to create a gender differentiation between simplified, iconographic figures in the late 1950s, many designers in western Europe and North America adopted the graphic convention of using a woman's skirt to differentiate between the conveyance of "female" from "male," and thus forever changed the way many people interpret human icons in visual signage. Whereas the male gender was assigned the graphically neutral iconic form, female restroom icons were *gender-marked* with a skirt to make them look *'different.'* As a result, viewers are now so pre-conditioned to delineating between male and female whenever they see human iconic forms that they automatically assume the neutral figure is almost *always* male. The unintended corollary to this now universally accepted norm is that assigning the neutral iconic figure to solely represent *man* precludes its even greater iconographic potential for representing the whole of *mankind*.

80

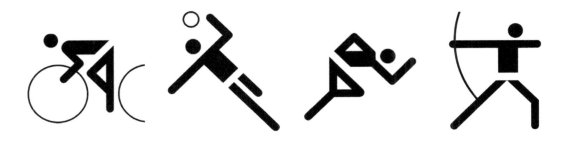

FIGURE 12: Aicher's anonymous figures representing the athletes who competed in the 1972 Olympic Games in Munich were supposed to be inclusive of everyone. Even though his geometric body alphabet represents sports played by both genders, why is it that viewers ONLY see male competitors, rather than women athletes? www.http:// aicher-pictograms.com (accessed May 25, 2016).

Challenging Discriminatory Conventions

Roland Barthes' approach to semiotics questioned the tacit agreement of the things we take for granted in our visual culture. He coined the term 'myths' to draw attention to the misconceptions between the properties and meanings we attach to images of the things around us. David Crow defines conventions as agreed upon systems of understanding that allow us to interpret what is happening: "All that is necessary for any language to exist is an agreement amongst a group of people that one thing will stand for another."[27] Semiotician Sean Hall, points out how "The rules that we use are important to reflect upon directly because we often fail to see just how much our behavior and our actions depend upon them.... In failing to notice these rules, we also fail to see the opportunities for questioning them and thereby for creating new codes and forms of meaning."[28] Meredith Davis summarizes that "If the relationship between form and what it means is arbitrary (merely a matter of cultural agreement), then it is open to renegotiation as a means of social reform."[29] Given the amount of mainstream cultural and political dialogue around restrooms and signage in the United States right now, the authors tested this theory in a series of social design projects. The first *'Gender Agenda'* project framed the problem with the following design question: *If public bathrooms no longer need to discriminate by gender identity, how can graphic restroom signage be transformed into a more preferable solution, by design?*[z] For this exercise, the female figure was reassigned with the graphically neutral iconic form, and undergraduate graphic

27
Crow, D. Visible Signs: An Introduction to Semiotics in the Visual Arts. Switzerland: AVA Publishing, 2nd Edition, 2010, p. 18.

28
Hall, S. This Means This: This Means That: A User's Guide to Semiotics. London, UK: Laurence King Publishing, 2nd Edition, 2012, p. 142.

29
Davis, M. Graphic Design Theory: Graphic Design in Context. New York, NY: Thames & Hudson Publishing, 2012, p. 131.

z Inspired by the Nobel Prize-winning economist, Herbert Simon who defined the process of design thusly: "Everyone designs who devise courses of action aimed at changing existing situations into preferred ones." Herbert Simon, Sciences of the Artificial. Cambridge, Massachusetts, USA: MIT Press, 1969, p. 130.

Gerd Arnz
Isostat, 1930

Otto Neurath
ISOTYPE, 1936

Otl Aicher
Olympics, 1972

Cook & Shanosky
D.O.T./AIGA, 1974

Unknown
Unisex, 2012

FIGURE 13: The Evolution of Indexical Restroom Figures: The convention of exaggerating the woman's skirt to gender-mark the female restroom figure forever changed the way we interpret human icons in visual signage.
Source: Dobson, T. 2016.

FIGURE 14: 'Gender Agenda 1': Challenging Discriminatory Conventions. This Loyola Marymount University undergraduate social design project was intended to challenge students to graphically differentiate between genders without using the stylized reference of a skirt. It became an experiment in how gender role-reversal could be effectively depicted in restroom signage. Source: Dobson, T. 2016.

FIGURE 15: O'Gender Agenda 2': Gender Neutral. This Loyola Marymount University & Azusa Pacific University undergraduate social design project challenged students to engage in sketch explorations as a means to reimagine transgendered restroom signage. *Source: Dobson, T. & Dobson, S.C. & Kirkpatrick, G. 2016.*

design students were challenged to design other ways to graphically differentiate between genders without using the stylized reference of a skirt (see fig.14).

The resulting exploration revealed how designers can proactively help bring attention to the often-invisible influence of the graphic artifacts they create. It also inspired these emerging designers to challenge the accepted rules and reconsider the conventions they have, in many cases, unwittingly inherited and often used unquestioningly. The second 'Gender Agenda' project required students at two different universities to reimagine transgendered restroom signage by framing the problem as a more focused design question: *How will public restroom signage change its 'function' in the future?* (see fig.15).

Teams were encouraged to expand their thinking beyond merely examining the accepted convention of marking to visually communicate gender, and initially visualized solutions that focused on *function* rather than *gender* through variations of pictograms destined for use just outside restrooms. However, this exemplified how difficult it becomes to *unlearn* the meanings inherent in signs already imbued with long-ago learned associations after societal norms change, or begin to change. Furthermore, it pinpointed the heretofore unmet need to communicate *'All-Inclusive'* and *'Gender-Friendly'* as equally important messages. Perhaps most significantly, the existing male and female iconic figures are already visually identifiable and indexically synonymous with restrooms. This compelled the designers of this learning experience to reframe the design question by asking: *How can we expand upon the existing 'indexical' connotation of restroom figures?*

83

FIGURE 16: Gender-friendly, Socially Symbolic, Indexical Restroom Signage Figures. By replacing the anticipated gender-marked restroom icons with a gender-neutral figure, our pre-conditioned tendency to automatically delineate between male and female is instead rewarded with the discovery that both figures are the same. Subverting the expectation for gender-marking becomes a socially symbolic act in gender neutrality. *Source: Dobson, T. 2016.*

In order to avoid a binary solution that singles out or excludes anyone, the project designers explored new ways to graphically reset neutrality expectations. By replacing the anticipated gender-marked restroom icons with a gender-neutral figure, the aforementioned pre-conditioned tendency among viewers to automatically delineate between male and female is instead rewarded with the discovery that *both figures are the same.* In other words, subverting the expectation for gender-marking now becomes a socially symbolic act in its gender neutrality (see fig.16).

Gender-Neutral Restroom Figures

To fully comprehend the simple efficiency of this solution, the project designers referenced the pioneering work of communication theorists Philip Emmert and William Donaghy as centermost to the articulation of the concept. Meredith Davis explains that according to the Emmert/Donaghy model of communication, "...our interpretation of a single message is influenced by all our previous experiences." Furthermore, "...meaning is constructed in the mind of the interpreter and is not controlled solely by the originator of the message," and "The best we can hope for, as designers, is to put in place the appropriate elements and conditions that help an audience arrive at a similar interpretation to the one we intend." [30] Accordingly, both color and shape become crucial

30
Davis, M. Graphic Design Theory: Graphic Design in Context. New York, NY, USA: Thames & Hudson Publishing, 2012, pgs. 17-20.

31

White, A. The Elements of Graphic Design. New York, NY, USA: Skyhorse Publishing, 2011, p. 59.

design elements in manipulating the viewer's decoding of the intended meaning. Even though Marshall McLuhan's *'hierarchy of communication'* puts color at the bottom of human perception, functioning in the viewer's subconscious, [31] it becomes the foremost characteristic of this signage system to compete for the viewer's attention. Since the colors pink and blue together are connotatively 'loaded' with preexisting gender associations, they automatically trigger the anticipation of a gender difference between the iconic figures within the shapes. [A] The Emmert/Donaghy principle—that argues for a deeper understanding of cognitive processes as fundamental to design practice—is thus effectively harnessed to influence the viewer's mental processing of stimuli to lead them to the desired conclusion. This subtle reformulation of existing restroom signage components provides a solution that focuses on the most important design deliverable: to transform a basic, human-centered experience—everyone has to use the restroom every day—into a more preferable one for *all users.*

Conclusion

The results of this visual inquiry into the issues created by culturally problematic signs culminated in the exploration of non-verbal solutions for the now-pressing issue to redesign transgendered restroom signage. [B] Articulating the complexities surrounding the circle-slash prompted the need to define a new model for describing signs, which resulted in an updated hybrid typology based on Peirce's original triad of icon, index and symbol. The subversion of the seemingly objective qualities of neutral iconic forms in ways that become socially-symbolic acknowledged the complicit function of graphic design to make what is and has become socially and culturally accepted appear natural. Thus, by translating graphic and historical analysis into a critical reading, writing and making of sign systems today, this research reframes an aspect of design thinking towards a reimagined role for the future of socially-symbolic, indexical restroom figures (see fig. 17).

[A] *The first to illustrate a pedigree with males represented as squares and females as circles seems to have been Pliny Earle, physician to the Bloomingdale Asylum for the Insane in New York in 1845.* Extracted from Schott, G. "Sex, Drugs, And Rock And Roll. Sex symbols ancient and modern: their origins and iconography on the pedigree," BMJ, 22 December, 2005. Online. Available at: http://www.bmj.com/content/331/7531/1509 (Accessed 27 October 2016).

[B] *California's Governor, Jerry Brown, signed a bill in September 2016 establishing the nation's most inclusive restroom-access law. It requires businesses and government buildings to post non-gender-specific signs on single-occupancy restrooms by March 1, 2017.* Extracted from Associated Press, "California governor Brown approves gender-neutral restroom bill," PBS Newshour, 29 September, 2016. Online. Available at: http://www.pbs.org/newshour/rundown/california-governor-brown-approves-gender-neutral-restroom-bill/ (Accessed 31 October 2016).

The primary contribution to ongoing study in the field of visual semiotics yields the classification of a new "sign" type: the 'symbolic-index.' This particular "sign" type is useful in both describing and creating signs that simultaneously harness symbolic and indexical qualities as predominant connotations. The result of this work makes a compelling case for new models in design education to unpack the historical and historiographic ideas that helped form and frame it, in order to provide a pedagogical path forward to guide its reform. However, this is just the tip of the icon. Signs and signage systems will

FIGURE 17: Socially Symbolic Indexical Signage: 'Faux' television news graphic depicting the 'reimagined' all-gender-friendly bathroom signage solution. *Source: Dobson, T. 2016.*

FIGURE 18: 'Faux' television news graphic depicting the 'alternative' exclusionary signage solution, which reduces the information using default visual language into a sign that's pragmatically clear but culturally unacceptable. *Source: Dobson, T. 2016.*

always be subject to variable social and cultural interpretations depending on their contexts of use. Unless we sensitize and educate ourselves to design signage with a higher and more broadly informed degree of iconographic empathy, designers are likely to repeat the socially and culturally insensitive "mistakes" of the past. Without greater discernment about how we perceive and use signifiers of supposedly neutral universal form, our signage systems will continue to perpetuate exclusionary social and cultural ideas. Further, the power our symbols carry to mark members of society with 'otherness' will remain as stereotypical of our future information landscape as it was of European design's often ignoble, heraldic past. The resulting alternative, as figure 18 predicts, depicts an effective reduction of information into a single unmistakable sign that's pragmatically clear but culturally unacceptable.

References

Abdullah, R. & Huber, R. Pictograms, *Icons & Signs*. London, UK: Thames & Hudson Publishing, 2006.

Associated Press, "California governor Brown approves gender-neutral restroom bill," PBS Newshour, 29 September, 2016. Online. Available at: http://www.pbs.org/newshour/rundown/california-governor-brown-approves-gender-neutral-restroom-bill/ (Accessed 31 October 2016).

Atkin, A. "Peirce's three categories of Signs: icon, index, symbol," Stanford Encyclopedia of Philosophy, 15 November, 2010. Online. Available at: http://plato.stanford.edu/entries/peirce-semiotics (Accessed April 14, 2016).

Barnard, M. *Graphic Design As Communication*. London, UK & New York, USA: Routledge, 2013.

Barthes, R. *Mythologies*. New York, NY, USA: Hill & Wang, 1995.

Crow, D. *Visible Signs: An Introduction to Semiotics in the Visual Arts*. Lausanne, Switzerland: AVA Publishing, 2nd Edition, 2010.

Cordua, G. et al. "Doctor or Nurse: Children's Perception of Sex Typed Occupations." *Child Development*, Vol.50.2 (Jun., 1979), pgs. 590–593.

Davis, M. *Graphic Design Theory: Graphic Design in Context*. New York, NY, USA: Thames & Hudson Publishing, 2012.

Dumbar, G. & Dumbar, D. "A Safe Place: International System of Disaster Diagrams." Originally presented at *The Utrecht Manifest: Second Biennale for Social Design,* November 3, 2007, in Utrecht, NL. SIGNS4DISASTER, 30 October, 2013. Online. Available at: https://signs4disaster.word-press.com/2013/10/30/a-safe-place-international-system-of-disaster-pictograms/ (Accessed November 9, 2016).

Eco, U. "Towards a Semiotic Inquiry Into the Television Message." *Working Papers in Cultural Studies,* University of Birmingham, 3 (1972): pgs. 103–21.

ERCO Piktogramme, 1972. Online. Available at: www.http://aicher-pictograms.com (Accessed May 25, 2016).

Eskilson, S. *Graphic Design: A New History.* New Haven, CT, USA: Yale University Press, 2007.

Fry, D. & Fry, V. "Continuing the conversation regarding Myth and Culture: An alternative reading of Barthes." *American Journal of Semiotics,* 6.2/3 (1989), pgs.183–197.

Friedman, K. "Theory construction in design research: criteria: approaches, and methods." *Design Studies,* 24.6 (2003), p. 507.

Griffin, E. *A First Look at Communication Theory.* New York, NY, USA: McGraw-Hill, 9th Edition, 2015.

Jury, D. *About Face: Reviving the Rules of Typography.* London: RotoVision (1996).

Hall, S. *This Means This: This Means That: A User's Guide to Semiotics.* London, UK: Laurence King Publishing, 2nd Edition (2012).

Jansen, W. *The Journal of Design History,* 22: 3: (2009), 229.

Kelly, Rob Roy. "The Early Years of Graphic Design at Yale University." *Design Issues* 17. 3 (2001): pgs. 3–14.

Kirkpatrick, G. *1+1=3: The Sum of the Parts is Greater Than the Whole.* Forthcoming research (2005).

Krampen, M. "Signs and Symbols in Graphic Communication." *Design Quarterly,* 62 (1965), pgs. 1–31.

Krampen, M. "Icons of the Road." *Semiotica: Journal of the International Association for Semiotic Studies,* 43.1–2 (January 1983), pgs. 33–164.

Lupton, E. *Design Issues,* MIT Press, 3.2 (Autumn, 1986), pgs. 50–51.

Lupton, E. & Miller, A. *Design Writing Research: Writing About Graphic Design.* New York, NY, USA: Kiosk Publishing, 1996.

Maldonado, T. Uppercase 5: HfG Ulm. Tonbridge, Kent, UK: Whitefriars Publishing (1961).

Meggs, Philip B., and Alston W. Purvis. *Meggs' History of Graphic Design.* Hoboken, NJ, USA: John Wiley & Sons, 2016.

Neurath, M, & Cohen, R. Otto Neurath: From Vienna Method to *ISOTYPE*. Dordrecht, Germany: Reidel Publishers, 1973.

Robb, A. "How gender-specific toys can negatively impact a child's development," *Women In The World,* 12 August, 2015. Online. Available at: http://nytlive.nytimes.com/womenintheworld/2015/08/12/how-gender-specific-toys-can-negatively-impact-a-childs-development/ (Accessed 1 November 2016).

Schipper, F. "Unraveling hieroglyphs: Urban traffic signs and the League of Nations." Métropoles: 87 (2009).

Schott, G. "Sex, Drugs, And Rock And Roll. Sex symbols ancient and modern: their origins and iconography on the pedigree," *The British Medical Journal,* 22 December, 2005. Online. Available at: http://www.bmj.com/content/331/7531/1509 (Accessed 27 October 2017).

Simon, H. *Sciences of the Artificial.* Cambridge, MA, USA: MIT Press (1969), p. 130.

Skaggs, S. "Visual Design Semiotic Primer," 27 July, 2011. Online. Available at: http://stevenskaggs.net/VDSP%20Chapt%201.pdf (Accessed 30 October, 2016).

Skaggs, S. *Zed 4: Semiotics: Pedagogy and Practice.* Richmond, VA, USA: Virginia Commonwealth University Press (1997).

Storkerson, P. "Antinomies of Semiotics in Graphic Design." *Visible Language,* 44.1 (2010): pgs. 6–37.

"Tie a Yellow Ribbon Round The Ole Oak Tree" by Dawn featuring Tony Orlando, written by Irwin Levine and L. Russell Brown, recorded 1973. New York City, New York, USA: Bell Records, 45 rpm.

Torres, E. "The three kinds of Signs in Linguistics," Linked-In SlideShare, 24 November, 2014. Online. Available at: http://www.slideshare.net/durakusnation/the-three-kinds-of-signs-in-linguistics (Accessed 17 September 2016).

White, A. *The Elements of Graphic Design.* New York, NY, USA: Skyhorse Publishing, 2011.

Biogarphies

Terry Dobson is Director of Design Programs and Associate Professor of Graphic Design at Azusa Pacific University. Terry earned an MFA in Graphic Design from Yale University. His creative direction at Disney for more than two decades won him a Themed Entertainment Industry Award with Walt

Disney Imagineering; an Interactive Academy Award with Disney Interactive Studios; and four online gaming awards with Disney Parks and Resorts Online. Terry was inaugurated into Disney Inventor's Hall of Fame, and awarded a patent for design and technological innovation for Disney's first multiplayer online theme park, Virtual Magic Kingdom. As a design scholar his research focuses on the making of symbolic visual meaning, and as a design curator, his gallery shows raise awareness for issues of social import. *tdobson@apu.edu*

Saeri Cho Dobson is a tenured Associate Professor of Graphic Design at Loyola Marymount University. Her social and moral design responsibility to educate the whole person are artistic hallmarks of her inclusive teaching pedagogy. In 2012, she founded BySaeRi, Inc., to pursue stories of amazing human lives through design and fashion typography. Saeri received a BFA in Communication Design from Parsons' The New School for Design in New York. She graduated with a MFA from Art Center College of Design in Pasadena, CA. Her experimental typography expands the boundaries between type as text and type as texture, and has been exhibited in galleries in New Zealand, South Korea, Mexico, Santa Monica, and Los Angeles. *saeri.dobson@lmu.edu*

Dialectic Volume I, Issue I: Position Paper

On Web Brutalism and Contemporary Web Design

AARON GANCI[1] AND BRUNO RIBEIRO[2]

1. Indiana University Herron School of Art and Design (IUPUI), Indianapolis, Indiana, USA
2. California Polytechnic State University, San Luis Obispo, California, USA

SUGGESTED CITATION: Ganci, A., & Ribeiro, B. "On Web Brutalism and Contemporary Web Design." *Dialectic,* 1.1 (2016): pgs. 91-110.
DOI: http://dx.doi.org/10.3998/dialectic.14932326.0001.107

Abstract

This paper acknowledges and frames the controversial Web Brutalism movement in and around contemporary web-based interaction design, and subsequently raises critical questions about its influence on present and future web design strategies and practices. This inquiry is informed and facilitated by a comparison of two distinct perspectives.

Professor Ganci contends that this movement has the potential to have a generally positive affect, and that it is a welcome response to the homogenization of a limited set of aesthetic conventions and practices that have become pervasive across the web. Professor Ganci further argues that because it has become fairly easy to create websites that "fit the mold and that look great," this type of idle, sans-design-thinking approach will eventually lead to web design failures, as it coerces web designers to engage in formulaic processes that sacrifice real invention and innovation centered on meeting well-understood user and audience needs and desires. The ability to make, rather than design, web-based interactions that are derived from various templates and other one-size-fits-all approaches is posited as a severe limitation, with Web Brutalism posited as a counter to this, and as an effective, relatively new type of catalyzer to web design strategies and tactics.

Professor Ribeiro contends that Web Brutalism is nothing more than a momentary distraction from a more crucial set of issues contemporary and near-future web designers face, such as usability, scalability, adaptability, and, especially, broad accessibility. Twenty-plus years into its development, the web is still fairly inaccessible to people who have physical disabilities, or who must access the internet through slow connections and underpowered devices, or who have limited access to internet connectivity or electricity.

This paper raises questions regarding perception, usability, effective communication, meaningful innovation, and what added and evolved responsibilities designers should assume in the context of contemporary web design. The discourse that has been initiated here needs to continue in order to reveal the expansive potential of design across the web.

On Web Brutalism and Contemporary Web Design

AARON GANCI

BRUNO RIBEIRO

Introduction

As we pass the twenty-year mark of visual design on the web, a new trend has emerged over the course of the last two to three years: *Web Brutalism.* This movement, or trend, in web design is guided by design processes that ensure the interface design of given websites are anything but user-friendly and aesthetically appealing. Websites like *Bloomberg Businessweek Features, Lifeaction-revival, The Drudge Report* and, perhaps most well-known of all, *Craigslist* have been designed purposefully to inhibit ease-of-use and to *not* appear professionally polished. Brutalist websites are also intentionally built to be rough, to be coded so that they appear to be uncomfortable for many audiences and users to interact with. Aesthetically and functionally, web brutalism can trace a portion of its roots to the mid 1990s and a time when web interfaces were much less affected by template-based design and functionalities that seek to manipulate particular types of user behaviors. (The term "brutalism" originated in the 1970s as a means to describe mostly institutional architecture that featured large, aesthetically heavy buildings that featured vast expanses of exposed concrete.)

For the moment, Web Brutalism is a niche movement, but it gives us pause and challenges the discipline of interaction design, and, more specifically, web design to reflect on the following questions: What roles does visual design play in the creation and evolving life of a website? What kind of place in the web design process should innovation and best practices have? How should we

93

Deville, P. Brutalist Websites. Online. Available at: http://brutalistwebsites.com/. (Accessed 25 May 2016).

define what constitutes quality in web design processes and their outcomes? As designers, these are important questions that we must confront effectively, or risk creating interactive experiences that inhibit usability, create misperceptions, or that waste our users precious time. The central ideas articulated in this paper will begin to examine these questions by reflecting on what the existence of Web Brutalism says about the design processes that inform and guide the look and feel of much of the contemporary web.

Akin to the architectural movement that gave rise to the term, Brutalist websites reject the polish and formulaic structures that have become ubiquitous across an increasingly homogenized web. The blog *Brutalist Websites* [1] showcases sites that its creators believe effectively demonstrate the Brutalist aesthetic and the often handmade, or "crude" coding that facilitates the delivery of the content of these websites. Pascal Deville, the site's editor, defines the movement as follows: "In its ruggedness and lack of concern to look comfortable or easy, Brutalism can be seen as a reaction by a younger generation to the lightness, optimism, and frivolity of today's web design." Moreover, while the borders and concrete definitions of this movement are inexact, Brutalist websites can be broadly defined by their general rejection of the ostensible drive toward perfection that permeates so much of contemporary web design through the use of repeatable visual patterns and standardized layout conventions.

Labeling the sites Deville has identified as Brutalist feels like a bit of a stretch—its parameters, if they can be called that, and aesthetic signifiers, are difficult to define specifically—and the movement is still relatively small. While these sites embrace the utilization of raw material (in this case primitive HTML and aesthetically rough graphic form), and they also reject the formula of contemporary design—just as the original Brutalist architects of the 1970s rejected Modernism and the International Style—many of them could be described as fitting the descriptions of the following variety variety of labels: Minimalist, Avant-garde, or one of several flavors of Postmodern. That stated, websites like these are unified in that those who have created them have made a conscious effort to distinguish both their visual appearance and the nature of their interactivity from the conventional. Brutalist websites are designed to engage the viewer in a hostile way. They frequently utilize the rough aesthetics of the early web, circa 1994–98, in raw and dissonant ways. Their formal configurations and facilitation of interactive functions break nearly every commonly held modern design convention, which forces the viewer to be fully present during his/her engagement with one of these websites in order to comprehend

FIGURE 1: Deadly Sports Tragedy (deadlysportstragedy.com) fits the profile of a Brutalist website. According to its designer, Ben Patterson, the site "capture[s] the intensity and coarseness of professional sports broadcasts."

2

Budds, D. "The Internet's 10 'Ugliest' Websites." Fast Company, 25 May 2016. Online. Available at: http://www.fastcodesign.com/3060196/the-internets-10-ugliest-websites. (Accessed 25 May 2016).

3

Arcement, K. "The hottest trend in Web design is making intentionally ugly, difficult sites." The Washington Post, 9 May 2016. Online. https://www.washingtonpost.com/news/the-intersect/wp/2016/05/09/the-hottest-trend-in-web-design-is-intentionally-ugly-unusable-sites/. (Accessed 25 May 2016).

their content. This tends to elicit strong reactions and opinions from both users and members of the design community. These types of websites also often do not utilize traditional navigation, and often mask the placement of the cursor. Perhaps most interestingly, they invite us to question the viability and efficacy of many well-established aesthetic and functional conventions that guide the design of so many modern web interfaces.

While Web Brutalism has been relatively quiet during its short life simply due to its limited scope (most of the sites on *Brutalist Websites* are personal in nature, and there are just not that many of them out there), the approach is starting to move into the view of the general public with sites like *Adult Swim* and *Bloomberg*. Some of these websites have also been gaining attention in the popular press, [2] with articles like "The hottest trend in Web design is making intentionally ugly, difficult sites" recently appearing in The Washington Post. [3] So—how should we think about these discordantly

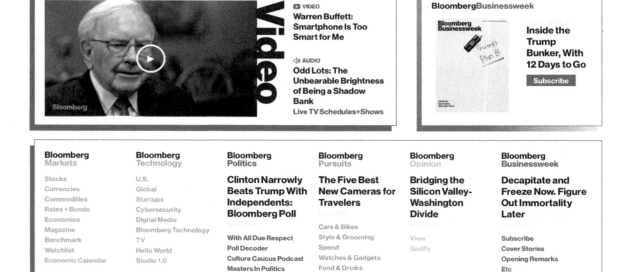

FIGURE 2: Bloomberg utilizes hints of a Brutalist aesthetic on their site, http://bloomberg.com

designed interfaces that sit at the fringe of web design? What do they say about the utility of particular aesthetic approaches and frameworks? What do they reveal about how and why the practice of designing websites has evolved as it has, specifically as it relates to an increasing reliance on broadly accepted conventions and patterns? Do Brutalist websites mark a renaissance of innovation, or are they merely an ostentatious distraction?

We argue that the Brutalist Web movement is both good and bad for contemporary web design. Each co-author of this piece has come to this inquiry with a distinct point of view: Professor Ganci contends that this movement can have a generally positive affect on the evolution of web design, with Professor Ribeiro contending that it is nothing more than a momentary distraction. In the following sections of this piece, we will each argue to promote our relative positions. The discourse that follows is purposefully provocative, and is intended to raise and contextually frame more questions than it answers. In the end, we will summarize our respective analyses and describe how we believe they can begin to help the web design community move effectively forward across common ground.

Brutalism is here to save us by Aaron Ganci

Most web design that exists across the internet of 2016-17 is boring. Too many of us who practice and teach it have become complacent, or, worse, merely efficient. Web Brutalism is here to show us the error of our staid, formulaic ways. It is a necessary intervention for us, a shrill wake-up call designed to shock us out of our current state of complacency.

It is easy to look at examples of Brutalist websites and opine that their creators are naïve or self-interested. While I agree with this assessment on some levels, I argue that their approaches have a good deal to teach us about the current state of our industry, if we would simply take the time to examine these more closely and critically. It is not easy to look upon these sites as types of saviors that can redeem us from the pervasive banality that now affects so much of contemporary web design, but, in ways that mirror the behavior of an individual undergoing a psychological or social intervention, web designers have gotten good at denying that we have a problem. Before I address how I think Brutalism can save us, I will quickly discuss the current state of the discipline, and explain how we developed the need for an intervention in the first place.

Uniformity within contemporary practice

When encountering a Brutalist site, a viewer will likely have a strong-but-justified emotional or even visceral reaction. Aesthetically, as was often the case with many websites that were designed and operated during the 1990s, today's Brutalist sites are often not good by contemporary aesthetic or functional standards. We have that strong reaction today because of a prevailing, fairly rigid set of ideas about how "good" websites should look and perform. This has become especially true in recent years because of the assertion of two primary factors. First, the act of building a website has become much easier due to advances in both the design and development arenas. This has resulted in broad cross sections of websites becoming much more formulaic in their appearance and behavior. UI (user interface) frameworks, like Bootstrap, Foundation, and Semantic UI allow designers to build a site quite quickly but have, in turn, systematized layout conventions and the appearance and functionality of many design elements in the process. The satirical website *Every Bootstrap Website*

97

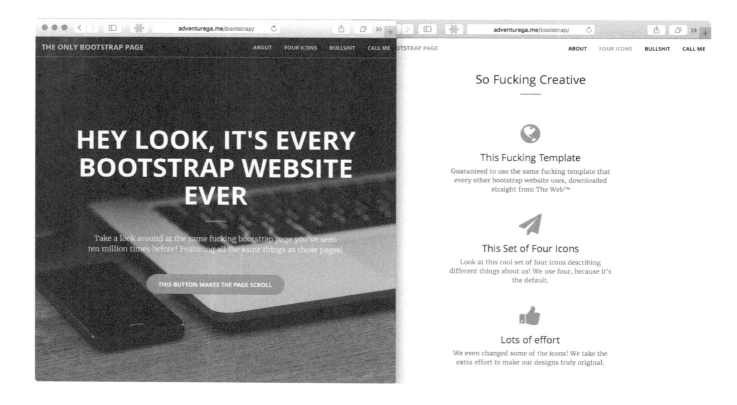

FIGURE 3: Every Bootstrap Website Ever summarizes and lampoons the uniformity of modern websites.

Ever[4] lampoons this reality by exposing this ubiquitous formula. Additionally, services like Squarespace enable anyone to build a polished site that automatically conforms to the norm with almost no effort. The second factor is the homogenization of a limited set of aesthetic conventions and practices on the web. Today, many websites use the same visual patterns, layout configurations and icon systems. This is partly due to the influence of the aforementioned UI frameworks, and partly due to the popularity of services like *Dribble* and *Pinterest* that tend to reward designers (with a high volume of views of their work) for sharing work that fits within broadly accepted trends.

In many ways, this working environment has created a sweet and comfortable spot for web designers. It has become fairly easy for us to create work that fits the mold *and* that also looks great *and* that we can also get paid for. I believe that this type of idle approach will eventually lead to widespread failure, as it coerces web designers to engage in processes that sacrifice real invention an innovation to meet user/viewer needs with only a limited array of "one size fits all" approaches. The kind of cyclical, critical inquiries that inform user experience-centered web design processes cannot occur. So many of the formulaic web design approaches that are prevalent today turn out to

4

Every Bootstrap Website Ever.
Online. Available at:
http://adventurega.me/bootstrap/.
(Accessed 26 May 2016).

5

Buchanan, R. "Branzi's Dilemma: Design in Contemporary Culture." Design Issues, 14.1 (1998): pgs. 3-20.

6

Roth, S.P, et al. "Location matters, especially for non-salient features-An eye-tracking study on the effects of web object placement on different types of websites." International Journal of Human—Computer Studies. 71.3 (2013): pgs. 228-235.

yield "good enough" solutions [5] for many contemporary UI designs, but that is all they are, and they tend toward the predictable, the banal, the "'been there, done that." By breaking away from these current, prevalent-yet-conventional approaches, we position ourselves and the design processes we devise and operate more effectively to resolve many of the communication and interaction problems we encounter now, and will encounter in the near future.

The thoughtfulness of Brutalism

There are many aspects of Brutalism that will not—and should not—translate into popular web design vernacular. However, we should consider borrowing some its most effective aesthetic and functional features as we move forward. Doing so will help more web designers break away from the trend of template-based uniformity and allow us to continue to innovate in tangible, meaningful and productive ways. In this context, two aspects of Web Brutalism are most pertinent: adopting and operating a skeptical approach to the design process, and a rejection of the type of banal, visual polish that has become all too ubiquitous across the modern web.

Questioning conventions with a skeptical approach

The web design conventions so many of us use today have been contextualized and defined through a continuous process of two decades' worth of testing and refinement. This is a good thing—it exemplifies the action research-based, dynamically iterative aspects of the web design process. Along the way, a diverse array of user-centered studies have been conducted to examine the specific effects of particular types of form and texture arrangements in interface designs. Their findings have been published to help web designers refine how they should configure the forms that constitute given user interfaces in ways that have become well-established conventions. Breaking these conventions tends to be strongly discouraged, and has been cited as a causal factor that negatively affects usability. [6]

With that stated, the conventions we so often utilize today that inform and guide how web-based content should be laid out or formatted should not be taken as gospel. Web designers—and our HCI counterparts and collaborators—are sometimes too quick to implement a validated solution to merely increase efficiency, to save time, as the design process evolves. However, if we rely on these accepted conventions too heavily, we may miss opportunities to engage in more broadly informed, deeply examined and original design decision-making. Even Jakob Nielsen, one of the definitive voices on web usability, warns us that usability guidelines cannot remain valid forever.[7] The web is simply too dynamic and too fluid a communication medium to allow its design conventions to remain as fixed as some would have them. By encouraging radical exploration, as the Brutalists do, we position ourselves to constantly re-evaluate what is working or not working, or what could potentially work (or not), given the design challenges at hand.

Rejecting visual polish and the effect of visual design on fluency

One critique that Brutalism has leveled at contemporary web design is that today's popular, template-based aesthetic has become overly polished, minimalistic and (generally) not tailored enough to meet the needs and desires of particular users. Usability experts have argued for roughly 20 years that reducing the complexity of a website will usually improve its overall usability.[8] Counter to this, literature from cognitive psychology suggests that the polish and predictability of so many contemporary websites may have a negative effect on certain aspects of user experience. Specifically, when content is presented in expected, overly fluent, or intuitive ways, readers have a more difficult time engaging with information.[9] Because the prevailing graphic styles on the web are so widely used, readers may *anticipate* the meaning of content based on its common visual presentation and then not fully engage with it. This is a very different reading experience than one that challenges a reader to actively engage with web-based content in ways that would allow them to effectively interpret its meaning.

By rejecting aesthetic polish, the Brutalists are promoting a disfluent approach, one that diverges from the normalized presentation of content. Studies from cognitive psychology indicate that content presented with disfluent characteristics enables readers to process information "more carefully, deeply, and abstractly."[10] While these studies incorporate only minor variations in typographic style or color, they still hint at an overlooked idea within contemporary practice: that utilizing a polished, ubiquitous visual style might not be the best way to address or resolve a given visual communication design problem. Exploring divergent aesthetics might be a way for us to more fully understand the correlation between the presentation of web content and a given individual's ability to process that information.

Brutalism pushes disfluency theories to their extreme, and may very likely lead to frustration on the part of the user,[11] or fatigue or other

7

Nielsen, J. "Durability of Usability Guidelines." Nielsen Norman Group (blog). 17 January 2005. Online. Available at: https://www.nngroup.com/articles/durability-of-usability-guidelines/. (Accessed 25 May 2016).

8

Whitenton, K. "Minimize Cognitive Load to Maximize Usability." Nielsen Norman Group (blog). 22 December 2013. Online. Available at: https://www.nngroup.com/articles/minimize-cognitive-load/. (Accessed 25 May 2016).

9

Alter, A.L, et. al. "Overcoming Intuition: Metacognitive Difficulty Activates Analytic Reasoning." Journal of Experimental Psychology. 136.4 (2007): pgs. 569-576. Available online at: https://pdfs.semanticscholar.org/526d/fb9f8715d-48fa79d0f766caa5cd9151cf074.pdf. (Accessed 1 September 2016).

10

Alter A.L. "The Benefits of Cognitive Disfluency." Current Directions in Psychological Science. 22.6 (2013): pgs. 437-442.

11

Diemand-Yauman, C., Daniel M. Oppenheimer, and Erikka B. Vaughan. "Fortune favors the bold (and the italicized): Effects of disfluency on educational outcomes." Cognition. 118.1 (2011): pgs. 111-115.

12

Alter A.L. "The Benefits of Cognitive Disfluency." Current Directions in Psychological Science. 22.6 (2013): pgs. 437-442.

13

Tuch, A, et al. "The role of visual complexity and prototypicality regarding first impression of websites: working towards understanding aesthetic judgments". International Journal of Human-Computer Studies. 70.11 (2012): pgs. 794-811

14

Maeda, J. Twitter post. 7 January 2014, 8:04 a.m. Available at: https://twitter.com/johnmaeda/status/420541336060575744. (Accessed 25 May 2016).

physiological issues. [12] This seems to us to indicate that the idea of utilizing disfluent visuals needs to be informed by applied research that examines how these types of visuals affect user behavior. This could be especially true regarding how the use of disfluent visuals affects a given user's initial impression of a website or User Interface. Research that has examined how various visual factors affect general website appeal indicates that users decide very quickly—within fractions of a second—whether they find the graphic configuration of a given website too complex and, as a result, unappealing. [13] This is where Brutalism fails. By encouraging an aesthetic that is so disfluent, Brutalistic websites often inhibit the specific types of communication and messaging. It is exciting to think about how web designers might use disfluent strategies and tactics to enhance how various types of interface components and systems could be freshly configured to enhance visual communications and functionality. Rather than resigning ourselves to the idea that the currently dominant array of visual tropes, patterns and layout templates are immovably cemented into the structure of the web, those of us who design in this arena need to continue to critically examine and question how and why these affect not only user perceptions and actions, but our own design processes.

Saving us from ourselves

On the surface, Web Brutalism looks like a regression from the formal and functional knowledge and understandings many web designers have worked thoughtfully and diligently to construct and cultivate since the 1990s. If we can effectively challenge ourselves to look past the initial rawness inherent in these designs, they have the potential to actually teach us some important lessons. They remind us that formal and process-based design conventions often need to be challenged for our discipline and the decision-making processes that inform it to evolve, and that a divergent aesthetic can sometimes be an effective means to achieve this. Whether or not it is the intended goal of the Web Brutalists, it might behoove us to appreciate their attempt to save us from ourselves.

Brutalism is here to distract us by Bruno Ribeiro

In early 2014, John Maeda wrote that "good design is about clarity over style, and accountability over ego". [14] Although Web Brutalists do not seem to be overly concerned with this approach to good design, I hereby state that I *am*. Good design is not merely rooted in understanding and achieving visually compelling and appropriate aesthetic forms and systems of forms, but it is also

15

"Dieter Rams: ten principles for good design." Vitsœ. Online. Available at: https://www.vitsoe.com/us/about/good-design. (Accessed 15 September 2016).

16

Hamilton, I. "A simple introduction to web accessibility." Creative Bloq (blog). 27 July 2011. Online. Available at: http://www.creative-bloq.com/netmag/simple-introduction-web-accessibility-7116888. (Accessed 25 May 2016).

17

"MYTH: Accessibility is "blind people." The A11Y Project (blog). 11 January 2013. Online. Available at: http://a11yproject.com/posts/myth-accessibility-is-blind-people. (Accessed 26 May 2016).

18

"Accessibility is hard." The A11Y Project (blog). 22 July 2014. Online. Available at: http://a11yproject.com/about.html. (Accessed 27 May 2016).

honest in terms of its intentions, and therefore is accountable and responsible to those users and audiences who are or may be affected by the outcomes of its processes. The possibilities to achieve real innovation in and around the ever-diversifying arena(s) of web design are far from being exhausted, and are likely still largely untapped and unrealized. And, as Dieter Rams opines in his ten principles for good design, "innovation can't be an end in itself." [15]

It is against this contextual backdrop that the promulgation and promotion of a deliberately ugly aesthetic for web design as "innovation," especially one that emulates the worst aesthetic and functional practices from the 1990s, is at best naïve and at worst insulting. Web Brutalism is a provocation that attempts to bring a specific type of egocentric design into the spotlight at the expense of clear communication and effective functionality. It distracts web designers and their collaborators from the more crucial issues they must confront, such as usability and, especially, accessibility.

We need to make the web* more *accessible to* more *diverse groups of people

The fact that a relatively small group of web designers have decided that too much of the design they are perceiving across the web is boring is a weak and fairly one dimensional rationale for infusing it with a new aesthetic. Focusing on how content is displayed across this dynamic medium diverts attention away from the need to confront more pressing concerns in web design, such as ensuring that the content it delivers can reach the broad cross sections of people who still have limited access to it. Twenty years into its development, the web is still fairly inaccessible to people who have physical disabilities, or who must access the internet through slow connections and underpowered devices, or who have limited access to internet connectivity or electricity.

According to user experience and accessibility consultant Ian Hamilton, one fifth of the world's population has some type of physical disability. [16] To help web designers more effectively address the concerns of users with limited access, he has typologized accessibility into four broad categories: visual, auditory, motor, and cognitive. This typology has been adopted by the A11Y Project, [17] an effort that a variety of web designers and developers have undertaken to make web accessibility easier for people who are affected by one or more physical impairments. Broadening the accessibility of the web has proved to be a difficult, time- and capital-intensive task. Even the A11Y Project admits that the design and functionality of their own website is limited in terms of how effectively it meets the needs of those with disabilities. [18] Designing a more universally accessible web will require the time and attention of a much greater number of web designers and developers than are currently working to improve accessibility. More research and development funding from national funding agencies around the world likely needs to be made available to university-based researchers and designers to address this deficiency, as this tends *not* to be the type of endeavor that private sector funding (like venture capital sources) has shown much interest in supporting.

In addition to designing web-based interactive experiences that meet the needs of those with physical disabilities more effectively, web designers should also attempt to improve usability experiences for the hundreds of millions around the world who are new to the internet and the web, and who often have limited access to them. According to *StatCounter*, 39% of worldwide web browsing during the first quarter of 2016 was facilitated through mobile devices. [19] A smartphone, or wireless mobile device (WMD), is the only computing device many people in the developing countries of the world have ever owned, and this trend of smartphones and WMDs penetrating the world's markets is continuing to grow. According to an article published in *Wired* magazine in February of 2015, "With pricing reaching an affordable $30 to $50 for some smartphones, people who have never before been able to afford a computing device now own one, and it fits in their pocket." [20] For many people living in places with limited access to electricity and the internet, a (relatively) cheap smartphone is their primary and often only means of accessing the internet. On May 19th, 2016, Tal Oppenheimer, a product manager on the Google Chrome team, gave a presentation at the Google I/O conference titled *Building for billions on the web*, during which she mentioned that 60% of globally mobile connections are facilitated using now-outdated—since roughly late 2010—second-generation, or 2G, wireless telephone technology. In India, where 108 million people connected to the internet for the first time in 2015, and 864 million people still do not have access to it, the cost of gaining and maintaining internet access is high (the equivalent of about $13 per month in a country where the average monthly wage is $295). Oppenheimer goes on to write that, for roughly two-thirds of India's population, 17 hours of minimum wage work is necessary to pay for 500MB of data at download speeds of between 2.5 and 5 mbps. If we consider the size of an average web page, that means that an hour's worth of minimum wage work in India yields about 15 pages worth of data. [21] Many contemporary web designers have yet to cultivate the understandings necessary to design effectively for these contexts of use. Designing Brutalist

19

"StatCounter Global Stats: Comparison from Jan to Mar 2016." StatCOunter Global Stats. Available at: http://gs.statcounter.com/#all-comparison-ww-monthly-201601-201603-bar. (Accessed 26 May 2016).

20

"In Less Than Two Years, a Smartphone Could Be Your Only Computer." Wired. 10 February 2015. Online. Available at: https://www.wired.com/2015/02/smartphone-only-computer/ (Accessed 1 November 2016).

21

Oppenheimer, T. "Building for billions on the web—Google I/O 2016." Google Chrome Developers. YouTube video. 19 May 2016. 37:13. Available at: https://www.youtube.com/watch?v=E6hGubMkNfM. (Accessed 27 May 2016).

FIGURE 4: BostonGlobe.com was one of the first large-scale responsive websites, in 2011.

web sites, and writing and talking about them, diverts too much of today's web designers' time and attention away from confronting the types of design and development issues that need to be addressed to evolve usability on behalf of much larger and more diversely constituted populations of users.

As design for the web evolves, the weight—or download size—of a website will continue to be one of its defining logistical features, and one over which designers will likely continue to exercise a good deal of control. One thing that Web Brutalism does seem to get right is its defense of handmade HTML, rejecting templates and web pages generated by Content Management and User Interface Formatting Systems that often make relatively simple pages unnecessarily heavy. This is not to argue that the websites featured on *Brutalist Websites* are necessarily light. Rather, many of them feature large images, which makes their homepages heavier than the (already heavy) average webpage. Again, Web Brutalism is not actually solving a relevant problem in this area, and is (again) a distraction from more relevant issues. Pascal Deville praises handmade HTML,[22] but bandwidth doesn't seem to be a concern for him.

22

Arcement, K. "The hottest trend in Web design is making intentionally ugly, difficult sites." The Washington Post, 9 May 2016. Online. https://www.washingtonpost.com/news/the-intersect/wp/2016/05/09/the-hottest-trend-in-web-design-is-intentionally-ugly-unusable-sites/. (Accessed 25 May 2016).

23

Marcotte, E. "Responsive Web Design." A List Apart. 25 May 2010. http://alistapart.com/article/responsive-web-design. (Accessed 26 May 2016).

24

Jehl, S. Responsible responsive design. New York: A Book Apart. 2014.

25

Norman, D. "Emotion & Design: Attractive things work better." Interactions Magazine. 9.4 (2002): pgs. 36-42. Online. Availabel at: http://www.jnd.org/dn.mss/emotion_design_at.html. (Accessed 25 May 2016).

26

Lidwell, W., Kritina Holden, and Jill Butler. Universal principles of design. Rockport: Gloucester, Mass:. pgs: 20-21. 2003.

We have plenty of room to innovate

As a medium that facilitates large scale, trans-global communication, the web is still relatively young, but its rise has been rapid and its reach has become widespread, aided greatly by the now decade-long worldwide advance in smartphone, or wireless mobile device, technology. The moniker Responsive Web Design, which represents the latest major innovation in web design, was only coined in 2010 by Ethan Marcotte in an article published on the website *A List Apart.* [23] (Responsive web design, or "RWD," refers to the practice of designing user interfaces for websites that alter their appearance and proportionality based on the size of the viewscreens upon which they are rendered. RWD is what causes the same site to configure itself differently as it viewed across different types of media platforms, as depicted in Figure 4.) In 2014, Scott Jehl expanded on the idea of Responsive Web Design on his book *Responsible Responsive Design,* after spending months using the Internet in developing countries in South and Southeast Asia. [24] What both Marcotte and Jehl were proposing were new ways to approach web design to meet the needs of users who were accessing web content in new ways. In their case, innovation occurred as a result of attempting to solve real problems that users attempting to access content across different types of viewscreens routinely confront.

Responsive Web Design is just one example of recent innovations that have affected the discipline of web design. A diverse array of designers and organizations have discussed developing and implementing new practices and standards to make the web more accessible to users with disabilities, bad connections, or underpowered devices. As the web and the means to access it evolves, designers will have to innovate, and, at times, *invent,* to meet new needs and desires.

Good aesthetics serve a purpose

Another consequence of Web Brutalism is that it emphasizes the personal, aesthetic style of an individual designer who created a particular site, or at least the unique stylistic decisions that affected the design of these types of websites. The product, then, becomes an end in itself, rather than a means to achieve a broader goal of effectively visually communicating specific content to a given audience on behalf of a particular organization or client.

Aesthetics play an important role in web design, but not for purely stylistic reasons. Beautiful pages are actually perceived to work better [25] and to be easier to use. [26] Because of this, web designers must continue to strive to create aesthetically well-resolved interfaces in our designs, and avoid creating gratuitous ugliness for its own sake. As is and has been the case with effective visual communications in print for the last couple of centuries (at least...), the visual style and configuration of elements designed for use in specific websites should be largely governed by what is deemed by a designer to be appropriate for a given user or audience, and that also effectively represents the interests and mission of a given organization or client. The assertion of distinct visual languages, styles and genres create different types of expectations and guide different types of experiences on given websites, much the same as they do in printed communications. Determining what is appropriate and what is not within and around a given context of use is as crucial a design consideration as it has ever been.

The old is not new

Whether you appreciate or reject the aesthetics that guide the physical and formal structure of Web Brutalism, we should avoid equating it with innovation. Applying outdated visual genres and styles purely for the sake of moving away from an established norm is not the same as moving forward. To praise these types of distractions rather than focusing attention on more prevalent issues currently confronting web designers—and their users and audiences—seems irresponsible now. There is so much more real work to be done to positively evolve web design to make it more accessible and more useful to broader populations than it currently serves. Those of us working in and around web design need to concentrate more of our efforts toward making the web more inclusive and less exclusive, and toward solving the problems that are rooted in the need to create and facilitate effective visual communications and functionalities that users deserve and expect from us.

Moving forward

While it may be a misnomer, the Web Brutalism movement—if it can actually be called that—has ignited an engaging and increasingly broadly informed discussion. The designers who are participating in it aim to expose weaknesses they see in what they perceive to be the far too predictable and banal approaches so often operated or defaulted to by so many of their peers. Are they right to do this? Have too many of us who practice and teach web design adopted processes that yield results that are too rigid, too uniform, too automatic? Critically grappling with these questions as we consider the future of our discipline, especially as it becomes more broadly informed and less exclusive, will be essential to our continued growth and well-being, and to the growth and well-being of future web and interaction designers.

In debating the usefulness and the affects—formal and psychological—of Web Brutalism, two discursive themes have emerged. Both raise valuable questions for web designers as our discipline evolves. First, the often heavy-handed role of utilizing standardized conventions within the discipline of web design has been called into question. These conventions originated during the days of the early web, and helped guide layout, sizing, and the facilitation of navigation, and stabilized the way information was presented and used by audiences. The viewpoints articulated in this narrative suggest a clear dichotomy regarding how web design opportunities might be contextualized and addressed: by using standard formal and functional conventions, web design is mired in unoriginality but retains its usability; when these standard conventions are ignored, usability is compromised. With that stated, we believe that this apparent dichotomy is false. Innovation and usability are *not* mutually exclusive. Rather, we suggest web designers explore ways to promote usability and innovation simultaneously, and in ways that are not mutually exclusive. We believe that standardized design conventions should be approached with open eyes, and that they should continue to be evaluated in terms of their contextual appropriateness. By engaging in this dualistic process, web design can evolve positively.

The second theme articulated in this piece addressed the need for web designers to carefully consider the ramifications of their aesthetic decision-making in the context of the contemporary landscape of visual design. As the web matures and the visual patterns, genres and styles that span it continue to solidify, we need to evaluate how specific approaches to visual design affect how the content that constitutes given websites is perceived and used. Deviating from these established norms could either help or hurt our ability to communicate clearly, depending on how these deviations are formulated and operated. Decisions about aesthetics also have implications for download size, and may impact low-bandwidth users' ability to access a given site.

Brutalism's provocation is further confirmation that a great deal of research is still needed to help designers understand the consequences of visual design on the web. As promised, this paper raised more questions than it answered: how does visual design affect the perception and usability of a given website? As web designers, where should we place the lion's share of our efforts

107

moving forward? How can we innovate and, if necessary, invent in meaningful and effective ways? Ultimately, how can we design complex visual systems that communicate distinctively, effectively, and responsibly across the web? These are difficult but pressing questions for web designers and their collaborators to confront as web design moves into its third decade. Failing to do this effectively could mean that we overlook the full potential of design on the web.

References

"Accessibility is hard." *The A11Y Project* (blog). Available at: http://a11yproject. com/about.html. (Accessed 27 May 2016).

Alter, A.L, et. al. "Overcoming Intuition: Metacognitive Difficulty Activates Analytic Reasoning." *Journal of Experimental Psychology.* 136.4 (2007): pgs. 569-576. Available at: https://pdfs.semanticscholar.org/526d/fb9f8715d-48fa79d0f766caa5cd9151cf074.pdf. (Accessed 1 September 2016).

Alter A.L. "The Benefits of Cognitive Disfluency". *Current Directions in Psychological Science.* 22.6 (2013): pgs. 437-442.

Arcement, K. "The hottest trend in Web design is making intentionally ugly, difficult sites." *The Washington Post,* 9 May 2016. Online. https://www. washingtonpost.com/news/the-intersect/wp/2016/05/09/the-hottest-trend-in-web-design-is-intentionally-ugly-unusable-sites/. (Accessed 25 May 2016).

Buchanan, R. "Branzi's Dilemma: Design in Contemporary Culture." *Design Issues,* 14.1 (1998): pgs. 3-20.

Budds, D. "The Internet's 10 'Ugliest' Websites." *Fast Company,* 25 May 2016. Online. Available at: http://www.fastcodesign.com/3060196/the-internets-10-ugliest-websites. (Accessed 25 May 2016).

Deville, P. *Brutalist Websites.* Website. Available at: http://brutalistwebsites. com/. (Accessed 25 May 2016).

Diemand-Yauman, C., Daniel M. Oppenheimer, and Erikka B. Vaughan. "Fortune favors the bold (and the italicized): Effects of disfluency on educational outcomes". *Cognition.* 118.1 (2011): pgs. 111-115.

"Dieter Rams: ten principles for good design." *Vitsœ.* Website. Available at: https://www.vitsoe.com/us/about/good-design. (Accessed 15 September 2016).

Every Bootstrap Website Ever. Website. Available at: http://adventurega.me/boot-strap/. (Accessed 26 May 2016).

Hamilton, I. "A simple introduction to web accessibility." *Creative Bloq* (blog). 27 July 2011. Available at: http://www.creativebloq.com/netmag/simple-introduction-web-accessibility-7116888. (Accessed 25 May 2016).

"In Less Than Two Years, a Smartphone Could Be Your Only Computer." *Wired.* 10 February 2015. Online. Available at: https://www.wired.com/2015/02/smartphone-only-computer/ (Accessed 1 November 2016).

Jehl, S. *Responsible responsive design.* New York: A Book Apart. 2014.

Lidwell, W., Kritina Holden, and Jill Butler. *Universal principles of design.* Rockport: Gloucester, Mass:. pgs: 20-21. 2003.

Maeda, J. Twitter post. 7 January 2014, 8:04 a.m. Available at: https://twitter.com/johnmaeda/status/420541336060575744. (Accessed 25 May 2016).

Marcotte, E. "Responsive Web Design." A List Apart. 25 May 2010. http://alistapart.com/article/responsive-web-design. (Accessed 26 May 2016).

"MYTH: Accessibility is "blind people." *The A11Y Project* (blog). 11 January 2013. Available at: http://a11yproject.com/posts/myth-accessibility-is-blind-people. (Accessed 26 May 2016).

Nielsen, J. "Durability of Usability Guidelines." *Nielsen Norman Group* (blog). 17 January 2005. Online. Available at: https://www.nngroup.com/articles/durability-of-usability-guidelines/. (Accessed 25 May 2016).

Norman, D. "Emotion & Design: Attractive things work better." *Interactions Magazine.* 9.4 (2002): pgs. 36-42. Online. Availabel at: http://www.jnd.org/dn.mss/emotion_design_at.html. (Accessed 25 May 2016).

Oppenheimer, T. "Building for billions on the web–Google I/O 2016." *Google Chrome Developers.* YouTube video. 19 May 2016. 37:13. Available at: https://www.youtube.com/watch?v=E6hGubMkNfM. (Accessed 27 May 2016).

Roth, S.P, et al. "Location matters, especially for non-salient features-An eye-tracking study on the effects of web object placement on different types of websites". *International Journal of Human–Computer Studies.* 71.3 (2013): pgs. 228-235.

"StatCounter Global Stats: Comparison from Jan to Mar 2016." *StatCOunter Global Stats.* Available at: http://gs.statcounter.com/#all-comparison-ww-monthly-201601-201603-bar. (Accessed 26 May 2016).

Tuch, A, et al. "The role of visual complexity and prototypicality regarding first impression of websites: working towards understanding aesthetic

109

judgments". *International Journal of Human-Computer Studies.* 70.11 (2012): pgs. 794-811.

Whitenton, K. "Minimize Cognitive Load to Maximize Usability." *Nielsen Norman Group* (blog). 22 December 2013. Online. Available at: https://www.nngroup.com/articles/minimize-cognitive-load/. (Accessed 25 May 2016).

Biographies

Aaron Ganci is UI/UX designer and an Assistant Professor of Visual Communication Design at Indiana University's Herron School of Art and Design (IUPUI). With professional experience in graphic, interaction, and user experience design, he is an expert in both the visual design of digital interfaces and in the translation of user needs into useful, usable, and desirable experiences. He is a frequent consultant on the design of websites and software interfaces, most recently for the IU School of Medicine, the Online Computer Library Center (OCLC), and The City of Indianapolis. In addition to professional creative activity, Professor Ganci also studies contemporary industrial practice and the use of technology to personalize design artifacts. *aganci@iupui.edu*

Bruno Ribeiro is an Assistant Professor of Graphic Design at the California Polytechnic State University, in San Luis Obispo. He received a Master of Fine Arts in design with a specialization in college and university teaching from The Ohio State University in the spring of 2012. He also holds an MBA in marketing from Fundação Getúlio Vargas–FGV (Rio de Janeiro), and a Bachelor of Science in both visual communication and industrial design, from Escola Superior de Desenho Industrial–ESDI (Rio de Janeiro). *ribeiro@calpoly.edu*

Dialectic Volume I, Issue I: Visual Essay

My Life as a Fake

JENNY GRIGG[1]

1. Royal Melbourne Institute of Technology (RMIT) University, Melbourne, Australia

SUGGESTED CITATION: Grigg, J. "My Life as a Fake." *Dialectic*, 1.1 (2016): pgs. 111-134. DOI: http://dx.doi.org/10.3998/dialectic.14932326.0001.108

My Life as a Fake

JENNY GRIGG

Introduction

The array of design work presented on the following pages is comprised of a set of images I created as part of my professional practice between 2003 and 2006. They emerged as I engaged in the process of designing covers for novels written by the contemporary Australian author Peter Carey.

Often considered merely catalytic to what will emerge as the final outcome of the design process, graphic explorations such as these are often discarded. However, when they are preserved and intentionally displayed, they constitute a visual and ontological representation of the ideas that occur during the design process and inform its progression. [1] Reflection on these various test pieces guided a form of analysis, "a designerly way of knowing," [2] that allowed me to examine how materially-led explorations with paper could enable the translation of abstract design concepts into visual forms.

The first half of this visual narrative depicts the design process that guided the development of the cover designs for the first Australian edition of Peter Carey's novel *My Life as a Fake* on behalf of Random House in 2003. The second half recounts my engagement in the design process that resulted in a more recent—2006—version of the cover design for the same novel, but this latter version was designed for Random House as an integral part of a series of nine covers for books authored by Peter Carey.

This visual narrative is an example of asserting the idea of transmediation, (transfer to a different medium), within the context of a specific graphic

[1]
Goldschmidt, G. (2003). "The Back-talk of Self-Generated Sketches." Design Issues, 19(1), 72-88; and Schön, D. A. (1983). The reflective practitioner : how professionals think in action. Aldershot: Avebury. doi:10.1162/07479360376266772

[2]
Cross, N. (2007). Designerly ways of knowing. Basel: London: Birkhäuser; Springer distributor.

design project. By intentionally changing the materials with which I was designing, I employed a strategy to promote ideatic renewal (Stamm, 2013). [3] As described in a 2007 article by Aaron Seymour that was published in 'Eye Magazine' about my design work for the covers of Carey's books, this intentional paradigm shift enabled me to "Do it again (Seymour, 2007)." [4]

My Life as a Fake, 2003

The plot of the novel is centered on a series of actions set in motion in the mid 20th century by a frustrated poet named Christopher Chubb, who perpetrates a literary hoax in Australia by creating poetry authored by a fictitious, working class Australian poet named Bob McCorkle. Chubb creates McCorkle and his work to demean and disrupt modernist poetic doctrine and to humiliate an editor who has rejected his work, and who Chubb regards as pompous. The poetry Chubb writes under McCorkle's name is compiled into a manuscript that, as the plot of the book progresses, becomes symbolic of the dubiousness and false pretention that pervades many of the characters and the world they inhabit. Eventually, amidst all of the posing and fakery, a man emerges who successfully and monstrously passes himself off as Bob McCorkle, and becomes the only character in the book who emerges as genuine.

When I first received the manuscript for *My Life as a Fake*, it came to me on approximately 250 sheets of A4-sized, 80gsm (grams per square meter) Bond typing paper. This is a ubiquitous tool in publishing in Australia, New Zealand and much of western Europe. Being cheap, available and conceptually relevant—Chubb typed the fictitious McCorkle's poetry on the same type of paper—I decided to experiment with white pages of Bond during my design process, and much of it involved my investigation of its physical properties and image-making potential.

Viewed as a sequence, the images signify depictions of the choices I made that guided the direction of the design for this piece and that also offer visual evidence of Schön's theory of "refection-in-action." [5]

Displayed more or less chronologically, the narrative begins with sketches (depicted in Figures 1 through 4) that recorded my thoughts [6] during my initial study of Carey's manuscript. Recording the iterative progression from literal to abstract concepts, the sketches reflect my intention to achieve an experimental result. For example, Chubb is initially rendered as a person with arms, legs and a face (as shown in Figures 1 and 2), and later, in order to express characteristics that are temperamental rather than physical, Chubb is

3

Stamm, M. (2013). Reflecting reflection(s)-Epistemologies of Creativity in Creative Practice Research. In J.V.a.B.Pak (Ed.): LUCA, Sint-Lucas School of Architecture (Ghent, Belgium).

4

Seymour, A. (2007). "Do it Again." Eye Magazine, 17(65).

5

Schön, D. A. (1983). The reflective practitioner : how professionals think in action. Aldershot: Avebury.

6

Goldschmidt, G. (2003). "The Backtalk of Self-Generated Sketches." Design Issues, 19(1), 72-88

114

7

Goldschmidt, G. (2003). "The Back-talk of Self-Generated Sketches." Design Issues, 19(1), 72-88; and Schön, D. A. (1983). The reflective practitioner : how professionals think in action. Aldershot: Avebury. doi:10.1162/074793603762266772

8

Cross, N. (2007). Designerly ways of knowing. Basel: London: Birkhäuser; Springer distributor.

9

Viray, E. (2011). Why Material Design? (Vol. Material Design, Informing Architecture by Materiality, pp. 8-10). Switzerland: Birkhåuser GmbH.

10

Cross, N. (2007). Designerly ways of knowing. Basel: London: Birkhäuser; Springer distributor.

realized as a smudge (as shown in Figure 3), and also as two characters to portray his schizoid nature (as shown in Figure 4).

Sketching my thoughts about various means to visually communicate the book's essential themes onto paper gave them visible presence, and made them physically tangible enough for me to manipulate and hybridize more easily. This aided my conceptual development process by providing evidence that could facilitate the process of critical appraisal.[7] Inspired by Carey's reference to "sparagmos,"a concept from Greek mythology that implies dismemberment, or tearing things apart, the later sketches are attempts to encode this concept visually[8] by allowing the composition to be dominated by an apparently haphazard arrangement of pieces of Bond paper (as shown in Figures 5–7). The pages appear to be thrown up and are being dismembered in mid-air.

Additional reflection on these sketches enabled me to realize that these falling pages could be encoded on a further level and composed to simulate[9] a despairing author's face (as shown in Figure 6). Satisfied that this concept was inherent to both the fictional themes being explored in Carey's narrative as well as in the material—the Bond paper—being tested, the second half of the narrative illustrates a transmediation process, from sketching to material testing (as shown in Figures 8–16).

These images demonstrate how haptic experiments (in this case, literally involving material handling) facilitated the creation of an abstraction of a face that I created from pieces of backlit Bond paper. Figure 8 depicts one of my tests that involved overlapping pieces of Bond paper to render this illusion. This type of test is an example of materially-driven visual encoding.[10] One piece placed horizontally at the top of the composition signifies the forehead, two splayed pieces placed in the midst of the composition signify the cheeks, and one piece placed below these implies a chin or a neck. The areas of overlap contribute two eyes, a nose and a mouth. The fact that none of the pieces is arranged in "perfect" vertical or horizontal alignment helps to visually communicate that the persona being rendered is anything but a well-adjusted citizen of a modernist society.

Subsequent experiments proved the paper's ability to hold a curl and cast a shadow when lit by a single source of light (as shown in Figures 10-12). These images demonstrate how particular placements of these curls within the abstract rendition of a facial structure could be used to encode various expressions.

11

Tyler, A. C. (1992). Shaping belief: The role of audience in visual communication (Vol. Design Issues 9, pp. 21-29).

Given its recognizable structure and long history of being abstracted in a variety of materials and across a diverse array of mediums, I surmised the face in these designs would be decoded quite easily by the intended audience [11] for this piece. I also surmised that this audience would be less apt to decode the reference to a literary manuscript typed on Bond paper, although I didn't consider this necessary to the success of the design. As this design is unpublished as of this writing, these predictions remain untested.

Typographic tests (as shown in Figures 11 and 12) provided an alternate design direction to my idea of arranging pieces of Bond paper to create the perception of faces. Starting with graphic representations of a spare, empty page, (as shown in Figures 14 and 15), I trialed overlaid placements of pieces of paper containing portions of letterforms and noticed that since they were the same color as the background, this gave the effect of corroding the page edges and fracturing the surface of the design (as shown in Figure 16). Decoding these material behaviors as I designed, I made an intellectual connection between the appearance of this fragmentation, the creative challenge of writing, and "sparagmos." Considering the sophistication of Carey's prose, this less figurative, more abstract option depicted in Figure 16 was the one proposed to the publisher.

ABOVE: *My Life as a Fake* (2003) Figures 1-2.

CLOCKWISE: *My Life as a Fake* (2003) Figures 3-7.

ABOVE: *My Life as a Fake* (2003) Figure 8.

My Life as a Fake (2003) Figures 19.

CLOCKWISE: *My Life as a Fake* (2003) Figures 10-12.

TOP TO BOTTOM: *My Life as a Fake* (2003) Figures 13-15.

My Life as a Fake (2003) Figure 15.

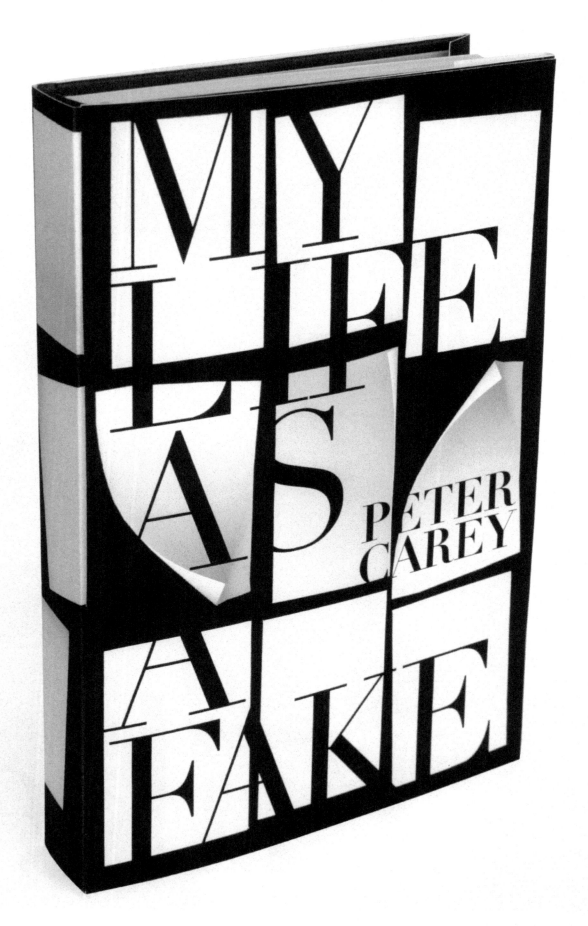

ABOVE: *My Life as a Fake* (2003) Figure 16..

My Life as a Fake, 2006

The client for this piece (Random House) required me to produce multiple, visually related design options, so I opted to construct a visual language of formally congruent shapes, textures and spaces, also known as a "relational (design) system," [12] from which nine, visually cohesive translations could be made. To do this, I revisited some unexplored results of tissue paper tests I had made in 2003 (as shown in Figure 17). The second array of design work described in this piece recounts aspects of the "operational testing" [13] that were undertaken to create this particular visual language. It includes evidence of which compositions were created and assessed, what the results of this process were, and, ultimately, how these were implemented.

The evolution of this concept was guided by my interest in constructing knowledge derived from examining the materiality of specific substances—in this case, tissue paper and other translucent materials—in this revisitation of the cover design for *My Life as a Fake*, as well as for a few other of Carey's more significant books. The results of this type of materialistic examination informing and guiding design processes are evident across the history of many design disciplines. Alvar Aalto sometimes featured burnt and mis-shapen bricks in buildings he designed, [14] fashion designers routinely craft garments based largely on their responses to the material qualities of specific types of fabric, plastics and sheeting, and graphic designers going back to Paul Rand, Saul Bass, Bradbury Thompson and several Russian Constructivists have experimented with allowing materialistic approaches like the simple overprinting of translucent areas of color inform their design processes. Printing a portion of a yellow area over a portion of a red area creates an orange area where they intersect, and can also create an opportunity to allow that area to signify a specific message.

As a sort of graphic design game, I often find myself mentally deconstructing graphic design compositions to try and decipher their technological and metaphoric make-up. A critical examination of a tissue-paper kite design by Ray and Charles Eames provided the inspiration for using overlaid areas of tissue paper to convey various effects of the interactions between some of the principal characters in *My Life as a Fake*.

To develop a set of test compositions that would allow me to experiment with different ways of doing this that effectively conveyed an essential theme from a given book, I progressively cut and arranged figurative shapes in various paper colors (as shown in Figures 18-26). As I engaged in this process,

[12]
Gursoy, B. (2015). Visualizing making: Shapes, materials, and actions. (Report). 41, 29. doi:10.1016/ j.destud.2015.08.007

[13]
Downton, P. (2003). Design research. Melbourne: RMIT Publishing.

[14]
Sennett, R. (2008). The craftsman. New Haven & London: Yale Universtiy Press.

15

Gursoy, B. (2015). Visualizing making: Shapes, materials, and actions. (Report). 41, 29. doi:10.1016/j.destud.2015.08.007; and Viray, E. (2011). Why Material Design? (Vol. Material Design, Informing Architecture by Materiality, pp. 8-10). Switzerland: Birkhäuser GmbH.

16

Walwin, J., & Krokatsis, H. (2006). You'll never know : drawing and random interference. London: Hayward Gallery.

I realized that overlaying transparent, shaped areas of color in these compositions could effectively signify particular ideas, or the personality traits of specific characters, or significant moments in a plot. For example, by placing a depiction of the outlaw character Ned Kelly's armored mask in orange over his black profile (as shown in Figure 20), we perceive both of Kelly's personas—a feared and "wanted" lawbreaker and a tragic human figure—simultaneously. This treatment of this legendary character from the fringes of Australia's rugged 19th century helps visually communicate Carey's choice to render the tale from a first-person perspective. I employed a similar tactic to signify the intimacy that slowly-but-surely evolves between the main characters of Carey's eccentrically rendered love story *Oscar and Lucinda*. In this composition, I placed a shape depicting Oscar underneath that of one depicting Lucinda, and designed his arms to be brought forward and literally fold around her waist. Manipulating their tissue paper shapes further, I learnt that if I brought his head forward of Lucinda's, their two forms became further entwined, merging their faces and increasing the perception of a disparate two becoming a cohesive one.

These experiments with over-lapping shapes of colored paper revealed ways to coax particular expressions of meaning from given images by concurrently exploiting the inherent transparency and pliancy of the material. [15] It also became apparent that it was necessary to combine colors that contrasted clearly to achieve graphic clarity. Because of its density and low value , black provided an effective background contrast when used as the base layer in a composition, and it was formally powerful enough to be perceived through two additional overlays (as shown in Figure 24). I proceeded to prioritize the use of a black component within the composition of each design.

Figure 26 depicts the version of this round of experimentation that was eventually published. It is the result of me using knowledge gleaned from engaging in a materialistic examination of overlaid tissue paper to inform my design decision-making. In this composition, Chubb is represented as a diminished figure crudely cut from blue tissue paper, at once embracing and being devoured by the towering, black menace of his creative aspiration. The "overprint effect" was achieved by manipulating the intersection of the blue and black shapes and this placement led to the chance creation of a gestalt-based form. Positioned underneath the blue layer, the black shape emerged to depict both Chubb's schizoid alter ego and a shadow cast by the Chubb *sensu*. [16]

The understandings I gained as I engaged in these materialistically informed design processes led me to the simple revelation that examining the material properties of given substances as an essential part of my working process could yield conceptually well-founded and aesthetically compelling results.

BELOW: *My Life as a Fake* (2006) Figures 17.

TOP TO BOTTOM: *My Life as a Fake* (2006) Figures 18-19.

CLOCKWISE: *My Life as a Fake* (2006) Figures 20-23.

My Life as a Fake (2006) Figure 24.

My Life as a Fake

as a

Fake

PETER CAREY

My Life as a Fake (2006) Figure 25.

References

Cross, N. (2007). *Designerly ways of knowing*. Basel : London: Birkhäuser ; Springer distributor.

Downton, P. (2003). *Design research*. Melbourne: RMIT Publishing.

Goldschmidt, G. (2003). "The Backtalk of Self-Generated Sketches." *Design Issues, 19*(1), 72-88. doi:10.1162/074793603762667728

Gursoy, B. (2015). *Visualizing making: Shapes, materials, and actions.*(Report). 41, 29. doi:10.1016/j.destud.2015.08.007

Schön, D. A. (1983). *The reflective practitioner : how professionals think in action*. Aldershot: Avebury.

Sennett, R. (2008). *The craftsman*. New Haven & London: Yale Universtiy Press.

Seymour, A. (2007). "Do it Again." *Eye Magazine, 17*(65).

Stamm, M. (2013). *Reflecting reflection(s)—Epistemologies of Creativity in Creative Practice Research*. In J. V. a. B. Pak (Ed.): LUCA, Sint-Lucas School of Architecture (Ghent, Belgium).

Tyler, A. C. (1992). "Shaping belief: The role of audience in visual communication" (Vol. *Design Issues* 9, pp. 21-29).

Viray, E. (2011). *Why Material Design?* (Vol. Material Design, Informing Architecture by Materiality, pp. 8-10). Switzerland: Birkhåuser GmbH.

Walwin, J., & Krokatsis, H. (2006). *You'll never know : drawing and random interference*. London: Hayward Gallery.

Biography

Jenny Grigg is an Australian graphic designer, a lecturer in visual communication at Monash University in Melbourne, Australia, and a Ph.D. candidate at the Royal Melbourne Institute of Technology (RMIT) University. Since graduating from the University of Technology in Sydney, Australia, Jenny has held several professional graphic design positions. These include stints as Art Director at Rolling Stone Magazine Australia, Art Director at HQ Magazine and MTV Australia. After a year in London designing for Pentagram and Faber & Faber, she became the Creative Director for Harper Collins Publishing in Sydney. Jenny continues to operate her design practice and is an Industry Fellow at RMIT University.

Designing graphic materials to support and promote the work of authors such as Peter Carey—Australia's best-known contemporary novelist—and on behalf of clients such as *Granta Portobello Books* in London, her creative inception begins with a deeply probative analysis of a given author's written words. As a Ph.D. candidate, she has begun to make use of the variety of epistemological understandings she has been able to cultivate by doing this.

She is currently conducting collective case study research about various forms of graphic design ideation (the formulation of ideas). Specifically, she is researching how professionals use materialistic approaches to guide regenerative, creative processes in graphic design practice.

"Doctoral Education in (Graphic) Design"

DOROTHY GRIFFIN[1]

1. Ohio University, Athens, Ohio, USA

SUGGESTED CITATION: Griffin, D. "Doctoral Education in (Graphic) Design." *Dialectic*, 1.1 (2016): pgs. 135–154. DOI: http://dx.doi.org/10.3998/dialectic.14932326.0001.109

Abstract

University-level graphic design education in the United States continues to struggle with the question of what academic designation should constitute the terminal degree: the MFA, or a doctoral degree such as a Ph.D., or a professional doctorate. In light of this question, the study described in this article has two primary goals: first, to gauge the contributions of graphic design educators to the scholarly literature that contextualizes the relationship between the design disciplines and doctoral education, and second, to critically review a broad cross section of the indexed scholarly literature on this subject. The results of this study reveal that the number of academics and professionals working in graphic design who have made significant contributions to this literature is negligible. This stands in sharp contrast to the comparatively higher number of academics and professionals working in architectural, industrial, product, and interior design, as well as the fine visual arts. This study argues that university-level graphic design educators—who are by definition members of the academy—should be familiar with the existing literature on this subject since it affects the academic standards that frame and guide their career achievement metrics and accreditation. In conclusion, this study calls for university-level graphic design educators to engage more fully in the continuing, inter- and trans-disciplinary conversations about doctoral education in design so that they might improve their abilities to contribute to the domains of knowledge that inform university communities, and, in so doing, advance their careers as they improve their students' learning.

"Doctoral Education in (Graphic) Design"

DORI GRIFFIN

Introduction

As it has in the U.S. since the 1960s, university-level graphic design education—sometimes referred to as communication design or visual communication design, and sometimes associated closely with interaction design
education—continues to struggle with the question of what academic designation should constitute the terminal degree. Should the MFA remain the
terminal degree of the discipline (as accepted by the National Association of
Schools of Art and Design, or NASAD, and by the regional accrediting author-
ities for postsecondary education that are recognized by the U.S. Department
of Education), or should it be supplanted by the Doctor of Philosophy, or Ph.D.,
or a professional doctorate, such as an Ed.D.? Should the American design
education community somehow make it possible to earn either a Ph.D. or an
Ed.D.? This study has two goals in response to these questions. First, it investigates the contributions that graphic design educators, researchers and scholars
have made to the indexed, scholarly literature that examines and interrogates
doctoral education in design, and argues that this group has failed to contribute to this literature in a sustained and meaningful way. Second, it reviews a
broad cross section of the indexed scholarly literature concerned with doctoral
education in design. Although the results of this study reveals that the number of academics and professionals working in graphic design who have made
significant contributions to this literature is negligible, this is *not* the case for

137

1

Davis, M. "Why Do We Need Doctoral Study in Design?" International
Journal of Design, 2.3 (2008), n.p.,
available online at http://www.ijde-
sign.org/ojs/index.php/IJDesign/ar-
ticle/view/481/223 (accessed 7 April
2014); M. Davis, M. et, al., "Making
Sense of Design Research: The Search
for a Database," Artifact: Journal
of Visual Design, 1.3 (2007),
pgs. 142-148.

academics and professionals working in architectural, industrial, product, and interior design, as well as the fine visual arts. This study will argue that university-level graphic design educators—who are by definition members of the academy—should be as familiar with the existing literature on this subject as their colleagues from disciplines outside design are about the respective educational standards of their academic disciplines. Further, in much the same way that university-level educators from disciplines outside design are expected to maintain understandings of the academic standards that frame and guide their career achievement metrics and accreditation, this study will argue that those who teach university-level graphic design should also maintain understandings of the academic standards that affect them their programs. This study will conclude with a call for university-level graphic design educators to engage more fully in the continuing, inter- and trans-disciplinary conversations about doctoral education in design.

The Loud Silence

To inform this study, the indexed literature pertinent to doctoral education in design was collected in the following manner. The abstracts of peer-reviewed, English-language scholarly literature in three major research databases were searched for the keywords "design" and "doctor/doctoral/doctorate" or "PhD." [a] An analysis of the search results across these databases—*Art and Architecture Complete, Art Full Text,* and the *Design and Applied Arts Index*—demonstrated a significant overlap in yields, although operating the search parameters using these keywords within each database broadened the spectrum of yields due to the ways that specific journals were covered within each one. This search returned a combined results list of sixty-five peer-reviewed, English-language articles written between January 1990 and December 2015 that pertained to the structural, philosophical, and/or pedagogical issues contextualizing and affecting doctoral education in design. Of these, only two were written by an author whose primary disciplinary affiliation was graphic design: Meredith Davis's 2008 article "Why Do We Need Doctoral Study in Design?" and her 2007 article "Making Sense of Design Research." [1] The remaining sixty-three articles in the sample emerge from other disciplines, ranging from architecture to education. Significantly, one additional article that directly addressed the need for doctoral education in graphic design was not returned as a result of searching the abstracts or keywords of peer-reviewed literature. Full-text searching for the terms "graphic design" or "visual communication design" in combination

[a] The search was conducted using the Boolean search term design*—thus including all possible variants of the word.

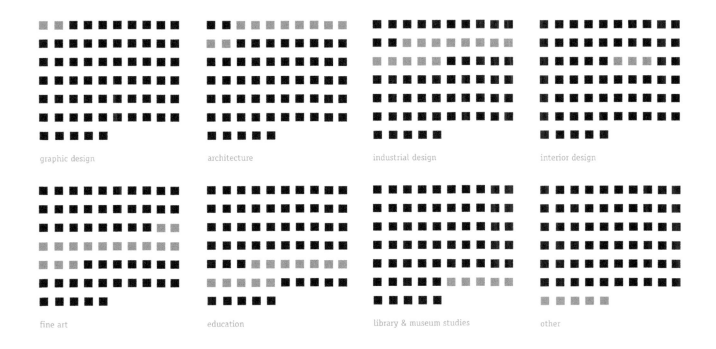

graphic design

architecture

industrial design

interior design

fine art

education

library & museum studies

other

FIGURE 1: Peer-reviewed literature contributions by discipline. Graphic design contributes 3% of the total.

with either "doctoral education" or "doctoral degree" in the three databases yielded over 5,000 combined results, but fewer than ten of these were written by authors with experience in graphic or visual communication design. Kate LaMere's excellent 2012 article "Reframing the Conversation about Doctoral Education in Design" is among them, although its affect is not as significant as it might be due to the effort and/or foreknowledge required to locate it. [2] This extensive literature search reveals that educators, scholars and researchers working in and around graphic or visual communication design have not made significant contributions to the indexed, searchable, scholarly literature on the subject of doctoral education in design.

Notably, much of the published, peer-reviewed, indexed literature emerges from scholarship that was originally made public during one of the international Doctoral Education in Design conferences, which have been held intermittently since 1998. Graphic design educators' relatively low participation rates in these well-respected, scholarly conference venues are indicative of a general lack of awareness of the level of scholarship and research that occurs at the doctoral level in academia generally and in and around design. At the

2

LaMere, K. "Reframing the Conversation about Doctoral Education: Professionalization and the Critical Role of Abstract Knowledge," Iridescent: Icograda Journal of Design Research, 2.1 (2012): n.p., available online at http://iridescent. icograda.org/2012/12/09/reframing_ the_conversation_about_doctoral_ education_professionalization_and_ the_critical_role_of_abstract_ knowledge/category16.php (accessed 1 March, 2014).

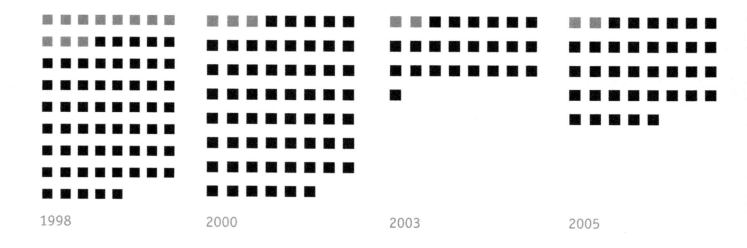

1998   2000   2003   2005

FIGURE 2: Graphic design contributions to Doctoral Education in Design conferences by year. The average participation rate of graphic designers across all four conferences with published proceedings is approximately 8.5%.

3

Buchanan, R., ed., Doctoral Education in Design: Proceedings of the Ohio Conference, October 8-11, 1998 (Pittsburgh USA: The School of Design at Carnegie Mellon University, 1999); Friedman, K. and Durling, D. eds., Doctoral Education in Design: Foundations for the Future, proceedings of the conference held 8-12 July 2000, La Clusaz, France (Stoke-on-Trent UK: Staffordshire University, 2000), 495-513; Durling, D. and Sugiyama, K. eds., Doctoral Education in Design: Proceedings of the Third Conference, Held 14-17 October 2003, in Tsukuba, Japan (Japan: Institute of Art and Design at University of Tsukuba, 2003); Giard, J. et al., Proceedings of the fourth conference Doctoral Education in Design: held 25-27 June 2005 in Tempe, Arizona, USA (Tempe USA: College of Design at Arizona State University, 2005).

inaugural 1998 Doctoral Education in Design Conference in Ohio, a record high 15.9% of the contributors were graphic designers. In 2000, in France, 4.8% were from graphic design. In 2003, in Japan, 8% were graphic designers. In 2005, in Arizona, 5.4% were from graphic design. [3] (The proceedings of the 2011 conference in Hong Kong are unpublished and therefore not relevant to this data set.) Although more graphic designers made scholarly contributions at the Doctoral Education in Design conferences since their inception in 1998 than in peer-reviewed publications, this is still not indicative of a significant rate of participation in the upper levels of scholarship, research and criticism of the discipline. The data also suggests that participating graphic design educators have not been engaged in the processes necessary to develop their contributions to academic conferences to meet the standards of rigor required for scholarly publication in the proceedings of these and other academic conferences, or in peer-reviewed journals. While dialogues at conferences are of course valuable, without publication in peer-reviewed journals, those dialogues often remain ephemeral and go unacknowledged by a broader academic audience.

The Existing Literature

Unlike graphic design, other disciplines have not remained silent regarding how and why doctoral-level education affects the construction and critical examination of the domains of knowledge that contextualize and inform their research, scholarship and professional practices. The extant literature on doctoral education in design may be modest in scope when compared to disciplines such as computer and political science, economics, and both the so-called "hard" and "soft" sciences, but its quality is becoming more robust, and its quantity is growing. A review of the extant scholarly literature reveals several themes that are applicable to expanding the bases of theoretical and practical knowledge that guide graphic design education, and these should not be overlooked as graphic designers begin to participate in broader, more inter- and trans-disciplinary discussions. This review organizes this literature around three central themes: 1) understanding and differentiating among degree structures backgrounded by some thoughts on negative academic perceptions about MFAs—as terminal degrees and in general; 2) examining obstacles to doctoral education in design; and 3) exploring distinct areas of concern for graphic design as it addresses essential questions regarding how doctoral-level education might or should affect its future development as a discipline.

Understanding and differentiating among degree structures

The MFA or MDES is not equivalent to a doctoral degree in any of the design disciplines. Generally, although there are some notable exceptions to this in more research-oriented design education programs, earning an MFA or an MDES does not require that those who earn them complete the rigorous scholarship or research necessary to construct the level or breadth of knowledge required to effectively complete a doctoral dissertation. An MFA or MDES is supposed to demand a higher level of critical rigor than earning an MA, and some MFA and MDES programs require that their students complete scholarly demanding thesis projects that entail both addressing a comprehensive, usually systemic design challenge *and* completing a written analysis of the theoretical frameworks and research methods that informed their design processes. As a terminal, professional master's degree, an MFA or an MDES was considered sufficient to prepare someone to embark on a career in university-level design education or their respective profession for the latter half of the 20th Century in the U.S. However, over the course of the last 15 years or so, degrees such as the Master of Architecture, Master of Industrial Design, and Master of Landscape Architecture no longer function as such for those who hold them. "Professional degrees [at the master's level] simply are [very different from doctoral degrees], and are intended to prepare students for very different roles upon graduation."[4] University-level graphic design education, particularly in the U.S.,

4
Kroelinger, M. "Defining Graduate Education in Interior Design," Journal of Interior Design, 33.2 (2007), pgs. 15-17.

5

Elkins, J. Artists with PhDs: On the New Doctoral Degree in Studio Art (Washington USA: New Academia, 2014); Newbury, D. "Foundations for the Future: Doctoral Education in Design," The Design Journal, 3.3 (2000), pgs. 57-61.

6

Richards, M. "Architecture Degree Structure in the 21st Century," Multi: The RIT Journal of Plurality & Diversity in Design, 2.2 (2009), pg. 46.

7

Kroelinger, M. 2007, p. 17.

8

Kroelinger, M. 2007, p. 17.

9

Jones, P. M. "The Doctor of Musical Arts in Music Education: A Distinctive Credential Needed at This Time," Arts Education Policy Review, 110:3 (2009), pgs. 3-8.

10

Macleod, K. and Holdridge, L. "The Enactment of Thinking: The Creative Practice PhD," Journal of Visual Art Practice, 4.2/3 (2005): pgs. 197-207; Millward, F. "The Practice-led Fine Art PhD: At the Frontier of What There Is—An Outlook on What Might Be," Journal of Visual Arts Practice, 12.2 (2013): pgs. 121-133; Melles, G. "Visually Mediating Knowledge Construction in Project-based Doctoral Design Research," Art, Design & Communication in Higher Education, 6.2 (2007): pgs. 99-111.

continues to widely acknowledge the MFA as a terminal degree, despite the fact that the disciplinary dialogue that has evolved in and around design since the early 2000s has long since moved beyond attempts to justify the master's degree as being the terminal degree of the discipline. Conversations around the idea of instantiating the PhD as the terminal degree in fine arts education, has been a persistent subject of inquiry during this span of time as well. [5]

Ignoring this state of affairs will not benefit university-level graphic design faculty or their students; at the very least, more of us must engage with the scholarly literature of our discipline, and offer well-reasoned, well-researched responses to the epistemological and ontological questions it raises. One of the foremost of these is how the perception of the MFA and MDES compare with the perception of the PhD within our broadly populated university, college and academy communities. Within the university system, a terminal master's degree often places faculty at a disadvantage among their peers from other disciplines, as many authors have observed. "The 'terminal master's' denotation is problematic when graduates [who hold this degree] attempt to teach courses or conduct research in a cross-disciplinary manner," and possessing an MFA or an MDES rather than a PhD can pose significant problems to grant writers who are attempting to secure funding for their research or scholarship from American federal or state-funding agencies. [6] Instead of perpetuating our structural disadvantage by clinging to a degree that no longer serves us well in the academy, the literature suggests that graphic design educators must come to grips with the need for the infusion of more doctoral education in our discipline.

Acknowledging the need for doctoral education in design is a first step toward ensuring that our discipline earns fuller participation across the span of disciplines that constitute the modern academy. To achieve this goal, proponents of doctoral education in design in general and in graphic design in particular must find ways to effectively confront questions about how this degree should be structured, and what domains of study it should encompass. Many design educators have raised "concerns about [having] one degree model supporting a professional practice (studio-based) path, [while another supports] a scholarship/research path, and [still another supports] a teaching path." [7] To address these concerns, many leading contributors to the literature have advocated for the broader adoption of the professional or practice-based doctorate. "The professional doctorate is worthy of exploration as a complement to the Ph.D.—the former with a professional practice basis and the latter with a research basis." [8] Proponents of the professional doctorate support both a research-based model (the PhD) and a practice-based model of doctoral education, perhaps akin to the EdD in Education. Generally speaking, they propose the PhD for historical studies, critical analysis, theory building, research, and methods development. Meanwhile, the practice-based doctoral degree prioritizes the production of design solutions. Both degree models include significant training in research methods and the theoretical frameworks that contextualize them, but the outcomes—roughly and sometimes falsely divided into "written dissertations" and "design solutions"—differ in both form and function.

As of this writing, how these complementary, practice-based doctoral degrees might eventually be designated remains subject to debate. For those practicing design within the fine arts tradition, "a studio doctorate of fine art (DFA) that operates within and as an extension to the conventions of the taught MFA might be more appropriate and valuable than the PhD." [9] Other doctoral programs in fine arts designate the degree as a practice-based PhD. [10] In architecture, the designation Doctor of Architecture (D.Arch.) is gaining traction. [11] Finally, the designation Doctor of Design (D.Des.) has been proposed for terminal degree candidates "motivated chiefly by the prospect of becoming a better designer." [12] In the United Kingdom, practice-based doctorates are increasingly being awarded in both the fine arts and design and, historically, they have been awarded as PhD degrees. [13] In Germany, doctoral degrees in design have been more recently introduced, but have gained traction rapidly. [14]

In the United Kingdom, some educators argue that differentiating between the traditional and practice-based PhD will "institutionalize existing [undesirable] divisions between theorizing and practicing, writing and making, intellectual activity and studio activity." [15] Meanwhile, in the United States, other educators argue that "the expectation for someone with a PhD in design should be that he or she is capable of designing something." [16] Both of these arguments propose that there should be multiple routes to the same terminal degree, rather than multiple research trajectories that conclude when distinct yet equally valued degrees are awarded. More commonly, however, the literature suggests that differing needs require differing degree structures. American graphic design educator Kate LaMere concludes that "the coexistence—and growth of—professional and philosophical doctorates for visual communication design" will "contribute meaningfully to the profession." She argues that "it is essential that both pathways for doctoral education in visual communication design be advanced," [17] so that knowledge can be constructed and shared in

11
Richards 2009, pgs. 56-7.

12
Pedgley, O. and Wormald, P. "Integration of Design Projects within a Ph.D." Design Issues, 23.3 (2007), p. 73.

13
Candlin, F. "Practice-based Doctorates and Questions of Academic Legitimacy," International Journal of Art & Design Education, 19.1 (2000), pgs. 96-101; Candlin, F. "A Dual Inheritance: The Politics of Educational Reform and PhDs in Art and Design," International Journal of Art & Design Education, 20.3 (2001), pgs. 302-311.

14
Melles, G. and Wolfel, C. "Postgraduate Design Education in Germany: Motivations, Understandings and Experiences of Graduates and Enrolled Students in Master's and Doctoral Programmes," Design Journal, 17.1 (2014): pgs. 115-135; Bredies, K. and Wolfel, C. "Long Live the Late Bloomers: Current State of the Design PhD in Germany," Design Issues, 31.1 (2015): pgs. 37-41.

15
Bell, D. "Is There a Doctor in the House? A Riposte to Victor Burgin on Practice-based Arts and Audiovisual Research," Journal of Media Practice, 9.2 (2008), p. 176.

16
Margolin, V. "Doctoral Education in Design: Problems and Prospects," Design Issues, 26.3 (2010), p. 76.

17
LaMere, n.p.

18
Candlin 2000, pgs. 97-8.

19
LaMere, n.p.

20
Pedgley and Wormald, p. 73.

21
Mottram, J. & Rust, C. "The Pedestal and the Pendulum: Fine Art Practice, Research and Doctorates," Journal of Visual Art Practice, 7.2 (2008), p. 149.

ways that benefit designers and their increasingly diverse array of collaborators from other disciplines in both the academy and in the private sector.

Even when the practice-based doctorate is offered as what some in and around the graphic design education community feel is an advantageous solution to the problem of how to evolve the terminal degree in design education, this type of degree raises problems its own unique set of problems. Among these, one of the most pressing is the issue of *equivalence*. Some proponents of the practice-based doctorate report, "an anxiety that if practice-based doctorates were acknowledged as such, they would undermine and devalue conventional doctorates." Therefore, it has been "important to ensure that art [and design] practice was not considered an easy route to doctoral status." [18] In arguing that graphic design practice can be a viable research trajectory for doctoral candidates, graphic designers and graphic design educators must articulate how and why an individual instance or set or system of instances of practice contributes to the broader development of knowledge that informs the further development of the graphic design discipline. "The primary goal [of doctoral research] is the improvement and gains to be had by the communities targeted by the research." [19] Thus, to support this conceptualization of the purpose of research, "the integration of design activity within a PhD must be as a means to an end, and not an end in itself." [20] As a relatively young academic discipline, graphic design cannot afford to regard practice as the easy route to a terminal degree. "A worrying tendency emerging in the field is the propensity of a claim for an activity [known as] 'practice-led' research to assume that this is all that needs to be said on the matter. That is not an acceptable model for use within an academic community that has only a short history of engagement with the responsibilities of the academic environment." [21] If graphic design as a discipline wishes to advance the practice-based doctorate as an alternative terminal degree to the PhD, it would be wise to heed the advice of those who—rightly concerned with false equivalency and/or equivocations—urge a higher level of rigor: methodological, pedagogical, theoretical and philosophical.

Obstacles to doctoral education in graphic design

As observations about the widespread lack of rigor in practice-based research models have warned, the design disciplines lag behind other professional fields in terms of considering and articulating the issues surrounding doctoral education: "our field has yet to undertake the deep consideration of form and structure [in doctoral education programs] that other fields have undertaken."[22] Design lags behind professional fields such as law, medicine, and even musical performance when it comes to the question of structuring the terminal degree.[23] Graphic design in particular is even less participatory than design writ large: "the communities of product and communication designers have not [by and large] been engaged in discussions about doctoral education in design."[24] Graphic design practitioners' and educators' lack of engagement with the broader disciplinary dialogue transpiring in and across other design disciplines is disturbing. To those in these other design disciplines, our lack of participation implies that graphic design is not concerned with building a body of significant disciplinary research and knowledge, or advancing the discipline as an academic activity. If graphic design practitioners and educators wish to claim that we are interested in design research, we must overcome the obstacle of non-participation in the research-based dialogues of the other design disciplines.

In order to participate in design as a research practice, "designers need explicit, quality education and experience in research methods."[25] Yet many contributors to the literature suggest that teaching research methods is highly problematic within many of the design disciplines because, "few design instructors that have the experience or educational qualifications to teach research methodology."[26] In design, there is a broadly noted "lack of an academic research tradition at [the doctoral] level."[27] Many observers of British practice-based doctorate programs are concerned by "the increasing number of studio-centered PhD graduates at UK universities who lack a proper foundation in research methods."[28] They express concerns that such graduates "are supposed to be qualified as tutors for the next generation of PhD students."[29] Graduates must, in other words, be "trained researchers."[30] These concerns underscore the fact that our field lacks a, "significant pool of experienced art and design supervisors available to pass on expertise to research students, [and also lacks] a readily available spectrum of exemplars of art and design practice-based PhD research from which faculty and students can learn."[31] Again, although there are exceptions, graphic design stands out among the design disciplines in its half-hearted approach to teaching research methods. "Graphic design has an even shorter history of experience with human-centered research [than other design disciplines]; courses in human factors are significantly absent from most graphic and communication design curriculums."[32] Formal training in research methods is absolutely critical to successful education at the doctoral level, and graphic design education cannot continue to

22
Durling, D. & Friedman, K. "Best Practices in Ph.D. Education in Design," Art, Design & Communication in Higher Education 1.3 (2002), p. 134.

23
Jones 2009.

24
Margolin 2010, p. 74.

25
Hanington, B.M. "Relevant and Rigorous: Human-Centered Research and Design Education," Design Issues, 26.3 (2010), p. 25.

26
Hanington, p. 21.

27
Hockey, J. "United Kingdom Art and Design Practice-Based PhDs: Evidence from Students and Their Supervisors," Studies in Art Education, 48.2 (2007), p. 157.

28
Hockey, J., p. 157.

29
Durling and Friedman, p. 135.

30
Newbury.

31
Hockey 2007, p. 157.

32
Hanington, p. 21.

33

Hockey 2007, p. 165.

34

Sato, K. "Perspectives of Design Research: Collective Views for Forming the Foundation of Design Research," Visible Language, 38.2 (2004), p. 235.

35

Macleod, K. and Holdridge, L. "The Doctorate in Fine Art: The Importance of Exemplars to the Research Culture," International Journal of Art & Design Education, 23:2 (2004), pgs. 155-168.

36

Hockey 2007, p. 169.

37

Hockey, J. "The Supervision of Practice-based Research Degrees in Art and Design," International Journal of Art & Design Education, 19.3 (2000), pgs. 345-355; Hockey, J. "Practice-Based Research Degree Students in Art and Design: Identity and Adaptation," International Journal of Art & Design Education, 22.1 (2003), pgs. 82-92.

38

Mottram and Rust, p. 144.

39

Mottram and Rust, p. 144.

40

Heynen, H. "Unthinkable Doctorates?" Journal of Architecture, 11:3 (2006): pgs. 277-282; Richards, M., 2009; Radu, F. "Inside Looking Out: A Framework for Discussing the Question of Architectural Design Doctorates," Journal of Architecture, 11.3 (2006), pgs. 345-351; Tai, L. & Myers, M. "Doctors: Here or There?" Landscape Review, 9.1 (2004): pgs. 215-221; Younes, C. "Doctorates Caught Between Disciplines and Projects," Journal of Architecture, 11.3 (2006), pgs. 315-321.

ignore questions involving theory, methodology and methods and scholarly knowledge creation if we wish to participate in and contribute to design (writ large) or graphic design as disciplines of study that can lay claim to being research-oriented or to having research-based foundations.

Research-based academic writing is also problematic for the design disciplines. A study of practice-based PhD students in the United Kingdom suggests that attaining proficiency in academic writing is a significant educational hurdle for doctoral students whose previous educational experiences have been more oriented toward the production of design solutions and/or art objects. In addition to a general lack of experience with academic writing, "the particular codified language form required for a doctoral thesis or dissertations appeared to [students] to be obscure, difficult to master, and rigid in terms of its form." [33] Art and design students, unlike students in the humanities or social and physical sciences, often fail to encounter academic writing as part of their discipline-specific program of study, because artifacts almost always trump texts as research outcomes. Furthermore, "research output remains inaccessible and underutilized because of the lack of a commonly understood categorization scheme, established dissemination media, and archival compilation." As an academic culture, design "puts little value on referencing other work or information sources, unlike other disciplines built upon an accumulated body of knowledge." [34] This evidence supports the rationale that the discipline of graphic design is in need of more rigorously structured and vetted scholarly exemplars such as peer-reviewed, indexed models of academic writing that address practice-based issues and incorporate making into the research paradigm. [35] A useful design research infrastructure must include ways to "expose students to [academic research] during their educational experiences prior to doctoral study." [36] Additionally, design students need professors and advisors who are familiar with the conventions of research-based writing. [37] Graphic design education, particularly in the U.S., needs to address the lack of coursework at the undergraduate and master's levels among so many of its university-level programs that effectively prepare students to pursue a terminal research degree. Those of us who constitute the graphic design education community also need to work more thoughtfully and diligently to develop in ourselves the research and writing skills that doctoral students will eventually need to learn from us.

146

41

Er, A.H., and Bayazit, N. "Rede-
fining the 'Ph.D in Design' in the
Periphery: Doctoral Education in
Industrial Design in Turkey," Design
Issues, 15.3 (1999), pgs. 34-45;
Jones J. C. & Jacobs, D. "PhD Re-
search in Design," Design Studies,
19.1 (1998), pgs. 5-7; Melles, G.
"Global Perspectives on Structured
Research Training in Doctorates of
Design—What Do We Value?" Design
Studies, 30.3 (2009), pgs. 255-
271; Pedgley & Wormald; Pizzocaro,
S. "Re-orienting Ph.D. Education in
Industrial Design: Some Issues Aris-
ing from the Experience of a Ph.D.
Programme Revision," Art, Design &
Communication in Higher Education,
1.3 (2002), pgs. 173-183.

42

Kroelinger 2007; Rabun, J. H. "Defining Graduate Education in Interior Design," Journal of Interior
Design, 33.2 (2007), pgs. 19-21.

43

Baxter, K., et. al., "The Necessity
of Studio Art as a Site and Source
for Dissertation Research," International Journal of Art & Design
Education, 27.1 (2008), pgs. 4-18;
Baxter et. al. 2008; Bell 2008;
Cabeleira, H. "The Politics and the
Poetics of Knowledge in Higher Arts
Education," International Journal of Education through Art, 11.3
(2015), pgs. 375-389; J. "Theoretical Remarks on Combined Creative and
Scholarly PhD Degrees in the Visual
Arts," Journal of Aesthetic Education 38.4 (2004): pgs. 22-31; Francis, M.A. "'Widening Participation'
in the Fine Art Ph.D.: Expanding
Research and Practice," Art, Design
& Communication in Higher Education,
9.2 (2010), pgs. 167-181; Hockey
2007; Jones, P.M. 2009; Knudsen, E.
"Doctorate by Media Practice," Journal of Media Practice, 3.3 (2002),
pgs. 179-185; Macleod, K. and
Chapman, N. "The Absenting Subject:
Research Notes on PhDs in Fine Art,"
Journal of Visual Art Practice, 13.2

Distinct areas of concern for graphic design education
as it addresses key issues at the doctoral level

In terms of how it will address the key issues that must affect the facilitation of education at its doctoral level, perhaps the most pressing question for graphic design education is not "How is our discipline special?," but rather "How is our discipline typical?" Mottrom and Rust observe that art and design faculties "are working across two realms, that of the professional context of creative practice and that of the academic context, and have the capacity to contribute significant value to both." [38] However, they caution that "this does not mean they should be treated differently [than those studying within] other disciplines, many of which also operate in such a manner." [39] By treating the need to effectively facilitate more research-based educational paradigms and practices in university-level graphic design programs as a special case, we run the risk of overlooking the ways in which our discipline is in fact quite typical. Within the design disciplines, architectural education [40] and industrial design education [41] are both well ahead of graphic design education in terms of how they have proactively addressed the development of workable structures to facilitate the delivery of content related to practice-based doctoral education. Educators facilitating graduate study in Interior design have made significant contributions in this area. [42] Additionally, the visual arts have established a robust discussion of the issues related to practice-based doctoral education. [43] To argue that graphic design education presents a special case to the extent that our discipline cannot model its approach on practice-based doctoral education based on any of these existing foundations is, at best, ill-advised and parochial.

In considering how doctoral education in design might best be conceptualized and structured, some contributors to the literature do warn that although Doctor of Fine Arts (DFA) programs offer some excellent structural models for incorporating making into the research process, it should be noted that pursuing graduate level education in design and the fine arts are vastly different undertakings. "It is important in any discussion of design to avoid becoming mired in debate about fine art, which may share some practical concerns with design but has some very different concepts of enquiry." [44] At its core, this observation points back toward the concern raised earlier in this discourse about the need to immerse graduate students in design in research methods training, and in the theoretical approaches and domains of knowledge that design used to uniquely frame and inform these. [45] Because all of the design disciplines must be concerned with the needs and aspirations of audiences,

147

(2014): pgs. 138-149; Malins, J. and Gray, C. "The Digital Thesis: Recent Developments in Practice Based PhD Research in Art and Design," Digital Creativity, 10.1 (1999): pgs. 18-29; Morgan, S. J. "A Terminal Degree: Fine Art and the PhD," Journal of Visual Art Practice, 1.1 (2001): pgs. 6-16; Mottram and Rust 2008; Paltridge, B. et. al., "Doctoral Writing in the Visual and Performing Arts: Issues and Debates," International Journal of Art & Design Education, 30.2 (2011), pgs. 242-255.

44
Rust, C. "Many Flowers, Small Leaps Forward: Debating Doctoral Education in Design," Art, Design & Communication in Higher Education, 1.3 (2002), p. 144.

45
Friedman, K. "Theory construction in design research: criteria: approaches, and methods." Design Studies, 24.6 (2003), pgs. 506-509.

46
Durling and Friedman 2002, p. 135.

47
Kroelinger 2002, p. 193.

48
Davis 2008, n.p.

49
Davis 2008, n.p.

users, and how and why the functionalities of components, products, and systems affect and are affected by these individuals and groups in ways that the fine arts most often do not, theories and methods that inform research in the fine arts may be inappropriate to inform research in design. While DFA programs can offer insights to inform some aspects of practice-based doctoral programs in design, it is wise to be aware of "the consequences of awarding a research degree to graduates who may be eminently competent artists or designers while being incompetent in research."[46] There is clear agreement across much of the literature that, regardless of whether or not it is practice-based, doctoral study in design must engage the questions that interrogate research theory, methodology and methods according to more traditionally accepted academic means. This will further the necessary work of promoting the intellectual development of the design disciplines.[47]

The conceptualization of graphic design education and practice as special case scenarios is problematic precisely because it prevents our discipline from engaging fully with well-established, critically rigorous academic and private sector research culture. In her discussion of why design needs doctoral study, Meredith Davis points out that designers on university faculties "spend much of their time making the case that they are special rather than integral to the overall research mission of the university."[48] Davis suggests that special treatment for faculty with MFA degrees, who make objects rather than conducting research, might make sense in the context of an art school but certainly does not in a research university. She concludes that the "dilution [by design faculty] of the traditional concept of university research stunts American efforts to launch a research culture in design and distracts faculty from the hard work necessary to move a discipline forward."[49] Instead of asking how our discipline is special, it seems much more useful to ask how we could fully participate in inter- and trans-disciplinary academic research culture, and to model our responses to this question on successful efforts undertaken by conceptually or structurally similar disciplines.

Moving Forward
University-level graphic design educators and practitioners have largely failed to participate in contributing to the peer-reviewed, scholarly literature that contextualizes, analyzes and interrogates doctoral education in and around design. This has resulted in discussions about doctoral education in graphic design being framed and developed largely by designers and/or fine artists with

other disciplinary affiliations. Failure to include the voices of university-level graphic design educators in dialogues emerging around this topic sends a distinct message to those outside our discipline that we are not key stakeholders in this discussion. It also implies that we are largely uninterested in positioning the scholarly work of our discipline as being worthy of making a viable contribution to either the present or the future of design research. While this is a conclusion with which I feel most American graphic design educators would probably disagree, many who teach in our discipline have fueled this perception by their inactions, and their lack of contributions or even participation in dialogue around this issue in respected academic forums such as peer-reviewed journals and books. Indeed, while many of us maintain a lively dialogue among ourselves about diverse aspects of postsecondary design education, including what constitutes its professional criteria and standards, this tends to occur outside the context of our scholarly literature. Because of this, these discussions are instead most often relegated to the usually-ephemeral context of conference presentations and panel exchanges. However, if graphic design wishes to continue to claim its place as a fully recognized design, and, beyond that, academic discipline, then we must join into the broader inter- and trans-disciplinary discussion regarding doctoral education in design. This is accomplished by participating in the recognized academic dialogue of studying and learning from indexed scholarly literature—an action most of us have not yet taken.

References

Baxter, K. et al. "The Necessity of Studio Art as a Site and Source for Dissertation Research." *International Journal of Art & Design Education,* 27.1 (2008): pgs. 4-18.

Bell, D. "Is There a Doctor in the House? A Riposte to Victor Burgin on Practice-based Arts and Audiovisual Research." *Journal of Media Practice,* 9.2 (2008): pgs. 171-177.

Bredies, K., & Wolfel, C. "Long Live the Late Bloomers: Current State of the Design PhD in Germany," *Design Issues* 31.1 (2015): pgs. 37-41.

Buchanan, R., ed. *Doctoral Education in Design: Proceedings of the Ohio Conference, October 8-11, 1998.* Pittsburgh, USA: The School of Design at Carnegie Mellon University, 1999.

Cabeleira, H. "The Politics and the Poetics of Knowledge in Higher Arts
    Education." *International Journal of Education through Art,* 11.3 (2015):
    pgs. 375-389.

Candlin, F. "Practice-based Doctorates and Questions of Academic Legitimacy."
    International Journal of Art & Design Education, 19.1 (2000): pgs. 96-101.

Candlin, F. "A Dual Inheritance: The Politics of Educational Reform and PhDs
    in Art and Design." *International Journal of Art & Design Education,*
    20.3 (2001): pgs. 302-311.

Davis, M. "Why Do We Need Doctoral Study in Design?" *International Journal
    of Design,* 2.3 (2008), n.p. Online. Available at http://www.ijdesign.org/
    ojs/index.php/IJDesign/article/view/481/223 (accessed 7 April 2014).

Davis, M., et. al. "Making Sense of Design Research: The Search for a Database."
    Artifact: Journal of Visual Design 1.3 (2007): pgs. 142-148.

Durling, D., & Friedman, K. "Best Practices in Ph.D. Education in Design." *Art,
    Design & Communication in Higher Education,* 1.3 (2002): pgs. 133-144.

Durling, D., & Sugiyama, K., eds. *Doctoral Education in Design: Proceedings of the
    Third Conference, Held 14-17 October 2003, in Tsukuba, Japan.* Japan: In-
    stitute of Art and Design at University of Tsukuba, 2003.

Elkins, J. *Artists with PhDs: On the New Doctoral Degree in Studio Art.* Washing-
    ton: New Academia, 2014.

Elkins, J. "Theoretical Remarks on Combined Creative and Scholarly PhD De-
    grees in the Visual Arts," *Journal of Aesthetic Education,* 38.4 (2004):
    pgs. 22-31.

Er, H.A., & Bayazit, N." Redefining the 'Ph.D in Design' in the Periphery: Doc-
    toral Education in Industrial Design in Turkey." *Design Issues,* 15.3
    (1999): pgs. 34-45.

Francis, M.A. "'Widening Participation' in the Fine Art Ph.D.: Expanding Re-
    search and Practice." Art, Design & Communication in Higher Educa-
    tion, 9.2 (2010): pgs. 167-181.

Friedman, K., & Durling, D. eds. *Doctoral Education in Design: Foundations for
    the Future, proceedings of the conference held 8-12 July 2000, La Clusaz,
    France.* Stoke-on-Trent, UK: Staffordshire University, 2000.

Friedman, K. "Theory construction in design research: criteria: approaches, and
    methods." *Design Studies,* 24.6 (2003), pgs. 506-509

Giard, J., et al. *Proceedings of the fourth conference Doctoral Education in Design:
    25-27 June 2005 in Tempe, Arizona, USA.* Tempe, AZ, USA: College of
    Design at Arizona State University, 2005.

Hanington, B.M. "Relevant and Rigorous: Human-Centered Research and Design Education." *Design Issues,* 26.3 (2010): pgs. 18-26.

Heynen, H. "Unthinkable Doctorates?" *Journal of Architecture,* 11.3 (2006): pgs. 277-282.

Hockey, J. "The Supervision of Practice-based Research Degrees in Art and Design." *International Journal of Art & Design Education,* 19.3 (2000): pgs. 345-355.

Hockey, J. "Practice-Based Research Degree Students in Art and Design: Identity and Adaptation." *International Journal of Art & Design Education,* 22.1 (2003): pgs. 82-92.

Hockey, J. "United Kingdom Art and Design Practice-Based PhDs: Evidence from Students and Their Supervisors." *Studies in Art Education,* 48.2 (2007): pgs. 155-171.

Jones, J.C., & Jacobs, D. "PhD Research in Design." *Design Studies,* 19.1 (1998): pgs. 5-7.

Jones, P. M. "The Doctor of Musical Arts in Music Education: A Distinctive Credential Needed at This Time." *Arts Education Policy Review,* 110.3 (2009): pgs. 3-8.

Jones, T.E. "The Studio Art Doctorate In America." *Art Journal,* 65.2 (2006): pgs. 124-127.

Knudsen, E. "Doctorate by Media Practice." *Journal of Media Practice,* 3.3 (2002): pgs. 179-185.

Kroelinger, M. "Issues of Initiating Interdisciplinary Doctoral Programmes." *Art, Design & Communication in Higher Education,* 1.3 (2002): pgs. 183-95.

Kroelinger, M. "Defining Graduate Education in Interior Design." *Journal of Interior Design,* 33.2 (2007): pgs. 15-17.

LaMere, K. "Reframing the Conversation about Doctoral Education: Professionalization and the Critical Role of Abstract Knowledge." *Iridescent: Icograda Journal of Design Research* 2.1 (2012): n.p. Online. Available at: http://iridescent.icograda.org/2012/12/09/reframing_the_conversation_about_doctoral_education_professionalization_and_the_critical_role_of_abstract_knowledge/category16.php (accessed 1 March 1 2014).

Macleod, K., & Chapman, N. "The Absenting Subject: Research Notes on PhDs in Fine Art," *Journal of Visual Art Practice,* 13.2 (2014): pgs. 138-149.

Macleod, K. & Holdridge, L. "The Enactment of Thinking: The Creative Practice PhD." *Journal of Visual Art Practice,* 4.2/3 (2005): pgs 197-207.

151

Malins, J., & Gray, C. "The Digital Thesis: Recent Developments in Practice Based PhD Research in Art and Design," *Digital Creativity,* 10.1 (1999) pgs. 18-29.

Margolin, V. "Doctoral Education in Design: Problems and Prospects." *Design Issues,* 26.3 (2010): pgs. 70-78.

Macleod, K., & Holdridge, L. "The Doctorate in Fine Art: The Importance of Exemplars to the Research Culture." *International Journal of Art & Design Education* 23.2 (2004): pgs. 155-168.

Margolin, V. "Doctoral Education in Design: Problems and Prospects." *Design Issues,* 26.3 (2010): pgs. 70-78.

Melles, G. "Global Perspectives on Structured Research Training in Doctorates of Design — What Do We Value?" *Design Studies,* 30.3 (2009): pgs. 255-271.

Melles, G. "Visually Mediating Knowledge Construction in Project-based Doctoral Design Research," *Art, Design & Communication in Higher Education,* 6.2 (2007): pgs. 99-111.

Melles, G., & Wolfel, C. "Postgraduate Design Education in Germany: Motivations, Understandings and Experiences of Graduates and Enrolled Students in Master's and Doctoral Programmes," *Design Journal,* 17.1 (2014): pgs. 115-135.

Millward, F. "The Practice-led Fine Art PhD: At the Frontier of What There Is— An Outlook on What Might Be." *Journal of Visual Arts Practice,* 12.2 (2013): pgs. 121-133.

Morgan, S. J., "A Terminal Degree: Fine Art and the PhD," *Journal of Visual Art Practice,* 1.1 (2001): pgs. 6-16.

Mottram, J., & Rust, C. "The Pedestal and the Pendulum: Fine Art Practice, Research and Doctorates." *Journal of Visual Art Practice,* 7.2 (2008): pgs. 133-151.

Newbury, D. "Foundations for the Future: Doctoral Education in Design." *The Design Journal,* 3.3 (2000): pgs. 57-61.

Newbury, D. "Doctoral Education in Design, the Process of Research Degree Study, and the 'Trained Researcher.'" *Art, Design & Communication in Higher Education,* 1.3 (2002): pgs. 149-160.

Paltridge, B., et. al. "Doctoral Writing in the Visual and Performing Arts: Issues and Debates." *International Journal of Art & Design Education,* 30.2 (2011): pgs. 242-255.

Pedgley, O., & Wormald, P. "Integration of Design Projects within a Ph.D." *Design Issues,* 23.3 (2007): pgs. 70-85.

Pizzocaro, S. "Re-orienting Ph.D. Education in Industrial Design: Some Issues Arising from the Experience of a Ph.D. Programme Revision." *Art, Design & Communication in Higher Education,* 1.3 (2002): pgs. 173-183.

Rabun, J.H. "Defining Graduate Education in Interior Design." *Journal of Interior Design,* 33.2 (2007): pgs. 19-21.

Radu, F. "Inside Looking Out: A Framework for Discussing the Question of Architectural Design Doctorates." *Journal of Architecture,* 11.3 (2006): pgs. 345-351.

Richards, M. "Architecture Degree Structure in the 21st Century." *Multi: The* RIT *Journal of Plurality & Diversity in Design,* 2.2 (2009): pgs. 44-59.

Rust, C. "Many Flowers, Small Leaps Forward: Debating Doctoral Education in Design." *Art, Design & Communication in Higher Education,* 1.3 (2002): pgs. 141-149.

Sato, K. "Perspectives of Design Research: Collective Views for Forming the Foundation of Design Research." *Visible Language,* 38.2 (2004): pgs. 218-237.

Tai, L., & Myers, M. "Doctors: Here or There?" *Landscape Review,* 9.1 (2004): pgs. 215-221.

Younes, C. "Doctorates Caught Between Disciplines and Projects." *Journal of Architecture,* 11.3 (2006): pgs. 315-321.

Biography

Dori Griffin is an Assistant Professor at Ohio University, where she teaches graphic design and design history. Currently, she is working on a book that contextualizes and illustrates the history of the type specimen for graphic design educators and students. The initial research for this project was funded by the Cary Fellowship at the Rochester Institute of Technology's Cary Graphic Arts Collection. In addition to writing about graphic design pedagogy, she researches and writes about popular images in relationship to the visual culture of twentieth century tourism. Her first book, *Mapping Wonderlands: Illustrated Cartography of Arizona, 1912-1962,* was published by the Univesity of Arizona Press in 2013. *griffid1@ohio.edu*

Defining Design Facilitation: Exploring and Advocating for New, Strategic Leadership Roles for Designers and What These Mean for the Future of Design Education

PAMELA NAPIER[1] AND TERRI WADA[2] (EDITED BY MICHAEL R. GIBSON)[3]

1. Indiana University Herron School of Art and Design (IUPUI), Indianapolis, Indiana, USA; Principal in Collabo Creative, Indianapolis, IN, USA

2. Indiana University Herron School of Art and Design (IUPUI), Indianapolis, Indiana, USA; Principal in Collabo Creative, Indianapolis, IN, USA.

3 The University of North Texas, Denton, Texas, USA; Producer and Co-Editor, Dialectic, a scholarly journal of thought leadership, education and practice in the discipline of visual communication design published by the AIGA Design Educators Community (DEC) and Michigan Publishing.

SUGGESTED CITATION: Napier, P. & Wada, T. "Defining Design Facilitation: Exploring New, Strategy Leadership Roles for Designers and What These Mean for the Future of Design Education." Edited by Gibson, M.R. *Dialectic* 1.1 (2016): 154-178. DOI: http://dx.doi.org/10.3998/dialectic.14932326.0001.110

Defining Design Facilitation:

Exploring and Advocating for New, Strategic Leadership Roles for Designers and What These Mean for the Future of Design Education

PAMELA NAPIER & TERRI WADA

(EDITED BY MICHAEL R. GIBSON)

Examining current prevalent trends in design practice and education
Over the past decade or so, design as a professional and academic discipline has seen much momentum and growth in interest from areas of both study and practice outside design. Over the course of the last decade, the buzz around design thinking as a transferable "method of creative action"[1] for developing and implementing innovative ideas has grown into broad assortment of executive education offerings and workshops. Professionals in arenas such as healthcare, business management and education have made concerted efforts to adopt designerly approaches[2] to identifying, framing, operationalizing, and, eventually, assessing the efficacy of new initiatives. Design processes and so-called 'design thinking' have been recognized widely as viable means to fuel innovative practices, and, in some cases, the invention of new ways of doing, making, distributing and communicating.

Additionally, there has been both an emergence and surge in university-level design education programs in many parts of the world offering degrees in design management, design strategy and design leadership. Much of this growth can be attributed to the recognition design has gained for being a "game changer" in the industrial, economic and social realms. As a result of this growth, contemporary designers are now being sought after as project partners and researchers by academics and professionals working in and

[1] Faste, R., Roth, B. & Wilde, D.J. "Integrating Creativity into the Mechanical Engineering Curriculum." In ASME Resource Guide to Innovation in Engineering Design, edited by C. A. Fisher. New York, New York, USA: American Society of Mechanical Engineers, 1993.

[2] Cross, N. "Designerly Ways of Knowing." Design Studies, 3.4 (1982): pgs. 221-227.

155

3

Cary, J. "What Is Design If Not Human-Centered?" Stanford SOCIAL INNOVATION Review, 25 June 2013. Online. Available at: https://ssir. org/articles/entry/what_is_design_ if_not_human_centered (Accessed 4 December, 2016).

4

Buchanan, R. "Human dignity and human rights: Thoughts on the principles of human-centered design." Design Issues, 17.3 (2001): pgs. 35-39; Norman, D. "Human-centered design considered harmful." Interactions, 12.4 (2005): pgs. 14-19.

5

Sanders, E. & Stappers, P. "Co-creation and the new landscapes of design." CoDesign, 4.1 (2008): pgs. 5-18.

6

Martin, R. The Design of Business: Why Design Thinking is the Next Competitive Advantage. Cambridge, MA, USA: Harvard Business Press, 2009: pgs. 57-78.

7

Fraser, H. M. A. "Designing Business: New Models for Success." In Design Thinking: Integrating Innovation, Customer Experience, and Brand Value, edited by T. Lockwood, pgs. 35-46. New York, NY, USA: Allworth Press, 2009.

across areas as diverse as healthcare, education, crime prevention, business instantiation and development, and urban and rural planning and revitalization. Designers are sought after because of their abilities to bring unique knowledge rooted in their understandings of creative processes to complex problems that require socio-cultural reframing, the empathetic inclusion of users in decision-making processes, and the invention of new processes and procedures for making and doing.

People-centered design has recently become synonymous with human-centered design, and has been promoted by the likes of IDEO and the d.school at Stanford University. [3] This advocacy builds upon earlier scholarship undertaken by Richard Buchanan and Donald Norman, [4] and continues to be examined and expanded in both design practice and design education. Despite its similarities with other, more established, design approaches—for example, "user-centered design"—people-centered design, as described in this paper, not only places potential users and stakeholders at the center of the design process, but additionally calls for and places value upon their active inclusion or participation in the identification and framing of problems, or problematic situations, within the particular communities that they live and work within, or that they routinely traverse. These communities can be actual, physical places, such as schools, healthcare facilities and neighborhoods, or virtual environments, such as online retail and news outlets, social media networks and data-delivery websites that provide information about the weather, sports and the financial markets. This approach also calls for users and stakeholders to be involved in the development and implementation of positive, efficacious changes that will or could affect their lives and livelihoods. This shift in approach to formulating and operating design processes that call for user or stakeholder participation during their so-called "front ends" changes the more established notion of "designers designing *for* users to designers designing *with* users." [5]

Involving people who possess different areas of expertise in thinking and decision-making that yield outcomes to design processes that are demonstrably more effective, or more desirable, or more efficient (or some combination of these) requires what has come to be known in some professional and educational design arenas as "design facilitation." This term describes a process that has been shown to aid and abet innovative practices within and between organizations and organizational cultures, and, in some cases, to help them gain competitive advantage in particular markets. [6][7] Design facilitation shifts the primary *intent* of the design process from yielding an artifact or set of artifacts—a branding system, a graphical user interface, a piece of furniture, a retail space—to yielding outcomes that identify needs, clarify goals or that help diversely populated groups decide where a given initiative should be started, what parameters should guide its evolution, and what should constitute "next steps." Effective design facilitators, especially those involved in design education, know that teaching and gaining understanding of these processes is often as crucial to what can be defined as "a successful outcome" as is achieving a hard, artifact-based deliverable like a logo, or a piece of furniture, or a user interface.

The trend toward design facilitation, and the need for broadly inclusive user participation in people-centered design projects has initiated many new and unique challenges for emerging designers. Today, designers who wish to sustain careers in many professional design arenas are being asked to construct and cultivate knowledge and experience with participatory design research approaches and methods to engage users *empathetically*, which involves attempting to deeply and broadly understand their experiences and socially, economically and politically contextualized viewpoints. This type of designing allows designers and their collaborators to create more desirable and useful means for people to effectively confront the challenges inherent in their everyday lives. These challenges can involve activities as diverse as shopping for groceries for people with dietary restrictions, engaging in family financial planning and the need to effectively juggle the demands of work, family and personal health for people who live from paycheck-to-paycheck. The complexity of the daily challenges individuals in contemporary societies must meet to live productive and—hopefully—meaningful lives is driving a need for emerging designers to learn to serve as *facilitators* of people-centered, participatory design research that effectively guides design decision-making processes.

A justification for and relevance of design facilitation

A description of the current landscape in design education and practice
The effective facilitation of human activity and aspiration is not a new concept or practice in design: its roots can be traced back to the *Wiener Werkstätte, The Bauhaus, The Ulm School of Design,* and the work of the so-called "design methodologists" of the 1960s. [8] Within the last 20 years, numerous books and white papers have been published around the topic of facilitation, or enabling significant positive change, and international associations and institutions have been created to critically examine and support scholarship to inform it. *The*

8

Bayazit, N. "Investigating Design: A Review of Forty Years of Design Research." Design Issues, 20.1 (2004): pgs 16–29.

157

9

Brewster, B., Dowse, E., Hogan, D., Wilkinson, M. & Woosley, B. "History [of INIFAC]," INIFAC, The International Institute for Facilitation, 28 September, 2006. Online. Available at: http://inifac.org/about-inifac.htm (Accessed 29 November 2016).

10

+Acumen. "Design kit: Facilitator's guide to introducing human-centered design." +Acumen. Online. Available at: http://plusacumen.org/courses/design-kit-facilitators-guide-to-introducing-human-centered-design/ (Accessed 12 October, 2016).

11

ibid.

International Association of Facilitators (IAF), was formed in 1994, has members in over 65 countries, and provides accreditation, certification and conferences worldwide. *The International Institute for Facilitation* (INIFAC) was created in 2003 "...when five facilitators came together to develop a certification program at the masters' level [and] developed a draft of competencies and sub-competencies specifically designed to define the knowledge and skills needed to achieve outstanding facilitated sessions." [9] Much of what the IAF and INIFAC exist and have existed to accomplish and promote parallels the need in contemporary design education to teach emerging designers to plan and operate at least portions of their careers as critical agents for positive social, technological, economic and political change.

Over the course of the last decade, the concept of *design facilitation* has been gaining traction. While the term itself is relatively new, hundreds of companies and organizations across the (mostly) developed world have begun offering workshops and training programs specifically designed to help people cultivate the ability to utilize design thinking as a means to engage in problem identification, framing and solving processes. In this context, design thinking refers to the process of developing, constructing, testing and assessing prototypical ways of doing, making or creating that yield innovative outcomes and, sometimes, inventive solutions to problems. One example of this is *The Design Thinkers Academy* (http://www.designthinkersacademy.com), which operates a series of service design thinking facilitation workshops in several countries in Europe. In the U.S., organizations like the *Next Design (NextD) Leadership Institute*—created and operated in New York City by *Humantific* co-founders Elizabeth Pastor and Garry K. Vanpatter—have offered innovation skill-building programs that teach skills specifically around facilitation. The recently founded "learn-by-doing community" known as The Design Gym in New York City offers classes and workshops with titles like *"Improv for Design Thinking," "Facilitation Bootcamps,"* and *"Facilitation Practice Labs."* And, more recently, IDEO.org and +*Acumen* teamed up to offer *"The Facilitator's Guide to Introducing Human-Centered Design,"* [10] a step-by-step guide to help "introduce new learners to this creative approach to problem solving." [11] AIGA (*the American Institute for Graphic Arts*, and the sponsor of the journal within which this article has been published) also began offering a series of *Facilitation: by Design* workshops at select locations across the U.S. in 2012, and which have since proven to sell out rapidly. These seminars provide training that "successfully leads diverse groups of stakeholders through design-thinking exercises and [helps them to] develop solutions to complex problems." [12] The popularity of these types of workshops in the U.S., western Europe and Australasia has seen a steady increase since the early 2000s. So has the variety of open-source tools designed to facilitate design thinking, design-led planning and management strategies, and design-led innovation. Viewed broadly, these are indicative of the recognition of the expanding roles designers now play as thought leaders, innovators and change managers across an increasing array of disciplinary boundaries, and the need (and desire) to have emerging designers develop new sets of skills that will allow them to successfully operate within these growing areas of design.

Examining the expansion of roles and the emergence of new skill sets for future designers

The logistical and intellectual complexities inherent in practicing people-centered design require the active, broadly inclusive participation and, at times, collaboration between designers, users and stakeholders throughout the design process. The processes (note the plurality of this term) are cyclic, and endeavor to overcome a wide variety of biases and assumptions that designers or design teams and their project partners may have about how given factors, conditions and the people involved in a given situation might affect each other. In order to practice people-centered design and participatory design research, designers must be able to effectively facilitate the perceptions and pursuant actions of others through a design process that is geared to yield new ways of thinking and doing, rather than being limited to yielding only artifacts or systems of artifacts. They must be able to develop, plan and *facilitate* activities that enable and empower people to collaboratively express, make, assess and reflect upon their progress in ways that allow them to collectively identify, frame and at least suggest improvements to problematic situations (or "solve the problems" inherent within these situations outright).

Designers who aspire to serve as facilitators of research, or the ability to engage in the kinds of systemic investigations that yield knowledge (that then guide design actions), need to actually be taught how to do this appropriately and effectively *by people who know how to do this themselves*. Facilitating learning experiences that can help emerging designers cultivate the understandings necessary to frame appropriate theoretical frameworks and effective data gathering and processing methods is not an easy one, especially in the U.S., given that so many design educators have *not* been effectively educated to do this. [13]

[12]
AIGA. "Register for Facilitation: by Design workshops." AIGA. Online. Available at: http://www.aiga.org/facilitation-by-design/ (Accessed 9 July, 2015).

[13]
Norman, D. "Why design education must change." Core 77, 10 November 2010. Online. Available at: http://www.core77.com/posts/17993/why-design-education-must-change-17993 (Accessed November 4, 2016).

14

Frascara, J. & Winkler, D. "Jorge Frascara and Dietmar Winkler on Design Research." Design Research Quarterly, 3.3 (2008): pgs. 5–6.

15

Ibid.

16

The authors have published another piece that describes these types of approaches to facilitating design and co-designing: Napier, P. & Wada, T. "Co-designing for Healthcare: visual designers as researchers and facilitators." Visible Language, 49.1–2 (2015). Online. Available at: http://visiblelanguagejournal.com/issue/161/article/961 (Accessed 2 December 2016).

16a

Dorst, K. & Lawson, B. Design Expertise. New York, NY, USA: Architectural Press, (an imprint of Routledge, an imprint of Taylor & Francis), 2009, pgs. 159-166.

Longtime North American design educator Jorge Frascara supports the need for design educators—particularly those working in graphic design—to endeavor to re-frame what they do and what they teach in ways that catalyze positive social, economic and public policy change: "There is a distinct difference between graphic design as useless styling and communication design as a way of supporting a social discourse between diverse segments of society." [14] He further advocates for contemporary design programs to:

- "develop efficient and supporting communication tools to promote solutions for problems;"
- "offer federal, state, and local governments their services to facilitate local, regional, national, and international efforts for developing and disseminating innovative plans for achieving...goals within reasonable timeframes;
- facilitate the adoption of their plans." [15]

Much of what of what Frascara is advocating for here has been advanced by those relatively few educators teaching and practicing design facilitation in the U.S., Canada and abroad over the course of the past decade.

Placing contemporary graphic (or visual communication or interaction) design students in learning situations that locates some portions of their learning experiences within these arenas can help ensure that they develop the ideological and practical tools necessary to facilitate design as a broadly transformative activity as their careers evolve. Too many students learn how to make, but not *why*, or *why not*, (to make), or how their making processes might help diverse communities address and resolve difficult social, economic, technological or public policy issues.

Contextual Approaches and Methodology

A set of broadly informed questions to guide possible approaches
In our research over the past few years—both as design educators and practitioners—we (the authors) have explored and tested several new approaches, tools and frameworks for teaching visual communication design students at both the graduate and undergraduate levels how to become effective *design facilitators.*

Our epistemological approach has been contextualized by the following research questions:

How does the changing role of visual communication designers (from more traditional "making" roles to "design facilitators" working to effectively implement people-centered design processes [a]) impact the curricular goals and experiences of visual communication design students, at both graduate and undergraduate levels?

How might understanding shifts/advancements in our discipline and the current practice of design facilitation positively inform/impact curriculum? How might new frameworks and tools positively affect students' abilities to plan and execute facilitated participatory design sessions?

[a] *Our definition of "people-centered design processes" is adapted from Jorge Frascara's chapter on the subject that appeared in a book he edited titled Design and the Social Sciences: Making Connections (Taylor & Francis, 2002, p. 33). In order for designers to effectively engage in people-centered design, he contends that, "We have to stop thinking of design as the construction of graphics, products, services, systems and environments, and think about those as means for people to act, to realize their wishes and satisfy their needs. It is the needs and the wishes we have to serve; the objects of design must be seen only as means. This requires a better understanding of people, of society, and of the ecosystem, and calls for an interdisciplinary practice."*

[b] *Participatory design, or co-design, emerged from ideas that originated in Scandanavia in the 1970s in and around the realms of software systems development. The idea that participants could cooperate with designers, researchers and developers during the evolution of inventive and innovative processes was eventually adapted into healthcare, information technology, human + computer interaction design, architecture and urban design as the 1970s gave way to the 1980s and 1990s. For more information about the origins of participatory design and co-design, the editors of Dialectic advise readers to reference the following scholarship:*
"Co-designing for Society" by Deborah Szebeko and Lauren Tan (Szebeko, D. & Tan, L. "Co-designing for society." Australasian Medical Journal, 3.9 [2010]: pgs. 580–590); and "Co-creation and the new landscapes of design" by Elizabeth Sanders and Pieter Stappers (Sanders, E. & Stappers, P. "Co-creation and the new landscapes of design." CoDesign 4.1 [2008]: pgs. 5–18.)

We have embarked on an ongoing process of research and practice in our quest to address these questions surrounding design facilitation. This has involved our attendance at design facilitation workshops, our working with various clients and partners as we engage in design facilitation, our testing and implementing new frameworks and approaches involving design facilitation in our design studio (as well as sharing those with educators in other institutions), and, ultimately, our public presentations on this topic, and our writing about these efforts in articles like this one. [16]

Establishing a methodological foundation

The work described in this piece is largely influenced by *participatory action research*, which is grounded in accounting for the experiences, reflections, and inclusive collaborations with others throughout the research and design process. This article is informed by both primary and secondary sources, and the author's own facilitations of participatory processes in classroom, workshop, and practice-based settings.

In our design practice, we have developed a process and methodology that focuses on the seminal axiom of participatory action research, or "co-design," which is to strive to design *with* people, rather than *for* them. [b] Initially, our process is comprised of three main phases: *Analysis, Synthesis and Evaluation.* These have been recognized as being necessary to engage in "the highest-level design processes"—meaning that considerable experience accrued through extensive practice is necessary to make effective use of these types of processes—by Bryan Lawson and Kees Dorst in their book *Design Expertise.* [16a] Each of these iterative phases is further broken down as follows: *Sensing* current conditions, *Understanding* behaviors and experiences, *Framing* insights & challenges, *Ideating* possible solutions, *Iterating* to test and refine,

161

17
Unger, R. Willis, D. & Nunally, B. Designing the Conversation: Techniques for Successful Facilitation. San Francisco, CA, USA: New Riders/ Peachpit, a division of Pearson Education, 2013, p. 6.

18
Thinkplace specializes in applying what they refer to as design thinking to a diverse array of complex, public sector challenges. More information about Thinkplace can be accessed online at http://www. thinkplaceglobal.com/#page (Accessed November 25, 2016).

19
Sanders, L. & Stappers, P. Convivial Toolbox: Generative Research for the Front End of Design. Amsterdam, The Netherlands: BIS Publishers, 2008.

and *Implementing* for final production. Each of these phases are affected by the critical input of those who will be affected by our design decision-making, so that a diverse array of audience members and potential users are allowed to have some affect across the entire design process. The ultimate goal of utilizing these methods is to empower those who use them to effectively communicate their experiences (of use, and that involve cognition and behavior/action). These communications can then be used to help identify and frame core problems in and around specific situations, and, in so doing, help contribute to the creation of meaningful impact, positive change, and innovation within the scope of a given project.

Examining means to effectively formulate and operate design facilitation

There are numerous scholarly and more publicly accessible resources (literally dozens are available through the *Design and Applied Arts Index* alone) that exist generally around the topic of facilitation as it has affected or can affect design processes, but far fewer that examine *why* the particular skills and traits necessary to effectively engage in or support facilitation are necessary—and uniquely suited—to designers. There is also only a paucity of resources that, given specific sets of circumstances, identify what types of facilitation practices are most appropriate and when, and what specific skill sets, professional traits and domains of knowledge are of paramount importance to bring to bear within a given social, economic or public policy context.

Design facilitation is an emerging type of design process that is fast becoming a core competency of designers who find themselves needing to engage in people-centered, participatory approaches to meet the intertwined demands of clients and the needs of particular groups of users and audiences. In their writings on design facilitation, Unger, Nunnally and Willis offer, "It takes skill and practice to be able to facilitate [on behalf of] people, and facilitation is truly the foundation of an effective design practice."[17] Education and training that might help emerging designers build this core competency has been largely unavailable in university-level design curricula in the U.S. until fairly recently (again, there simply aren't enough American design educators who have acquired the expertise in this area to teach it well). John Body, Nina Terrey and Leslie Tergas of the Australia-(and New Zealand-, Kenya-, and Singapore) based strategic design consultancy *ThinkPlace*[18] describe the increasing complexity of formulating and operating design applications within the context of

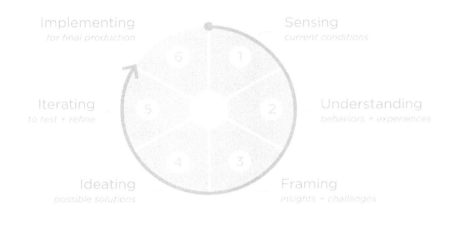

FIGURE 1: This diagram depicts Collabo Creative's People-Centered Design Process. (Collabo Creative is a strategy and service design consultancy based in Indianapolis, Indiana, USA founded and operated by the authors that also fosters workshops that immerse participants from a variety of disciplines in innovative activities.)

[c] *According to their website, "MakeTools offers consulting services and education to people and organizations that see the value in using collective forms of creativity to address the environmental, social and cultural challenges we face today."* More information about Maketools can be accessed online at: http://www.maketools.com/about.html (Accessed November 22, 2016).

20
Body, J., Terrey, N. & Tergas, L. "Design Facilitation as an Emerging Design Skill: A Practical Approach," in Proceedings of the 8th Design Thinking Research Symposium, 19–20 September 2010, University of Technology, Sydney, Australia, edited by Dorst, K., Stewart, S., Staudinger, I., Paton, B., & Dong, A. Sydney, Australia: DAB Documents, 2010: pgs. 64–65.

public sector organizations, and the increasingly complex requirements that must be met to effectively engage people within them over time. They state that design facilitation is "...a distinct and emerging role for designers," and they cite Liz Sanders, co-author of the book *Convivial Toolbox* [19] and founder of *MakeTools,* [c] to further explain that the role of the designer is now being extended from what was an exclusive, "sole expert" to what is now more of a participatory, inclusive facilitator. [20]

Due to this shift from a "designer-as-expert" mentality to that of "designer-as-facilitator," there is a need to also determine what types of facilitated engagements are most appropriate in particular learning situations. Unger, Nunnally and Willis differentiate between *group facilitation, one-on-one facilitation, and one-on-many facilitation*, describing different types of interactions and activities for facilitating conversations that can help guide positive transformations. [21] In the *Facilitation: by Design* (FxD) workshop series operated by Maggie Breslin and Martin Ratinam on behalf of the AIGA (American Institute of Graphic Arts) at the School of Visual Arts in New York in July of

21

Unger, R. Willis, D. and Nunally, B. Designing the Conversation: Techniques for Successful Facilitation. San Francisco, CA, USA: New Riders/ Peachpit, a division of Pearson Education, 2013, pgs. 19–31.

22

AIGA. "Facilitation: by Design workshops." AIGA, 16–17 July, 2017. Online. Available at: http://www. aiga.org/facilitation-by-design/ (Accessed 9–14 November, 2016). Material used in this piece was gleaned from dialogue that transpired during the AIGA Facilitation by Design Workshop, led by Breslin, M. and Ratinam, M., hosted by The SVA (School of Visual Arts) Branding Studio, NY, NY, USA, July 16–17, 2015. For further information, contact Mathan Ratinam at Parsons The New School for Design (mathan. ratinam@gmail.com) or Maggie Breslin at SVA (maggie.breslin@gmail.com).

23

Body, J., Terrey, N. & Tergas, L. "Design Facilitation as an Emerging Design Skill: A Practical Approach," in Proceedings of the 8th Design Thinking Research Symposium, 19–20 September 2010, University of Technology, Sydney, Australia, edited by Dorst, K., Stewart, S., Staudinger, I., Paton, B., & Dong, A. Sydney, Australia: DAB Documents, 2010: pgs. 66–68.

2015, a distinction was made between what they referred to as *Workshop Heavy* (a workshop as the project in-and-of-itself), and *Workshop Light* (a workshop that has no particular link to a larger project or to a specific point in the design process). [22] Breslin and Ratinam further articulated different types of "general workshop categories" that can be linked to different phases of the design process. These included workshops that were titled as follows: *"Definition," "Discovery & Synthesis," "Ideation," "Idea Refinement and Design Execution,"* and *"Deliverable."* Breslin and Ratinam further stressed the point that a designer-as-facilitator must possess, exhibit and master distinct skills and traits in order to successfully facilitate participatory design activities on behalf of diverse groups of people. These include the ability to engage in proactive listening, the ability to moderate and build consensus between competing individuals and groups, and the ability to account for and fairly balance disparate social, cultural, political and economic biases.

The practitioners at *ThinkPlace* (Body, Terrey and Tergas) and the facilitators of the AIGA *FxD* workshops (Breslin and Ratinam) also provide rationales for why designers are well-suited for and valued to fulfill roles as facilitators. Body, Terrey and Tergas [23] contrast *design facilitation* and *generalist facilitation*. They describe *generalist facilitators* as being focused on engaging in a highly structured series of predefined steps with the objective of arriving at a result that is "created, understood and accepted by all participants," and *design facilitators* as possessing the driving force necessary to iteratively develop and produce a designed outcome, with a heavy emphasis on making, and using a design thinking approach that is heavily influenced by observing specific groups of potential users or audience members as they interact with what has been made. They further articulate the personal qualities and key considerations that designers who fulfill the role of "design facilitator" must exemplify, such as maintaining a strategic, temporally located perspective, a human-centered, empathetic perspective and a perspective informed by the designer's need to make effectively. They then go on to describe techniques for planning and operating different stages of the design process in order to explore, innovate and evaluate. Similarly, embedded within the content delivered by Ratinam and Breslin during the AIGA FxD workshop are four key reasons designers are highly valued as facilitators: 1. designers are comfortable with ambiguity; 2. designers play an increasingly key role in planning and orchestrating activities within organizations; 3. the design profession is necessarily highly collaborative in nature; 4. designers increasingly infuse the work they do with a human-centered approach. [24] During the course of the AIGA *FxD* workshop, Ratinam and Breslin also stated that effective design facilitators are responsive, attentive, and reflective. [25] Within the context of people-centered design projects, they must be able to determine what type of planning, preparation, and execution of participatory engagements are most appropriate and when they should occur during whatever iterative steps constitute a given design process.

This discourse helps contextualize and inform a pressing question for visual communication design education: how should the changing role of visual communication designers (from roles that involve more traditional "making" processes those that involve comporting themselves as "design facilitators" of a people-centered design process) affect the curricular goals and learning experiences of visual design education programs geared toward meeting the needs of graduate and undergraduate students? These questions will be addressed throughout the remainder of this piece.

Introducing research facilitation and design facilitation into design education and practice

Preparing designers to assume roles as facilitators

The authors are proposing a new framework for distinguishing two emerging roles for those who teach and practice design. This framework is based on knowledge we have constructed and cultivated as we have taught, researched, and practiced people-centered design since 2009. Both require some level of expertise in and around facilitation. We refer to these two roles as *Research Facilitation and Design Facilitation*.

Research Facilitation is conceptually similar to Breslin and Ratinam's descriptions of *"Workshop Light"* during their presentation at the AIGA *FxD* workshop in New York, New York in July of 2015: "a workshop that has no particular tie to a larger project or point in the design process." [26] However, we distinguish this role slightly from their description in that the purpose of leveraging facilitation skills during *research facilitation* is to elicit data-cum-information through primary research by *engaging directly* with users or stakeholders. As such, to fulfill a research facilitation role, a designer should be able to satisfy the following goals:

1) *Identify and select* appropriate participatory design research methods; and

24

AIGA. "Facilitation: by Design workshops." AIGA, 16–17 July, 2017. Online. Available at: http://www.aiga.org/facilitation-by-design/ (Accessed 9–14 November, 2016). Material used in this piece was gleaned from dialogue that transpired during the AIGA Facilitation by Design Workshop, led by Breslin, M. and Ratinam, M., hosted by The SVA (School of Visual Arts) Branding Studio, NY, NY, USA, July 16–17, 2015. For further information, contact Mathan Ratinam at Parsons The New School for Design (mathan.ratinam@gmail.com) or Maggie Breslin at SVA (maggie.breslin@gmail.com).

25

Ibid.

26

AIGA. "Facilitation: by Design workshops." AIGA, 16–17 July, 2017. Online. Available at: http://www.aiga.org/facilitation-by-design/ (Accessed 9–14 November, 2016). Material used in this piece was gleaned from dialogue that transpired during the AIGA Facilitation by Design Workshop, led by Breslin, M. and Ratinam, M., hosted by The SVA (School of Visual Arts) Branding Studio, NY, NY, USA, July 16–17, 2015. For further information, contact Mathan Ratinam at Parsons The New School for Design (mathan.ratinam@gmail.com) or Maggie Breslin at SVA (maggie.breslin@gmail.com).

27

Sanders, E. & Stappers, P. "Co-creation and the new landscapes of design." CoDesign, 4.1 (2008): pgs. 5-18.

28

Ibid.

29

Almegaard, H. "Problems in Problem Analysis," in Proceedings of the Third International Workshop on Design in Civil and Environmental Engineering, 21–23 August 2014, The Technical University of Denmark, edited by Jensen, L. B., & Thompson, M.K. Kongens Lyngby, Denmark: The Technical University of Denmark, 2014: pgs. 97–102.

2) *Execute* whatever participatory design research methods were selected; and

3) *Develop and adapt* these as needed—all the while accounting for changing user/stakeholder input—as the project evolves iteratively.

A designer who is *not* engaged in a research facilitation approach to a given project can approach a potential initiative very differently, and not account for user/stakeholder input. She could begin by choosing to identify a problematic situation, contextually and theoretically frame it, and then initiate her research process by formulating, operating, and then gathering, analyzing and assessing data by enacting particular research methods. She could then use this data to support her design decision-making, and ultimately exit that process or project, with no other commitment to or role within it. These types of processes have been practiced by a graphic, industrial, interior, architectural and fashion designers for more than a half a century, and exemplify what has come to be described as "designing for rather than with."[27] Research facilitation operates quite differently than this more traditional approach, as it strives to meet the three goals articulated earlier in this paragraph.

Design Facilitation can be compared to the concept presented by Breslin and Ratinam as *"Workshop Heavy,"*[28] which describes a situation wherein a "workshop is the project in-and-of-itself."[29] When fulfilling a role as a design facilitator, the designer's main goals are to: 1) *Enable* a design process that addresses a specific problematic situation that is broadly inclusive and collaborative; 2) *Develop and effectively* operate an appropriate participatory design research methodology or set of methods with which to do this; and 3) use the results of this research to *affect outcomes* to design processes that create appropriate and desirable results, changes and/or actions on behalf of the users and stakeholders who are most affected by the social, economic, technological or political variables at play within the afore-mentioned problematic situation. Designers who plan and implement design facilitation processes tend to need to operate multiple, iterative engagements with users and stakeholders as these processes evolve, and as the users and stakeholders gain knowledge and—often—shift their essential opinions and viewpoints regarding key issues.

Despite the differences in purpose, we propose that effectively fulfilling both types of facilitation roles require that designers construct and cultivate knowledge of and about:

1) the planning and preparation of research and design facilitation engagements (i.e. workshops, participatory sessions, etc.);

2   several means to effectively plan and manage their interactions with the people who constitute the groups of users and stakeholders with whom they must glean data-cum-information from; and

3) exhibiting and mastering the distinct skills and traits of design facilitators.

A suggestion for a new pedagogical framework for design education

The authors suggest that the current foundation for visual communication design curricula needs to expand so that it can encompass the need to immerse students in learning experiences wherein they will gain the knowledge and skills necessary to plan, operate, and derive effective results from *Research Facilitation* and *Design Facilitation*. Examining the relationship between these two approaches has caused us to conclude that students should initially be exposed to the core experiences and knowledge that inform Research Facilitation, which provides the foundation necessary to then introduce students to Design Facilitation. The rationale for this sequence is supported by the ways that basic, applied and clinical approaches to research can and have effectively informed design processes. [30] A people-centered approach to engaging in design processes allows these broader approaches to be guided by *participatory* design research methods. Gaining familiarity with fundamental research frameworks and methods provides the foundation upon which research that accounts for the accrued knowledge and viewpoints of users and stakeholders can be built.

At the Indiana University Herron School of Art and Design, we have coordinated processes for familiarizing graduate students with (first) general approaches to understanding the thinking and methods that frame and guide effective research, and then (second) using these to guide more designerly approaches to knowing [31] across a two-year program of study. As part of their first year experience, graduate students are exposed to a wide range of research approaches and methods that can inform design processes. They then draw upon the knowledge and understandings they gain from these first-year experiences to help them effectively formulate and operate participatory research methods during the evolution of specific assigned or student-initiated projects during their second year of study. This experience involves graduate students spending approximately 30 weeks (two North American semesters of study) learning to plan and operate Design Facilitation processes inside the classroom

30
Friedman, K. "Theory construction in design research: criteria: approaches, and methods." Design Studies, 24 (2003): pgs. 507–522.

31
Cross, N. "Designerly Ways of Knowing." Design Studies, 3.4 (1982): pgs. 221-227

167

and in projects that involve users and stakeholders from communities outside the university. By studying within this structure, these graduate students are provided with ample opportunities to explore, practice, and refine their abilities to facilitate interactions between diverse individuals and groups in iteratively structured, participatory frameworks. To provide viable learning settings within which our students can learn to do this, we have forged and sustained working relationships with area-based, governmental and non-governmental organizations, consultancies and service institutions that we have found to be in need of participatory, facilitated engagements. The activities that our students have been involved in include but have not been limited to strategic planning meetings operated on behalf of various campus committees, charrettes that have incorporated knowledge and insights from community organizations relative to broad and specific problems they are attempting to confront, and "envisioning" workshops aimed at helping groups develop and effectively implement new programs or initiatives. These partners emerge from these interactions with a wide variety of outcomes, including transcriptions and visual syntheses of data-cum-information gleaned and assessed from their interactions with us, and, in some cases, clearly articulated means to plan and operate strategic initiatives.

Addressing challenges to incorporating these approaches into undergraduate and graduate curricula

The authors have refined and iteratively developed classroom exercises and coursework over the past four years, and continue to encounter significant challenges regarding how to effectively teach students to fulfill roles as research and design facilitators. We have found that immersing students in experience-based learning opportunities is necessary for them to effectively construct the knowledge and grasp the skills necessary to engage in both research and design facilitation. The challenge arises with finding and creating optimal learning environments where the students can feel safe to practice 'new' or 'unfamiliar' skills in 'real' contexts.

In most previous courses students have either been tasked with initiating their own contexts, or the instructor ahead of time set up their community partnerships. Given that these facilitated exercises and activities often times occur outside of class periods the assessment of these engagements then becomes increasingly challenging as well.

Additionally, a recurring challenging area that appears to be a serious concern for students is in dealing with difficult participants during an actual engagement or session. These kinds of situations can easily be a challenge for even seasoned professional facilitators, therefore it is necessary to determine appropriate ways to enable or simulate high stress environments without 'high stakes,' which is essential for students to practice conflict management and resolution tactics.

The last challenge area that we've encountered deals with teaching and assessing skills (and the knowledge that informs them) that can't necessarily be seen, or are difficult to notice. For example, attunement—or a person's ability to 'read the atmosphere and attitudes in a given room' and then comport herself accordingly as a facilitator—is not only difficult to teach, but is also difficult to assess given the diverse nature of contextual factors that have to be considered to do this with reasonable accuracy. Despite creating exercises and teaching and learning activities that afford students opportunities to develop this skill, the ability to assess a student's attunement becomes evident over a period of time and through noticing specific patterns or lack thereof.

A description of how specific curricular tools can enhance the teaching of research and design facilitation

The authors have developed a set of tools to address some of the challenges associated with teaching emerging designers to effectively formulate and operate research and design facilitation. These tools were first developed and tested during the authors interactions with specific clients and partners of *Collabo Creative,* our professional design practice. Prominent among these tools is a strategic framework that can be used to aid the planning and preparation necessary to facilitate collaborative, participatory design sessions. This planning framework has also been incorporated into the design education curriculum at the Herron School of Art and Design.

Based on their experiences planning and operating design facilitation experiences within their classrooms at Herron and in their professional practice at Collabo Creative, the authors contend that preparation and planning are two of the most important factors in being able to successfully engage in Design Facilitation. These ideas have been incorporated into the strategic framework the authors have implemented across the design education curriculum at Herron, which are validated by the tenets of Breslin and Ratinam's workshop. These articulate that, "preparation is key to facilitating a successful workshop"

169

32

Forlizzi, J. & Lebbon, C. "From Formalism to Social Significance in Communication Design." Design Issues, 18.4 (2002): pgs. 3–13.

d Zoe Strickler articulates several ways for design research to be formulated and conducted to positively benefit visual communication design processes in "Elicitation Methods in Experimental Design Research" (Strickler, Z. "Elicitation Methods in Experimental Design Research." Design Issues, 15.2 [1999]: p.27).

An examination of how design research approaches and methods can positively affect research practices in other disciplines through "problem framing" has been articulated by Kees Dorst in his article "Frame Creation and Design in the Expanded Field" (Dorst, K. "Frame Creation and Design in the Expanded Field." She Ji, 1.1 [2015]: pgs. 22–33).

e The objectives of a session can be widely varied, from gathering groups of doctors, nurses and other hospital personnel together with patients and patients' family members to discuss ways to improve patient's psychological comfort during hospital stays, to gathering groups of educators, educational administrators and students together to discuss ways to improve learning experiences in particular types of classrooms.

and "the more preparation you're able to do, the better." We (the authors) have utilized interviews and interactions with our students, our collaborators and others who practice design facilitation to educate ourselves about the value and importance of engaging in broadly informed, comprehensive planning prior to operating design facilitation sessions. We have also found that attending to logistical details—factors such as seating arrangements for participants, the types of drawing and writing materials that are made available for them to use during facilitation sessions, and the orchestration of the scaffolding of information sharing activities—make for more responsive, attentive, and reflective interactions.

Once logistical details are resolved, design facilitators can then advance their planning processes in ways that move them away from their traditional tendencies toward relying predominantly on intuition to guide their interactions with clients, users and audience members. Design facilitators *also* need to comport themselves in ways that help them build and positively utilize empathetic and sympathetic understandings of and about those who will be affected by the outcomes of design processes in which they are involved. These types of approaches are supported by the scholarship of Forlizzi and Lebbon[32] (among others),[d] who have written that, "[designers] also must be concerned about the interaction between the audience, the content of the communication, and the outcomes of the design."

The strategic framework the authors have developed to teach visual communication design students at Herron to effectively formulate and operate design facilitation is comprised of six sections—plus whatever the objectives of a given research or design facilitation session are[e]—that feed into and inform each other. These sections are titled *People, Time, Environment, Methods, Tools (to make)* and *Supplies (to take)*. This structure of this strategic framework is depicted in Figure 2.

The *"People"* portion of this framework refers to cultivating empathetic and sympathetic understandings of the audience(s) or users who will be affected by the outcomes of a given set of design processes. This requires that design facilitators develop broadly informed and deeply plumbed knowledge about the different types of personalities and roles that individuals and subgroups assume during interaction sessions, and the types of socio-cultural biases and value systems that inform these. Making the most of the *Time* available to operate a given interactive session is crucial, as design facilitators need to be able to set realistic expectations for what they can accomplish with a given

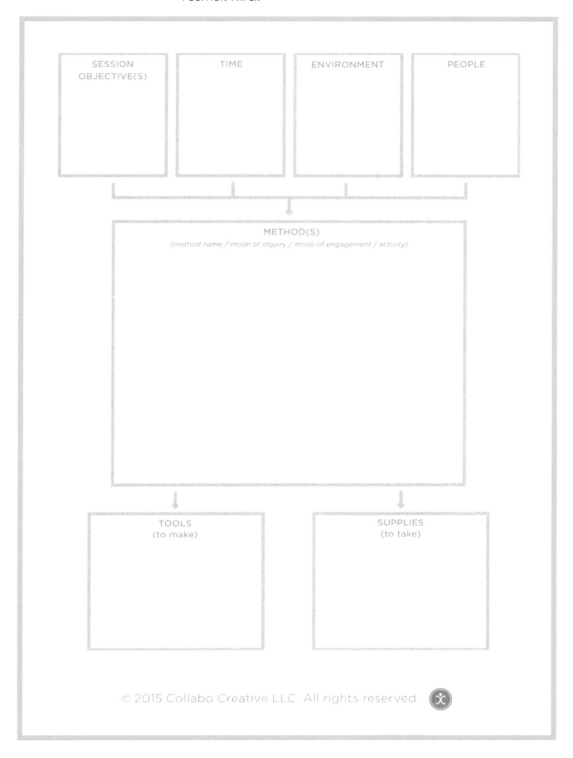

FIGURE 2: The strategic framework depicted here was developed by the authors during a series of interactions with various clients and user and stakeholder groups between 2013 and 2016 at their Indianapolis, Indiana-based design consultancy, Collabo Creative. This framework has also been used to guide learning experiences that introduce design facilitation to visual communication design students at the Herron School of Art and Design.

171

group of session participants in a set time frame, and not have the goals of the session be derailed by unexpected exchanges.

The authors have found that it is helpful to think about the *Environment* within which a data gathering or design facilitation event occurs in terms of its *tangible* and *intangible* qualities. These have to be designed, or at least accounted for, in ways that promote rather than inhibit meaningful interactions between participants and researchers or facilitators. *Tangible qualities* are most often physical: they include the attributes of the space people respond to viscerally, such as how it is lit, how the furniture within it has been arranged to afford physical comfort, and how wall, floor and ceiling surfaces have been treated. *Intangible qualities* describe the attributes of a space that affect how it performs to affect people's behavior: research and design facilitation participants tend to feel socially uncomfortable in spaces wherein they feel hot or cold, do not have easy access to refreshments or lavatories, or wherein they are made to feel "out of place."

Once information and understandings pertinent and relevant to the sections *Time, People* and *Environment* have been gathered, analyzed and documented, the knowledge gained from this is funneled into the section titled *Methods*. The activities that must be planned for and articulated in this section involve marrying the information and understandings that populate the *Time, People* and *Environment* sections with specific methods for gathering, analyzing and assessing data from participants during their interactions with designers and (sometimes) researchers from disciplines outside design. (The authors reference the contents of two books with undergraduate and first-year graduate students to begin to familiarize themselves with a range of design research methods that could potentially be effectively operated within particular time-, people-, and environment-based parameters: Bruce Hanington and Bella Martin's text *Universal Methods of Design: 100 Ways to Research Complex Problems, Develop Innovative Ideas, and Design Effective Solutions* [33] and *Vijay Kumar's volume 101 Design Methods: A Structured Approach for Driving Innovation in Your Organization.* [34]) The *Methods* section of this strategic framework is also the place within it where whatever specific methods for gathering and processing data that have been chosen for design researchers and facilitators to operate with users, audience members and other stakeholders are formulated into an agenda that can actually be met within the given time, personnel-based and environmental constraints.

33

Hanington, B. & Martin, B. Universal Methods of Design: 100 Ways to Research Complex Problems, Develop Innovative Ideas, and Design Effective Solutions. Beverly, MA, USA: Rockport Publishers, 2012.

34

Kumar, V. 101 Design Methods: A Structured Approach for Driving Innovation in Your Organization. Hoboken, NJ, USA: John Wiley & Sons, Inc., 2013.

Successfully operating methods for gathering useful and usable data during activities that involve interactions between designers and potential users or project stakeholders requires researchers and facilitators to perform a kind of balancing act. Contributions from particular individuals and groups must be effectively mediated to ensure that specific voices are neither too assertive nor too diminished, documentation must occur within the time allowed, and care must be taken to ensure that the design of a given space promotes rather than inhibits critical exchanges and movement. The final two items in the strategic framework—*Tools to make* (i.e. worksheets, visuals, etc. to facilitate interactions) and *Supplies to take* (i.e. post-its, chart paper, markers, food, etc. to aid in documentation and the creation of a collaborative atmosphere) are informed by the knowledge and understandings gleaned from analyzing and assessing the contents of the *Time, People, Environment* and *Methods* sections. A well-constructed strategic framework enables a high level of *sustained, constructive* participation from the greatest possible array of potential users and stakeholders—and the designers they are interacting with—within given specific environmental and temporal constraints.

Areas for Future Research

As of this writing, the authors are engaged in further research in the area of Design Facilitation, as we continue to apply the knowledge and skills described in this article to new iterations of frameworks and tools that can effectively inform design education and practice. We will continue to develop and test these frameworks and tools in both of these arenas, and assess their relative efficacy in terms of how they might prove to critically affect at least some aspects of 21st century design education. We feel that further scholarly explorations that examine the distinct-yet-interdependent relationships between Research Facilitation and Design Facilitation are also warranted, as are exploring the specific domains of knowledge and skill sets that affect student learning outcomes in and around these areas.

Additionally, we are exploring a pedagogical approach to incorporating Research Facilitation and Design Facilitation into a broader context that involves educating People-Centered Designers. This will include investigations into university-level design education programs that address Design Facilitation in a broad sense, and thus include various aspects of and pertinent to Design Research, Design Management, Design Strategy, and Design Leadership.

To remain relevant in these new professional realities, a sought-after, and, more to the point, effective designer will need to be able to formulate, conduct, analyze and synthesize the results of research that informs design processes and design decision-making beyond the traditional, cursory client interview and a narrowly framed, shallowly plumbed survey of secondary resources. Rather, the contemporary designer will need to possess the ability to cultivate and effectively utilize meaningful input from the varieties of people who both affect and will be affected by the design processes that guide the development of these projects and their outcomes. Failing to broadly account for the social, economic and technological biases of eventual users and audiences will limit the designers' abilities to create useful, usable and meaningful artifacts, services and experiences *with*, rather than *for*, these groups.

References

+Acumen. "Design kit: Facilitator's guide to introducing human-centered design." *+Acumen*. Online. Available at: http://plusacumen.org/courses/design-kit-facilitators-guide-to-introducing-human-centered-design/ (Accessed 12 October, 2016).

AIGA. "Facilitation: by Design workshops." *AIGA*, 16–17 July, 2017. Online. Available at: http://www.aiga.org/facilitation-by-design/ (Accessed 9–14 November, 2016). Material used in this piece was gleaned from dialogue that transpired during the AIGA *Facilitation by Design Workshop*, led by Breslin, M. and Ratinam, M., developed by Al-Yassini, R., hosted by The SVA (School of Visual Arts) Branding Studio, NY, NY, USA, July 16–17, 2015. For further information, contact Mathan Ratinam at Parsons The New School for Design (mathan.ratinam@gmail.com), Maggie Breslin at SVA (maggie.breslin@gmail.com), or Renna Al-Yassini (renna@bydesignworkshops.com).

Almegaard, H. "Problems in Problem Analysis," in Proceedings of the Third International Workshop on Design in Civil and Environmental Engineering, 21–23 August 2014, The Technical University of Denmark, edited by Jensen, L. B., & Thompson, M.K. Kongens Lyngby, Denmark: The Technical University of Denmark, 2014: pgs. 97–102.

Bayazit, N. "Investigating Design: A Review of Forty Years of Design Research." *Design Issues*, 20.1 (2004): pgs 16–29.

Body, J., Terrey, N. & Tergas, L. "Design Facilitation as an Emerging Design Skill: A Practical Approach," in *Proceedings of the 8th Design Thinking Research Symposium*, 19–20 September 2010, University of Technology, Sydney, Australia, edited by Dorst, K., Stewart, S., Staudinger, I., Paton, B., & Dong, A. Sydney, Australia: DAB Documents, 2010: pgs. 61–70.

Brewster, B., Dowse, E., Hogan, D., Wilkinson, M. & Woosley, B. "History [of INIFAC]," INIFAC, The International Institute for Facilitation, 28 September, 2006. Online. Available at: http://inifac.org/about-inifac.htm (Accessed 29 November 2016).

Buchanan, R. "Human dignity and human rights: Thoughts on the principles of human-centered design." *Design Issues*, 17.3 (2001): pgs. 35-39; Norman, D. "Human-centered design considered harmful." *Interactions*, 12.4 (2005): pgs. 14-19.

Cross, N. "Designerly Ways of Knowing." *Design Studies*, 3.4 (1982): pgs. 221-227.

Dorst, K. "Frame Creation and Design in the Expanded Field." *She Ji*, 1.1 (2015): pgs. 22-33

Dorst, K. & Lawson, B. *Design Expertise*. New York, NY, USA: Architectural Press, (an imprint of Routledge, an imprint of Taylor & Francis), 2009.

Faste, R., Roth, B. & Wilde, D.J. "Integrating Creativity into the Mechanical Engineering Curriculum." In *ASME Resource Guide to Innovation in Engineering Design*, edited by C. A. Fisher. New York, New York, USA: American Society of Mechanical Engineers, 1993.

Forlizzi, J. & Lebbon, C. "From Formalism to Social Significance in Communication Design." *Design Issues*, 18.4 (2002): pgs. 3–13.

Frascara, J. *Design and the Social Sciences: Making Connections*. New York, NY, USA: Taylor & Francis, 2002.

Frascara, J. & Winkler, D. "Jorge Frascara and Dietmar Winkler on Design Research." *Design Research Quarterly*, 3.3 (2008): pgs. 5–6.

Fraser, H. M. A. "Designing Business: New Models for Success." In *Design Thinking: Integrating Innovation, Customer Experience, and Brand Value*, edited by T. Lockwood, pgs. 35-46. New York, NY, USA: Allworth Press, 2009.

Friedman, K. "Theory construction in design research: criteria: approaches, and methods." *Design Studies*, 24 (2003): pgs. 507–522.

Hanington, B. & Martin, B. *Universal Methods of Design: 100 Ways to Research Complex Problems, Develop Innovative Ideas, and Design Effective Solutions*. Beverly, MA, USA: Rockport Publishers, 2012.

175

Kumar, V. *101 Design Methods: A Structured Approach for Driving Innovation in Your Organization.* Hoboken, NJ, USA: John Wiley & Sons, Inc., 2013.

Martin, R. *The Design of Business: Why Design Thinking is the Next Competitive Advantage.* Cambridge, MA, USA: Harvard Business Press, 2009: pgs. 57-78.

Norman, D. "Why design education must change." *Core 77*, 10 November 2010. Online. Available at: http://www.core77.com/posts/17993/why-design-education-must-change-17993 (Accessed November 4, 2016).

Napier, P. & Wada, T. "Co-designing for Healthcare: visual designers as researchers and facilitators. *Visible Language*, 49.1–2 (2015). Online. Available at: http://visiblelanguagejournal.com/issue/161/article/961 (Accessed 2 December 2016).

Sanders, E. & Stappers, P. "Co-creation and the new landscapes of design." CoDesign, 4.1 (2008): pgs. 5-18.

Strickler, Z. "Elicitation Methods in Experimental Design Research." *Design Issues,* 15.2 (1999): p.27.

Szebeko, D. & Tan, L. "Co-designing for society." *Australasian Medical Journal,* 3.9 (2010): pgs. 580–590.

Unger, R. Willis, D. & Nunally, B. *Designing the Conversation: Techniques for Successful Facilitation.* San Francisco, CA, USA: New Riders/Peachpit, a division of Pearson Education, 2013, p. 6.

Biographies

Pamela Napier is a Co-Founder, Design Strategist & VP of Operations at Collabo Creative, a strategic design consultancy in Indianapolis, Indiana, U.S.A., and an Assistant Professor of Visual Communication Design at the Herron School of Art and Design, also in Indianapolis, Indiana, U.S.A. She has been teaching across both the graduate and undergraduate curricula there for the past seven years. Through both teaching and practice, Pamela has been invited to give presentations, facilitate workshops, and co-design events nationally and internationally, and has worked with an array of local, regional and national clients on a variety of design research initiatives. She has been an AIGA member since 2002, and was recently appointed as the AIGA Indianapolis Chapter Education Director. *pcnapier@iupui.edu*

Terri Wada is a Co-Founder, Design Strategist & President of Collabo Creative, a strategic design consultancy in Indianapolis, Indiana, U.S.A., and an and adjunct faculty member in the Visual Communication Design Department at the Herron School of Art and Design, also in Indianapolis, Indiana, U.S.A. Design thinking and research have informed her roles in both design education and practice for most of the past five years. Her work with Collabo has afforded her opportunities to engage in design research-based projects on behalf of a diverse array of organizations, including non-profits, start-ups and fortune 500 companies. Terri's expertise in design is evident in the numerous lectures and presentations she's been invited to give nationally and abroad. Her most recent speaking engagement includes facilitating a people-centered design workshop on behalf of the U.S. Army at the Pentagon in Washington D.C. *tawada@iupui.edu*

Developing Citizen Designers

Compiled and edited by Elizabeth Resnick (2016); published by Bloomsbury Academic,

an imprint of Bloomsbury Publishing Plc, New York, NY, USA; 432 pages, approximately

253 illustrations. ISBN: 9780857856203.

REVIEW BY ANN MCDONALD[1]

1. Associate professor, design, Northeastern University College of Arts, Media
   and Design, Boston, MA, USA

SUGGESTED CITATION: McDonald, A. "Developing Citizen Designers." Review of *Developing Citizen Designers,* compiled
by Elizabeth Resnick (New York: Bloomsbury Publishing Plc, 2016). *Dialectic,* 1.1 (2016): pgs. 179–184. DOI: http://dx.doi.org/10.3998/
dialectic.14932326.0001.111

Reviews

Developing Citizen Designers

Compiled and edited by Elizabeth Resnick (2016);
published by Bloomsbury Academic, an imprint of
Bloomsbury Publishing Plc, New York, NY, USA;
432 pages, approximately 253 illustrations.
ISBN: 9780857856203.

REVIEW BY ANN MCDONALD

Associate Professor, Design
Northeastern University College of Arts,
Media and Design, Boston, MA, USA

Developing Citizen Designers is a well-organized resource, designed to offer meaningful guidance on social design practices via a close, cover-to-cover read or quick access to individual, topic-specific, framing essays, interviews and case studies of university-level, socially and culturally transformative design assignment briefs.

The book can be viewed as an open-ended provocation and imperative to design educators to:

- acknowledge social, theoretical and historical precedents,
- build relationships and facilitate possibilities outside of the classroom,
- be mindful of assumptions and bias,
- strategically use shared methodologies and tool-kits,
- experiment and fail with consideration of community impact and
- be cognizant of student learning objectives,
- incorporate outcomes assessment.

BELOW: Book cover *Developing Citizen Designers,* edited by Elizabeth Resnick (2016).

While this may seem a daunting challenge, Developing Citizen Designers offers exemplary guidance.

Elizabeth Resnick's deep experience as a design curator, educator, author, facilitator, and instigator offers an ideal, passionate position from which to call upon, cull and synthesize the diverse array of national and international voices and project-based case studies on offer within Developing Citizen Designers. Her consistent advocacy for graphic design as a tool for social change is broadened through the thoughtful assertion of many expert voices who have been invited to define and reflect on expanded design practices, their histories and genesis in allied fields, and their pitfalls and potentials for positive social impact.

In her essay that prefaces the primary sections of this volume titled "What is Design Citizenship?," Resnick writes that "...designers have both a social and a moral responsibility to use their visual language training to address societal issues either within or in addition to their professional design practice." Later in the same piece she adds, "at its best, design can change, improve, renew, inspire, involve, disrupt, and help solve the 'wicked' problems of this world." These ideas form the foundation of Resnick's definition of what it means not only to be a citizen designer, but what it means to aspire to be one. They also provide guidance to those who wish to teach design students to engage in design processes in ways that account for the real needs and wants of diverse groups of people around the world. As Victor Margolin opines in an essay titled "Graphic

Design Education and the Challenge of Social Transformation" that immediately follows Resnick's, "…the cultivation of formal judgement—the use of typography, the organization of information, the creation of symbols and logotypes—must now be taught as a means of social communication rather than pure visual techniques." He goes on to argue that, "the greatest challenge facing design schools today…is contributing to clarifying and sorting out the multiple communication needs of people around the world."

Developing citizen designers is a complex and varied practice. The wide range of essays, interviews and case studies included in this book broadly communicate its central theme: that there is no one "right" way for practitioners and educators to achieve the goal of developing ourselves as citizen designers, or teaching our students to act as such. This well-edited collection of material makes clear the need for us to seriously consider the varied levels of engagement, commitment, and timeframes needed to initiate, sustain and grow socially responsible and responsive design practices and design education programs. Taken as a whole, the contents of this book effectively argue that the effort necessary to plan and then strive for these goals offers rich learning opportunities and outcomes that align well with the broad qualities recently called for by Meredith Davis in the design of learning experiences: open-endedness, situatedness, responsiveness, position, integration, and assessment. [1]

In the book's foreword, Bernard Canniffe notes the "urgency and need for design to move forward and accept

responsibility," and engage in and with a diversely populated, intricately structured world to address global challenges. This book offers an open-ended guide to those who choose to address this challenge and be among the emerging number of design educators, students, and practitioners whom he observes are able to comport themselves as a "mix of builder, designer, entrepreneur, and activist."

The bulk of Developing Citizen Designers is devoted to well-articulated, amply illustrated case studies and essays that are organized into three meta-level "Parts," each of which is divided into two to three sub-sections of between five and eight pieces. Each sub-section begins with an essay commissioned from one of a group of educators who teach across a wide variety of educational programs. These frame the contents of each sub-section with a critical backdrop that addresses key aspects of social design practice, offering contextual and historical connections and perspectives from relevant fields. Each framing essay, save the one that begins the final sub-section on "Resources," is further supported by an interview with a design practitioner or educator. These interviews offer more concrete ideas about and examples of what is more broadly described in the framing essays that precede them.

Many of the essays in Developing Citizen Designers point to a broadening of the practice of design for social good that extend beyond visual communication, advocating for the open-ended use of human-centered and participatory design methodologies to co-discover system-based,

[1] Davis, M. (2011). "Anatomy of a Student Learning Experience," AIGA Pivot Conference, Phoenix, Arizona, USA, October 2011. Online. Available at: http://educators.aiga.org/wp-content/uploads/2012/01/PIVOT.pdf (Accessed August 17, 2016).

clarifying strategies and outcomes that may or may not result in visual communication artifacts.

The first of the books three parts, titled "Part 1: Designing Thinking" investigates how design and the design process can contribute to positive social and cultural change. It is divided into three sections: "Socially Responsible Design," "Design Activism," and "Design Authorship," with introductory section essays by Andrew Shea, Natalia Ilyin and Steven McCarthy.

"Part 2: Design Methodology" emphasizes active, empathetic methodologies for designing, particularly designing with rather than for, in order to better understand the needs of diverse stakeholders. It is comprised of three sections: "Collaborative Learning," "Participatory Design," and "Service Design," with introductory section essays by Teal Triggs, Helen Armstrong and Michael Gibson.

"Part 3: Making a Difference" offers reflections on fostering responsible, sustainable and equitable engagements. It is divided into two sections: "Getting Involved," with section essays by Eric Benson, Myra Margolin, and Elisabeth Tunstall and "Resources," with section essays by Audra Buck-Coleman, Cinnamon Janzer and Lauren Weinstein, Penina Acayo, Gunta Kaza, and Scott Boylston. The Resources section includes a list of downloadable toolkits and frameworks.

The use of the term 'Design Thinking' as the title of Part 1 likely refers to design thinking's use of the design process to further the goal of

better future socio-cultural, economic, political, environmental and technological conditions. But one could readily argue for the inclusion of it as one of the design methodologies situated within Part 2. The author acknowledges that many of the case studies could easily have been "housed" under multiple sections, and that the section classifications "exist primarily for guidance and ease of use."

The interviews that occur in all but one of the book's sub-sections reflect the perspectives and approaches of designers from different parts of the world who have incorporated social design initiatives into their professional practice or teaching. Many of their stories point to a particular experience that helped them understand the positive affect that well-framed and actuated, socially transformative design can have in different places in the world. Additionally, the book concludes with a Bibliography that provides significant texts on social design and related topics. The book's essays present the reader with a contextualization of theories and frameworks related to design for social change, such as the 1964 First Things First manifesto, Movement Action Plan (MAP), Design Anthropology, Service Design, and Collaborative Learning, among others.

Case studies of education modules and projects from a wide range of countries and design education programs include process and outcome visuals accompanied by summaries written in response to the following prompts: Description, Research, Challenges, Strategy, Effectiveness and Assessment. Each case study identifies the

members of its Project Team and the Duration of the Project, and provides critical analysis of the design processes that guided its evolution in ways that reveal both its contextual framework and the strategies employed to address key issues. More logistical specifics regarding Client, Project Title, and Budget are also included in each case study. The projects described vary in scale and scope from individual student projects to single and multi-term (i.e., semester) team projects, through grant-funded projects operated under the authority of research centers that involved faculty and staff who have established and grown sustained connections within communities. Some teams engaged at a hyper-local scale, within the environs of a campus or in close-by neighborhoods, while others worked across universities, cities, cultures and time zones.

The call for case study submittals for possible publication in this book stated the following selection criteria: "case studies [will be considered] that address the belief that design can illuminate a viable pathway as a counter balance to business and commercial objectives while providing the impetus for students to become inspired and enabled to employ their visual and critical thinking skills as a vehicle for social change."

The quality of the reflections offered throughout the book, and the admission in some cases that project outcomes led to more questions, or that time was too short, or direct access to primary source information or key partners and audiences was limited, provide eye-opening alerts to others who might wish to plan and operate related initiatives. The reflexive sharing of logistical and outcome successes and failures allow the potential for these case studies to be used as realistic models by other educators. Additionally, the inclusion of the category "Assessment" in each of the case studies is a good first step toward providing the reader with understandings about the actual efficacy and affect(s) of the projects . A useful extension of this type of project reporting and analysis would have involved allowing individual authors to further detail and assess the social, technological, economic, environmental or political impact each project had on design students' learning outcomes, community partnership missions, community perceptions of the role of design as an effective catalyst for social change, individual end-users' goals, and design curricula.

The verb 'Developing' in the book title suggests an unclear impression beginning to come into focus as pilot projects are developed iteratively, are better understood, assessed longitudinally, shared and finally used as models for multiple approaches and methods for practicing socially transformative design and socially engaged design education. Developing relationships, projects and frameworks demands fluidity, resourcefulness, planning and outreach beyond the educational or professional experiences of many designers. However, if we are challenging students to become citizen designers as a means to improve various aspects of the worlds we and they inhabit and affect, we need to model behaviors informed by thoughtfulness, preparedness, organization, and broadly constituted connections. We need to

scale timeframes to pursue both small and large-scale sustained partnerships, that enable us to listen and learn, cultivate values, design with rather than for, collaborate across disciplines, measure impact and share insights.

As design educators, we need to work more effectively to cultivate understandings of what our students know, do not know, and then encourage learning experiences in fields and disciplines related to design to help them expand and extend their abilities to construct, rather than merely perform, new knowledge. We need to be calculated risk-takers, and realize that the pilot projects completed within a given term or semester may have longer trajectories, both in helping to expand the way emerging designers choose to practice in the future, and to increasing the diversity of the types of projects they engage with and the topics they investigate. The people-centered design and research skills imparted in the various methodologies outlined in the essays, interviews and case studies in Developing Citizen Designers comprise the spectrum of understanding and knowledge needed by future designers, regardless of how, when and whether they define themselves as citizen designers.

Leap Dialogues:
Career Pathways in Design for Social Innovation

Edited by Mariana Amatullo, with Bryan Boyer, Liz Danzico and Andrew Shea (2016);

published by Design Matters at ArtCenter College of Design, Pasadena, CA, USA

REVIEW BY ANNABEL PRETTY[1]

1. Senior Lecturer, Academic Leader, Architecture; Unitec Institute of Technology, Auckland, New Zealand

SUGGESTED CITATION: Pretty, A. "Leap Dialogues: Career Pathways in Design for Social Innovation." *Review of Leap Dialogues: Career Pathways in Design for Social Innovation,* edited by Mariana Amatullo (Pasadena: Design Matters, 2016). *Dialectic,* 1.1 (2016): pgs. 185-188. DOI: http://dx.doi.org/10.3998/dialectic.14932326.0001.112

Leap Dialogues:
Career Pathways in Design
for Social Innovation

Edited by Mariana Amatullo, with Bryan Boyer, Liz Danzico
and Andrew Shea (2016); published by Design Matters at
ArtCenter College of Design, Pasadena, CA, USA

REVIEW BY ANNABEL PRETTY

Senior Lecturer, Academic Leader,
Architecture; Unitec Institute of Technology,
Auckland, New Zealand

"'Take the leap. Take the leap.' And I kept on thinking, 'Easy for him to say.' Take the leap where? Don't I have to know where I am going? The wisdom, in hindsight of course, is that you don't have to know where you're going, you only have to know that you want to start the journey. In fact, you can't know where you are going—that's the point."

Heller, C. & Polak, P. (2016). "Taking the Leap," in M. Amatullo, B. Boyer, L. Danzico and A. Shea (eds.) Leap Dialogues: Career Pathways in Design for Social Innovation, Pasadena, CA, USA: Designmatters: ArtCenter College of Design, p. 238.

Leap Dialogues: Career Pathways in Design for Social Innovation is undeniably a comprehensive tome of a book, which covers the vast array of the typologies of dialogue one might expect to come across when discussing and analyzing design and design processes: Generative Dialogue—involving flow and space-collapsing boundaries; Reflective Dialogue—involving inquiry, empathetic listening, and changing one's point of view; Talking Nice—listening, engaging in polite, cautious exchanges; Talking Tough—

ABOVE: Book cover *Leap Dialogues: Career Pathways in Design for Social Innovation,* edited by Mariana Amatullo with Bryan Boyer, Liz Danzico and Andrew Shea (2016).

engaging in or facilitating debate, rule-revealing, clashing. Indeed, it is the thoughtfully asserted presence of all of these which makes for a truly didactic approach to the consumption of the book.

So we take the metaphorical "Leap" into the book, firstly with an excellent written introductive precis by the editor Amatullo, (p. 10), in which she offers, "…it is purposely ambivalent and pluralistic in its use of definition about the social design practices it illustrates and describes." This declaration sets the stage for the forthcoming chapters. These chapters derive their structure from the design methodology of "Why," "What," "How," (plus "How-based case studies"), and "Futures."

Amatullo's introductory essay "Why: Why Designers Practice in Social Innovation" leads us through the storytelling of each author. The chapter quickly reveals that the common language of social innovation is a multi-faceted diamond—each author/contributor/actor has their own way of interpreting social innovation. The noise of "Talking Tough" thrives and ambiguity abounds. In the face of this murk, the chapter provides sure navigation through and interpretation of diverse soliloquy, monologue and aside.

Danzico's introductory essay "What: What Designers Need to Practice in Social Innovation" draws the threads of the various conversations around the metaphor of modal jazz, especially in relationship to the roles that "improvisation" plays in the effective development of both. It is a charming introduction and leads effortlessly into the various repartees. Danzico reveals herself to be especially cognizant to the requirements necessary for designers to engage in socially innovative endeavors as she opines that, "[to be a] good improviser is to be very comfortable with ambiguity." However, as Sarah Lidgus quotes from Alejandro Aravena's caveat, "There's nothing worse than answering well the wrong problem," the reader is reminded of how this book is intended to be used as an exemplar, or a guide to more precedent study. Just as highly skilled modal jazz musicians must listen as effectively as they play to ensure an inclusive-but-oppositional musical narrative, designers working to instigate positive social change must effectively engage in oppositional dialogues to fuel inclusive design decision-making.

In the essay "How: How Designers Practice in Social Innovation," Boyer's initiatory words bring an imperceptible smile to those who truly and experientially understand the hard work involved with fomenting change. This occurs especially as one reads lines like "the elusive line that distinguishes the social impact designer from the do-gooder who just happens to be a designer," and "here's the secret: social impact is an outcome—not a thing—and so it can only be sought, never designed." In this last section, the main editor Boyer interviews/moderates the authors, which gives it greater cohesiveness, or stickiness, to the main ideas addressed and expressed within this section.

The sub-section titled "How: Case Studies" leads the reader through the American paradigm of Social Innovation, particularly within the context of working within large organizations. Frog's "The Humanitarian Data Exchange" is a fascinating case study with complex scaling issues and co-design across multi-organizational situations. It is unfortunate that the duotone photographs that are embedded within this narrative are difficult to understand as presented in this context. They fail to offer the reader further insights into or about how frog developed or operates its Humanitarian Data Exchange. (Sadly, this ineffectiveness of supporting imagery to help the reader gain further understanding of ideas presented in the text recurs throughout much of the book—a disappointment given the quality of its written content.)

The "Future Outlooks" section is the culmination of this volume, and

ABOVE: Image compilation *Leap Dialogues: Career Pathways in Design for Social Innovation*, edited by Mariana Amatullo with Bryan Boyer, Liz Danzico and Andrew Shea (2016).

begins with an essay from Allan Chochinov. His idea that, "…it's all about fluencies. I believe that designers are the connective tissue of any constructed system…" is a charming-albeit-sometimes-wishful reference, and sets the scene for a series of notable quotes from a diverse multitude of design educators and practitioners as to the essential qualities necessary in a student.

Although conceding that the four-part chapter structure is eminently prudent, being the rather deviant reader that I am, I do wonder as to the veracity of this. Perhaps instead of having the case studies presented as being the culmination and the summit of journey, introducing them earlier would have set the scene for the reader more effectively, and thus given the whole book more of a united structure, which would have facilitated a more cohesive read. As it is, the dialogues that frame and form the content presented in the various chapters slips and slides about rather like kelp drifting and floating in the tide—some of offerings are exceptionally well-written, and the exchanges that unfold resonate effectively between the two authors/collaborators. Conversely, other pieces are largely impenetrable as context and meaning slip and slide off one another without really addressing each other's thoughts. At many points I wondered as to how the pairings of actor/author were chosen. Some are rendered eminently readable as collations of thoughts rather than actual conversations, while others allow the language of the writer to obfuscate the effective narration of the story.

In the closing pages of this book Natacha Poggio states, "Social impact work requires empathy, co-creation and collaborative skills." This quote exemplifies the primary message of this book. Rather than reading it from start to finish in one sitting, Leap Dialogues is a well to dip in and out of; it exists as a conduit through which to consider the many voices and personal strategies that together or individually can help facilitate social innovation. To consider its offerings is to consider the wide range of discourses around the subject and to attempt to conjugate meanings from these. Though some of the conversations presented in "Leap Dialogues" go "off piste," the bulk of the content presented here truly constitutes a dialogue that is dialectic in nature.

Are We There Yet?
Insights on How to Lead by Design

Written by Sam Bucolo

REVIEW BY HEATHER CORCORAN[1]

1. Director, College & Graduate School of Art, Jane Reuter Hitzeman & Herbert F. Hitzeman, Jr. Professor of Art, Sam Fox School of Design and Visual Arts, Washington University in St. Louis, St. Louis, MO, USA

SUGGESTED CITATION: Pretty, A. "'Are We There Yet?' Insights on How to Lead by Design." Review of *"Are We There Yet" Insights on How to Lead by Design,* written by Sam Bucolo. *Dialectic,* 1.1 (2016): pgs. 189-191. DOI: http://dx.doi.org/10.3998/dialectic.14932326.0001.113

ABOVE: Book cover *"Are We There Yet? Insights on How to Lead by Design",* by Sam Bucolo.

"Are We There Yet? Insights on How to Lead by Design"

Written by Sam Bucolo

REVIEW BY HEATHER CORCORAN

Washington University at St. Louis

In "Are We There Yet? Insights on How to Lead by Design," Sam Bucolo posits design process as a transformative agent for mid-sized businesses to become innovators. As a consultant to SMEs (small- to medium-sized enterprises, as he describes them), Bucolo documents his own experiences advocating for companies to understand their customers more deeply and systematically in order to reimagine business products, practices, and culture. He believes that mid-sized companies are ideally suited to engage design process, as they are small enough to have connections across all parts of the organization, and the potential for close contact with customers. Small and medium-sized businesses are also an economic powerhouse—comprising the largest employer category in the world's economy.

This book presents a framework for applying design process to business, and describes how design has affected a set of companies in Australia. It is a relevant read for design educators interested in design process as a tool of innovation, as well as the surrounding discourse about design thinking. It is also appropriate for design students who

may find themselves challenged by employers to apply their knowledge of design to innovation-seeking business practices.

To be clear, the book is written to business leaders. Bucolo speaks to them in a direct, informal style. Chapter 1 is entitled "can you tell me how innovative you are?" "You" is a person in business. The book concludes with a series of questions for CEOs to consider. Each chapter ends with reflections for decision-makers in business. A bright yellow book, peppered with abstracted, iconic illustrations and design process and structure diagrams, Are We There Yet? reads as a guidebook—a kind of conversation between Sam Bucolo and businesses who seek innovation. Designers, design educators, and students of design who read the book will witness a dialogue. They have a tool to imagine how design practice and design education should evolve, though the book does not address the role that they might play explicitly.

Bucolo argues that three questions should drive a company's self-assessment of potential for innovation. First and foremost is the idea of customer: Who is your customer and what problem are you solving for them? The second question is about how the customer's priorities impact the daily operations of a business: What business activities across the organization do you carry out on a daily basis, which ensure you're addressing your customer's problems? And the last question addresses building capacity and focus: What could you do less of that does not directly address your customer's problem? These questions loosely correlate to the three elements of design led innovation (DLI) that he views as critical—customer value, strategic alignment, and management mindset.

Examples of consulting projects conducted by Bucolo include Centor, a company that produces door components. Through a DLI process, with over 300 interviews with employees, Centor learned that it would join a bigger, more diverse and profit-bearing market if it began to manufacture doors and windows, instead of just components, where it would able to differentiate its brand and product more directly. Without the design process, Centor likely would have continued to grow modestly inside the components market. And then there is the case of Gourmet Garden, a fresh herbs company. Seeking more innovation from its tubed herbs product, it conducted observations of professional chefs and ordinary families, with assessments of shopping trips and everyday refrigerators. Gourmet Garden learned that they needed to refine the way that they combined convenience and freshness in their herbs. Their primary consumer is a person for whom cooking dinner is a time challenge, and freshness a top priority. Their "lightly dried" herbs—an idea they developed and tested as a prototype—was not viewed as fresh enough. As a result, they developed a new package which made fresh herbs easier to access, as well as a set of bowls for herbs, both of which were met with market success.

Bucolo's endorsement of design process is strengthened by several references to design literature. He links the open-ended brainstorming of design thinking to abductive reasoning, a concept introduced by early 20th century philosopher Charles Sanders Peirce. Bucolo sees Peirce's work as a precursor to Nigel Cross' description of the problem-solution loop that happens in design process, as solutions sometimes refine—and even redefine—problems. He categorizes levels of innovation impact according to a revised version of the Danish Design Ladder. He describes Doblin's Ten Types of Innovation, which are aspects of a business that can be innovative; these are grouped under the three categories—configuration, offering, experience.

While the book's content is communicated mostly through text, there are several structure and process diagrams that shape Bucolo's framework, including what he terms the "Design Led Innovation Matrix" and the "Deep Dive Framework." The "Design Led Innovation Matrix" is a four part-process, organized according to individual and company-wide growth, and tactical and competitive strategy. The steps, which describe a company's typical path toward full engagement with design process, include awareness, experimentation/prototyping, transformation reorganizing, and education capability. The deep dive framework is used in parallel to help companies to assess themselves in a customer-driven way.

"Are We There Yet?" provides a model for how small-and middle-sized businesses can use design process to innovate. While it is a book written for business, it also participates in the emerging design discourse, which values the application of a design process to complex problems (e.g., wicked problems, business challenges, collaborative research issues), which may or may not require artifact-based solutions. This book provides valuable on-the-ground knowledge and experience for business, and an important context for designers, educators, and students.

Mapping the Grid of Swiss Graphic Design: A review of 100 Years of Swiss Graphic Design

Compiled and edited by Christian Brändle, Karin Gimmi, Barbara Junod, Christina Reble,

Bettina Richter (hardcover, 2013); published by Lars Müller Publishers, Zurich, Switzerland;

384 pages, approximately 600 illustrations. ISBN: 9783037783528.

REVIEW BY RICHARD DOUBLEDAY[1]

1. Associate Professor of Art Graphic Design, Louisiana State University School of Art, Baton Rouge, LA, USA

SUGGESTED CITATION: Doubleday, R. "Mapping the grid of Swiss Graphic Design: a review of 100 Years of Swiss Graphic Design." *Review of Mapping the Grid of Swiss Graphic Design: A Review of 100 Years of Swiss Graphic Design,* compiled and edited by Christian Brändle (Zurich: Lars Müller Publishers, 2013). *Dialectic,* 1.1 (2016): pgs. 192–195. DOI: http://dx.doi.org/10.3998/dialectic.14932326.0001.114

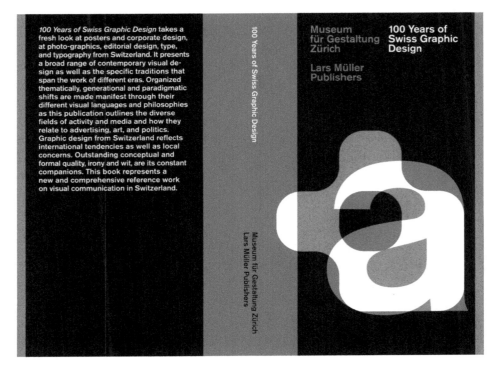

100 Years of Swiss Graphic Design takes a fresh look at posters and corporate design, at photo-graphics, editorial design, type, and typography from Switzerland. It presents a broad range of contemporary visual design as well as the specific traditions that span the work of different eras. Organized thematically, generational and paradigmatic shifts are made manifest through their different visual languages and philosophies as this publication outlines the diverse fields of activity and media and how they relate to advertising, art, and politics. Graphic design from Switzerland reflects international tendencies as well as local concerns. Outstanding conceptual and formal quality, irony and wit, are its constant companions. This book represents a new and comprehensive reference work on visual communication in Switzerland.

Mapping the Grid of Swiss Graphic Design: A Review of 100 Years of Swiss Graphic Design

Compiled and edited by Christian Brändle, Karin Gimmi, Barbara Junod, Christina Reble, Bettina Richter (hardcover, 2013); published by Lars Müller Publishers, Zurich, Switzerland; 384 pages, approximately 600 illustrations.

ISBN: 9783037783528.

REVIEW BY RICHARD DOUBLEDAY

Associate Professor of Art, Department of Graphic Design, Louisiana State University School of Art, Baton Rouge, LA, USA

100 Years of Swiss Graphic Design is a new, comprehensive reference work that presents a fresh perspective on Swiss graphic design and typography. It offers a behind-the-scenes look at the renowned graphic design collection of the Museum für Gestaltung Zürich, Switzerland's leading design and visual communication museum. However, as editor Christian Brändle explains in the foreword, the book offers more than a "mere inventory" of the museum's collection. Drawing from sources beyond the museum's collection, the book traces the origins of Swiss graphic design and typography, while also offering a wide range of examples of contemporary Swiss visual communication design. It provides a rich array of familiar Swiss classics as well as a broad range of material that is much less well known, including sketches, posters, packaging, stamps, maps, banknotes, design system manuals, and type specimens. According to editor Karin Gimmi, "The choice of the images was done together with the designers of the book. The studio NORM, with Manuel Krebs, Dimitri Bruni and Ludovic Varone, had a big share in defining the visual content of the book. We tried to find a good balance between eye-catching objects and such that are less known."

The publication is divided into eleven chapters that are sequenced thematically into important developments in the canon of Swiss graphic design and that feature several types of visual communication design artifacts. Many chapters begin with a short essay that serves to frame and place its topic in the historical conditions that existed within Switzerland and throughout Europe during specific spans of time. These are followed by explanatory case studies. Each case study adds new layers of depth by exploring the social, technological and political trends that helped bring new forms of visual communication design into existence. As Gimmi explains, "The thematic approach was indeed chosen to replace

ABOVE: Book cover *Mapping the grid of Swiss Graphic Design: a review of 100 Years of Swiss Graphic Desgn,* edited by Brändle, Gimmi, Junod, Reble, and Richter (2013).

a biographical one. While some of the entries profit from earlier research work, others are based on completely new material." The wealth of material spanning several generations is supplemented by comprehensive analysis by academics, historians, and a network of expert curators within the Museum für Gestaltung Zürich's poster and graphics collection. The aim of the editorial team, as Gimmi described, was to "try and set a new standard" for graphic design surveys.

The poster as a popular advertising medium in Swiss visual communication design is presented first, but continues to feature prominently throughout the rest of the book. The first chapter examines posters produced by Swiss designers, or designers working in the Swiss style, over the course of the twentieth through the early twenty-first centuries, beginning with the first Sachplakat ("Poster style") poster by Emil Cardinaux in 1908. The essays outline the medium's artistic evolution, universal visual language, distinctive approaches, and steady advancement in new directions. Most notable from the early period of the twentieth century are a number of posters advertising products and publicizing Swiss tourism. These include work from such prominent poster designers such as Emile Cardinaux, Niklaus Stoecklin, Herbert Leupin, Hans Erni, Otto Baumberger, as well as Swiss-born belle-époque Parisian artists Théophile-Alexandre Steinlen and Eugéne-Samuel Grasset. Despite these designers having diverse artistic backgrounds and careers, many shared a painterly style, and, from a conceptual standpoint, sought to create compositions of typography and imagery that concisely and effectively conveyed

essential meaning about the goods and services they had been designed to promote. Another important consideration for this group was using the medium of the poster to reach wider audiences as communication and transportation technology rapidly evolved across Europe.

The Swiss school, also referred to as the "International Style," materialized as a design movement during the 1950s and 1960s, sought what its practitioners believed to be a more universal and scientific approach to solving design problems. An entire chapter in this volume, "Swiss Style," is dedicated to examining this movement with a series of illuminating case studies: the first tracks its evolution, followed by pieces that analyze the perspective of the "Swiss Style" from abroad, the affect that the implementation of the J. R. Geigy AG corporate image had on corporate identity design in the United States, the influence the Ambassadors of Swiss design had in Italy, and culminating with a short history of the development and evolution of the typeface Helvetica. Richard Hollis' essay: "The New Graphic Design: Views from Abroad," details the individuals and publications that were influential in spreading the new "Swiss Style" to an international audience. Hollis' piece also provides a unique first-person perspective on how and why the aesthetic trends of the movement have remained stable, and that examine how the formal characteristics of Swiss graphic design distinguish it from other movements and styles that have affected graphic design over the last hundred years.

A broad range of modern Swiss graphic design—work designed from the late

twentieth century and the 2000s—is represented throughout the book. The final case study, "Autonomy and Assignment," provides interviews with five contemporary Swiss graphic designers: Ruedi Wyss, Natalie Bringolf, Kristin Irion, Tania Prill, and Manuela Pfrunder. These Swiss designers were asked to discuss their working history, design ideas, working methodology, and the importance of the reception of Swiss graphic design as communicated by exhibition institutions, the press, and publications. Although the designers interviewed indicated that their particular working methods varied—from approaches guided by methodically operated research and tightly defined frameworks to those informed by investigative analyses of "stuff lying around a table"—they were united in that almost all of them were design educators, and that they all believed in the importance of maintaining strong, dynamic relationships in their studios between design teams and those who guide their working processes.

The primary criticism of this book, as is so often the case with specifically located graphic design histories, concerns the weight of emphasis placed on individual (in this case, Swiss) graphic designers. Given that the process of selecting whose work should be included in a volume like this is made difficult due to the sheer volume of designers who have produced outstanding work from which to choose, it is unfortunately not surprising that the work of several important designers was not given sufficient emphasis. The contributions of Ernst Keller, considered an instrumental Swiss design educator and a key figure in the development of the Swiss design movement, is mentioned only sparingly in the text. Additionally, Siegfried Odermatt and Rosmarie Tissi, partners of the design firm Odermatt & Tissi, are given limited attention in the text, and are only granted page space for three images between them. As Odermatt and Tissi played a leading role in applying the International Typographic Style to corporate and cultural visual communications, they deserved more attention than they received in the book.

100 Years of Swiss Graphic Design was designed by Dimitri Bruni, Manuel Krebs, Teo Schifferli, and Ludovic Varone of NORM, an experimental team of graphic designers based in Zurich. Graphic design monographs are genuinely challenging for a designer to effectively develop and execute, due to the sheer volume of historical material and breadth of content they must accommodate, yet the design team at NORM has risen to the call as evidenced by their design of this book. Gimmi offered, "We had very close cooperation with NORM, with whom we [have worked] together on different occasions. There have been a lot of discussions both about content and form of the book." The book cover is made formally seductive by virtue of its elongated shape, minimalist color palette (black, white, red and blue), and sparsely rendered graphic and typographic forms. This composition is comprised of two graphically intersecting letterforms rendered large enough to occupy most of the available surface area. A slightly blurred and pixelated lower-case 'a' from the typeface FF Moonbase Alpha (designed by the Swiss-born designer

Cornel Windlin in 1991) is juxtaposed with the lower-case 'a' from the a revival version of the typeface Antique (designed by the Swiss typeface designer François Rappo in 2010-11). The carefully assembled cover image of overlapped shapes fittingly captures the elemental graphic-form language that evolved from a new generation of Swiss graphic designers in the 1950s. The well-balanced weight of images and text on the interior pages facilitates a simple and elegant reading experience throughout this volume. The pages are dense with information, but possess a high degree of graphic exactness clearly arranged according to an underlying grid-structure.

Overall, 100 Years of Swiss Graphic Design is an engaging and comprehensive historical survey, accompanied by numerous examples of the vast body of design work to have emerged from Switzerland in the past century. Showcasing visual design across a wide range of niche areas of expertise, this invaluable book demonstrates how many Swiss designers' use of modernist elements along with their considerate graphic deployment of constructivist ideals continue to exist as an indelible part of today's graphic design language. It is essential reading for design students, or anyone interested in Swiss graphic design and its larger effects on the discipline worldwide. It is a salient contribution to the development of graphic design history as a scholarly discipline, and a comprehensive account of a period of significant artistic creativity.

The typographic structure of *Dialectic* employs typefaces from four different families: Fira (Sans and Mono), Freight, Idealista, and Noe Display.

Fira Sans was introduced in 2013 as Feura Sans, and was designed by Erik Spiekermann, Ralph du Carrois, Anja Meiners and Botio Niktoltchev of Carrois Type Design. Fira Sans and Fira Mono (the latter was designed as a monospaced variant of the former) are based on Speikermann's typeface designs for the FF Meta family of typefaces, which originated in the 1980s. Fira is classified as a humanist, sans-serif typeface family.

The Freight family of typefaces—"Big," "Display," "Sans," and "Text— was designed by Joshua Darden in the early 2000s and is comprised of over 100 styles. The Freight families are currently licensed through Darden Studio, and, with the exception of the "Sans" variants, may be classified as a display, serif typefaces.

The Idealista family was designed by Tomáš Brousil and released in 2010. It is comprised of ten style variations and five weights. It may be classified as a geometric, sans serif typeface, and is available from MyFonts.com.

The Noe Display family was designed by Lauri Toikka in 2013 and is available through the Schick Toikka digital foundry. It is comprised of four Roman and four italic variants, ranging in weight from "regular" to "black." It may be classified as a display serif typeface, and shares some formal characteristics (sharp, angled serifs, high contrast between thick and thin strokes) with the Noe Text family.

CPSIA information can be obtained
at www.ICGtesting.com
Printed in the USA
FSOW04n2214060417
32835FS

9 781607 854159